Sonja Lyubomirsky is a professor of psychology at the University of California, Riverside. She received her BA from Harvard University and her PhD in Social Psychology from Stanford University. In 2002, Dr Lyubomirsky and her research were awarded the 2002 Templeton Positive Psychology Prize. Currently, she is an associate editor of the *Journal of Positive Psychology* and (with co-PI Ken Sheldon) holds a 5-year million-dollar grant from the National Institute of Mental Health to conduct research on the possibility of permanently increasing happiness. Her research has been written up in dozens of magazines and newspapers and she has appeared in multiple TV shows, radio shows and feature documentaries in North America, Europe and East Asia. She lives in Santa Monica, CA with her family.

D0814651

THE HOW OF HAPPINESS

*A Practical Approach to Getting
the Life You Want*

Sonja Lyubomirsky

sphere

SPHERE

First published in Great Britain in 2007 by Sphere

Copyright © Sonja Lyubomirsky, 2007

The moral right of the author has been asserted.

All rights reserved.
No part of this publication may be reproduced, stored in a retrieval
system, or transmitted, in any form or by any means, without the prior
permission in writing of the publisher, nor be otherwise circulated in any
form of binding or cover other than that in which it is published and
without a similar condition including this condition being imposed
on the subsequent purchaser.

A CIP catalogue record for this book
is available from the British Library.

ISBN 978-1-84744-193-5

Typeset in Bembo by M Rules
Printed and bound in Great Britain by
Clays Ltd, St Ives plc

Sphere
An imprint of
Little, Brown Book Group
100 Victoria Embankment
London EC4Y 0DY

An Hachette Livre UK Company

www.littlebrown.co.uk

Contents

Acknowledgements

Somewhere in the Introduction I wrote that the star of this book is science. Well, there would be no science without scientists. My deep gratitude goes to my collaborators, my students and colleagues far and wide who have laboured on the research depicted in this book. First and foremost I am infinitely grateful to Ken Sheldon, who is an equal collaborator on the empirical research I describe, and who was central to the development of the pie-chart model. I thank Ken for our fruitful and rewarding collaboration and hope it will continue for many years to come. David Schkade also deserves major credit for helping develop several ideas at the heart of this book. I am also grateful to Marty Seligman for providing Ken, David and myself with the sublime setting, the funding and the feedback to germinate and propel our ideas forward, and for introducing me to Richard Pine (more on him later).

I am privileged to be mentored and championed by several very special individuals. Lee Ross kindled in me an enduring interest in happiness. I am indebted to his brilliance and warmth, and the many intellectually provoking and thoroughly enjoyable discussions we have had over the years. When it comes to the greater part of my research today, all roads lead back to Lee. My wonderful mentor and friend, Susan Nolen-Hoeksema, has taught me much about how to do science and has always been an unflagging supporter of myself and my work. Barry Schwartz has been a treasured friend and I am grateful for his encouragement, wisdom and wit and for giving me copious sage advice about how to shepherd this book from the earliest spark of an idea to the end.

I would like to acknowledge my appreciation for my many

friends and fellow psychologists, for being there intellectually and emotionally: Andrew Ward (first as always), Larry Rosenblum, Shelly Gable, Ed Diener, Becky Collins, Robert Biswas-Diener, Danae Aitchison, Terry Johnson, Carol van Heerden, and many others. Countless thanks are also due to my fabulous students, current and former, without whom none of this research would have been possible (in chronological order): Kari Tucker, Fazilet Kasri, Lorie Sousa, Allison Abbe, Chris Tkach, Rene Dickerhoof and Julia Boehm. Finally, I am indebted to two friends and department chairs who have supported me unreservedly: David Funder and Glenn Stanley.

Writing this book was a (surprisingly) painless experience and oftentimes even a fun and thrilling one. This was undoubtedly true because of the fantastic direct and indirect help and encouragement I reaped from the terrific team at Penguin Press - the most talented, expert, professional and supportive group of individuals. The only place to start is by acknowledging my immense gratitude to my US editor at Penguin Press, the unparalleled Ann Godoff, who is brilliant, irreverent and wise. I also had the great fortune to work with four senior editors: Joanne Dickinson and Sarah Rustin, my thoughtful UK editors at Little, Brown; Emily Loose, who was the first to recognize the promise of my ideas and to help launch them, and especially Vanessa Mobley, who has been indefatigable in her efforts towards improving the book and unstinting with her assistance, advice and a bounty of thoughtful and penetrating feedback. Late in the publishing process, but certainly not least, Tracy Locke has been a superb Associate Publisher.

Richard Pine deserves his own paragraph. I know lots of people say that theirs is the best agent in the world, but they are wrong. Richard *is* the best agent in the world. Without his manifold virtuosity, this book would have been a figment of my imagination and I would certainly not have stumbled on the fabulous Penguin Press.

A number of individuals read drafts of chapters and made valuable suggestions. My sincere thanks go to Dianne Fewkes and Lisa

Terry, for giving me honest and discerning feedback from the layperson perspective; to Jennifer Aaker, for her astute suggestions, always made with humility and humour; to Julia Boehm, Irene Chang and Crystal Schmidt, for conducting and writing up interviews; to the students of my Fall 2005 Psychology 148 class ('The Psychology of Happiness and Virtue'), for sharing their stories and insights; and to a score of incredibly smart, capable and industrious research assistants, starting with Jessica Geleng and Andrea LaPlante and continuing with Danielle O'Brien, Sapna Mendon, Kimberly Hazelwood, Adrienne Grant, Valerie Laws, Nesha Sharma, Ligia Ceja, Lisa McMoran and Yazmin Perez.

Although money may not make people as happy as they might think, it positively improves research. I extend my gratitude to the National Institute of Mental Health, the Templeton Positive Psychology Prize and the University of California for their generous funding for a great portion of my work.

Finally, some extra special thanks. To my parents and brother, for always being there for me, and to my two awesome sisters-in-law. To Peter Del Greco: Although my appreciation, love and admiration may go without saying (at least publicly), I say them anyway. Peter is many things, but, with respect to the writing of this book, he has been my editor, my moral support, and, most of all (as some of my friends have pointed out), the greatest husband ever. Finally, saving the best for last, I thank my two young children, who will understand one day that they are not just the hows of my abundant happiness, but the whats, whens, wheres and whys.

Introduction

All of us want to be happy, even if we don't admit it openly or choose to cloak our desire in different words. Whether our dreams are about professional success, spiritual fulfilment, a sense of connection, a purpose in life, or love and sex, we covet those things because ultimately we believe that they will make us happier. Yet few of us truly appreciate just how much we can improve our happiness or know precisely how to go about doing it. To step back and consider your deep-seated assumptions about how to become a happier person and whether it's even possible for you – what I hope this book will spur you to do – is to understand that becoming happier is realizable, that it's in your power, and that it's one of the most vital and momentous things that you can do for yourself and for those around you.

What are the meanings and mysteries of happiness? Is it possible to acquire more of it, and can new happiness ever endure? These are fundamental questions to which I have devoted my entire career as a research psychologist. When I was beginning my investigations, as a twenty-two-year-old psychology graduate student, the study of well-being wasn't a well-regarded choice, the subject matter considered elusive, unscientific, 'soft' and 'fuzzy'. But recently happiness has exploded as a hot topic in the social science community – a symptom, perchance, of the Western twenty-first century individualistic zeitgeist.

Alas, has happiness today become a fad, like hula hoops, big hair-dos and Fonzie? It can certainly appear so, with the market saturated with newspaper and magazine pieces, television documentaries, books, quotes, blogs and podcasts on the topic, the vast majority of which are relatively uninformed by empirical data. Not infrequently, this frenzy drives researchers like myself to want to keep a distance, yet I think it's essential to engage in the discussion about happiness and insist that it abide by strict scientific standards. Why? Because I believe deeply in the importance and consequence of the scientific study of happiness and well-being. The majority of people in the world, across vast continents and cultures, profess that being happy is one of their most cherished goals in life – for themselves and, above all, for their children. What's more, happiness offers myriad rewards – not just for the happy person, but for his or her family, workplace, community, nation and society. Working on how to become happier, the research suggests, will not only make a person *feel* better, it will boost his or her energy, creativity and immune system, foster better relationships, fuel higher productivity at work and even lead to a longer life.[1] Happiness, in my humble opinion, is the Holy Grail – 'the meaning and the purpose of life', as Aristotle famously said, 'the whole aim and end of human existence.'

The science of happiness deserves to be more than a fad. Striving to be happy is a serious, legitimate and worthy aim. If you consult the ancient texts in history, literature or philosophy, you'll also find that it's eternal. Many of us suffer, and many more feel empty and unfulfilled, yet to attain more joy, less anguish, more tranquillity and less insecurity is a venerable goal. I have been conducting research in this field for eighteen years, initially as a doctoral student at Stanford University and then and now as a professor at the University of California, Riverside. In the intervening years, I have seen the science of happiness grow as part of a movement called 'positive psychology', the psychology of what makes life worth living. The label comes from the conviction that empowering people to develop a positive state of mind – to live the most rewarding and happiest life they can – is just as important as psychology's traditional focus on repairing their weaknesses and healing their pathologies. The focus on flourishing and fulfilment may seem like a wise and obvious choice, yet psychology for the last half of the twentieth century had been fixated on disease, disorder and the negative side of life.[2]

The goals of today's psychologists are grander and more ambitious. During the past ten years, psychological science has made tremendous advances in knowledge not only about how to treat depression, that is, how to lift people from feeling terrible to feeling good, but also how to elevate them to *feeling great*. We're in a new era, each month witnessing hot-off-the-presses publications about how to achieve and sustain happiness, how to make life more fulfilling, more productive and more enjoyable. Unfortunately, these findings are typically disseminated formally and informally only among scientists, or else published in technical academic journals subscribed by universities and lying beyond the reach of the non-expert. In this book, I have assembled and interpreted the discoveries about how to become happier, using them as jumping off points to teach skills that people can use to shift to a higher and sustainable level of well-being.

Allow me temporary licence to make some lofty claims. First, the star of *The How of Happiness* is science, and the happiness-increasing strategies that I and other social psychologists have developed are its key supporting players. My story is that of a research scientist, not a clinician, life coach or self-help guru. To my knowledge, this is the first 'how-to-become-happier' book authored by someone who has actually conducted research revealing how people can achieve a greater sense of happiness in their lives. Friends and colleagues have urged me to write this book for many years, but only now do I believe that the scientific advances in the field are solid and rigorous enough to interpret and translate into specific recommendations. As a result, *The How of Happiness* is different from many self-help books as it represents a distillation of what researchers of the science of happiness, including myself, have uncovered in their empirical investigations. Every suggestion that I offer is supported by scientific research; if evidence is mixed or lacking on a particular subject, I plainly say so. Notes and references are provided for all theories, statistics or original research. If you are interested in any specific topic area in these pages and aspire to pursue it more deeply, the notes will tell you where to go. If you find such interruptions distracting, feel free to disregard them.

Why should readers care about whether the advice they read in self-help books is supported by science? Because empirical research holds multiple advantages over anecdotal or clinical observations. By applying the scientific method, researchers have the ability to disentangle cause and effect and to study a phenomenon systematically, without biases or preconceptions. Thus, if a magazine article proclaims that daily meditations make people happier or that a natural herb alleviates headaches, only with a true double-blind experiment in which participants are randomly assigned to the 'meditation' (or 'natural herb') condition and others to a control group can it be determined whether these claims are true. Although science is imperfect, we can be much more confident in its conclusions than those of a single individual proffering advice based on his or her limited experience and assumptions.

A newspaper reader once wrote the following eloquent letter to the editor, on the subject of science:

> There are questions of faith, such as 'Does God exist?' There are questions of opinion, such as 'Who is the greatest baseball player of all time?' There are debate questions, such as 'Should abortion be legal?' And then there are questions that can be answered to a degree of certainty by the application of the scientific method, which are called empirical questions – in other words, those that can be largely settled by the evidence.[3]

Whether it's possible to learn how to become lastingly happier and how exactly you can go about doing so turns out to be just such an empirical question. My friend and research collaborator, Ken Sheldon, and I received a grant for over $1 million from the National Institute of Mental Health to fund research on the possibility of becoming happier. Along with a team of gifted graduate students, Ken and I have been using this grant to conduct so-called 'happiness interventions' – a scientific term we use to refer not to confrontations with addicts but to experiments that aim to find out which happiness-boosting strategies are effective, and how and why. (Incidentally, both types of 'interventions' share the notion that for major change to happen, a break with the status quo must be achieved.) Our research from such experimental interventions suggests, as you will soon learn in these pages, that enjoying a real increase in your own happiness is in fact attainable, *if* you are prepared to do the work. If you make a decision to be happier in your life – and you understand that this is a weighty decision that will take effort, commitment and a certain amount of discipline – know that you can make it happen.

Merriam-Webster's Collegiate Dictionary (eleventh edition) lists the first, second and third definitions of the word *how* as follows: 1) In what matter or way; 2) for what reason: why; and 3) with what meaning: to what effect. *The How of Happiness* embraces each of these definitions in full. Above all, this is a book about *how* to become a happier person, supplying you with a roadmap – a dozen happiness-increasing strategies – for the manner or *way* to get there and for *how* to choose the strategies that fit you best. Further, understanding the precise *reasons* why the strategies are successful is just as important as knowing what they are and how to apply them optimally. Finally, the *meaning* and *effects* of being happier is another vital theme that I address.

Backed by the results of our work with thousands of research participants, I deliver in *The How of Happiness* a theory of the determinants of happiness, a unifying theory of a sort, which encapsulates for you, in one take, everything that scientists currently know about what makes people happy and the implications for attaining ever-greater well-being. In a sense, the many dribs and drabs you may have picked up about the subject of happiness from other sources converge meaningfully in this book into a single integrated whole. And essential to my idea that we can maximize our own happiness is the notion of the 40 per cent solution.

As it happens, 'The 40 per cent Solution' was one of this book's original titles, because it is effectively the tool that under-lies the promise of becoming happier – the answer to the question of *how* the realization of greater happiness is possible and what this book is essentially all about. Why 40 per cent? Because 40 per cent is that part of our happiness that it's in our power to *change* through how we act and how we think, that portion rep-resenting the potential for increased lasting happiness that resides in all of us. It's not a small number and it's not a huge number, but it's a reasonable and realistic number. *The How of Happiness* shows you *how* to apply that number to your own circumstances. However, instead of showing you how to move from the nega-tive range towards a neutral point – the aim of most therapies and treatments for depression – I will spotlight how to advance from your current (perhaps unrewarding) state (be it –8, –3 or +3) towards +6 or +8 or even higher.

This is how to read this book. Chapters 1 and 2 introduce you to the foundations of the how-to-be-happier programme described here – the theory behind the 40 per cent solution. These chapters lay out the principles and empirical evidence behind two funda-mental questions that we ask ourselves – how can we decide what will make us happier and how precisely should we go about making it happen? You will learn what most of us believe will make us happier, and in what ways we're wrong, and what scientists have shown *actually* determines happiness. In the 40 per cent solution lies a bounty of possibilities. Part I of the book will deliver you to that starting line.

At that point, you'll be geared up to begin introducing the thoughts and behaviours that will make you happier, but where to start? This is where Chapter 3 plays a decisive role. In this brief but important chapter, you will complete a diagnostic test that will flag which particular strategies will work to make you hap-pier. Establishing this outright will direct you to what to take away from the next part of the book, from Part II, which presents detailed analyses and concrete illustrations of twelve specific happiness-enhancing activities. The 'fit diagnostic' will lead you to those chapters detailing activities that apply specially to your personality, resources, goals and needs. Contrary to popular belief, there is no one secret to happiness, just as there is no one miracle diet that works for all. Each of us needs to determine which strategy, or set of strategies, will be most valuable, and once you have completed the fit diagnostic in Chapter 3, you are prepared and equipped to carry on. Find your best-fitting activities in Part II and begin the challenging but rewarding process of becoming a happier person.

That's not all. The last part of the book contains two vital chapters. Chapter 10 describes five important 'hows' behind abiding happiness, offering you insight into how and why the happiness strategies 'work'. We know from the field of medicine that patients who have a good understanding of the thinking behind a treatment are more likely to comply with the treatment and to benefit from it. The same logic applies here. Some of you might be tempted to skip this chapter, but you will be more successful in improving your own happiness, not to mention more erudite, if you read on. A final chapter worth reading, the Postscript ('If you are depressed'), is reserved for those of you who have been feeling sad or down during the last weeks. If this describes you, you may even want to read the Postscript first.

I must also pre-empt an observation I made while writing about the twelve happiness-enhancing strategies and it is this: Why do many of the most powerful happiness activities sound so, for lack of a better word, 'corny'? To be sure, some of us find exhortations to 'count your blessings', 'live in the present', 'commit random acts of kindness', 'look on the bright side' or 'smile!' trivial at best and corny at worst. Yet, as I will plainly illustrate, these strategies, when practised in effortful and optimal ways, have been borne out in numerous studies to be incredibly effective. Why aren't they hip then? Why don't people shout them from mountain peaks and rooftops?

One reason, perhaps, is that such potent and complex happiness recommendations are not easily condensed or drawn down to their essence. *Of course*, we would all be happier if we truly and sincerely felt gratitude for our health, our families, friends, homes and jobs, even when those things are imperfect. But, somehow, boiling down this behaviour to 'you'll be so much more content if you just counted your blessings' makes the suggestion sound like a silly platitude. Alternatively, it may be that when we translate into a universal maxim something so personal, so close to the bone as how we wish to be or how we behave towards our loved ones, the outcome sounds clichéd.

Last but not least, some people associate happiness-enhancing strategies with people who seem to be too cheery to be real. When I was in high school, I had a friend whose bedroom was adorned (to the horror of my fifteen-year-old self) with Pollyanna-like assertions ('I ♥ Life', 'Never Give Up', etc.) beneath photos of cuddly kittens and dazzling sunsets. Of course, now I look at some of those quotes, which I used to think were so trite, and notice that they are powerful enough to include in my book. My point is that you don't have to hang quotations about happiness on your walls or agree with the exact locution of some of the phrases I employ here to experience the impact of what I am trying to impart. Above all, understand that there are many faces of happiness aside from the ubiquitous smiley face and the inspirational poster. The face of happiness may be someone who is intensely curious and enthusiastic about learning, it may be someone who is engrossed in plans for his next five years, it may be someone who can distinguish between the things that matter and the things that don't, it may be someone who looks forward each night to reading to her child. Some happy people may appear outwardly cheerful or transparently serene, and others are simply busy. In other words, we all have the potential to be happy, each in our own way. Yet what I hope you'll come to appreciate from reading this book is the notion that the basic strategies for improving happiness in our day-to-day lives are less daunting than you might once have thought.

Growing up in both Russia and the United States, I've known some very unhappy people in my life. I've also witnessed more than one friend become – and remain – genuinely happier as she grew, changed and matured. This book is the product of years of thinking, reading and conducting research on how each of us can accomplish this feat. Whether you personally yearn to become happier, or know someone who does, or you are intellectually curious about what scientists currently understand about the causes and potential for abiding well-being, I hope you will be enriched and enlightened by these pages.

PART I

~

'To change one's life, start immediately, do it flamboyantly, no exceptions.'

WILLIAM JAMES

~

Chapter 1

Is it possible to become happier?

What do you think would make you happier? Take a moment to consider. Might it be:

- A relationship?
- More flexibility at work?
- A new job that better provides for you and your family?
- An extra bedroom?
- A more attentive spouse?
- A baby?
- Looking younger?
- Relief from your bad back?
- Losing weight?
- Your child excelling at school?
- Knowing what you really want to do with your life?
- More supportive, loving parents?
- Cure from a chronic illness or disability?
- More money?
- More time?

If your answers look anything like these, all of which friends have confided to me over the years, you're in for a surprise. None of these things will make you substantially happier. But this doesn't mean that the goal of finding lasting happiness is unrealistic or naïve. The catch is that we tend to look for happiness in the wrong places. What we *believe* would make a huge difference in our lives actually – scientific research shows – makes only a small difference, while we overlook the true sources of personal happiness and well-being.

In almost every nation – from the United States, Greece and Slovenia to South Korea, Argentina and Bahrain – when asked what they want most in life, people put happiness at the top of their lists.[1] Learning how to be happier is critical for those of us who are currently depressed or low, and it may be invaluable to everyone. In this book, I will show you why our desire to be happier isn't just a pipe dream.

A programme for lasting happiness

You may have picked up this book because you believe that you are not living up to your potential in your personal or working life, or perhaps you are not as happy and fulfilled as you yearn to be. Nationally representative samples of adults in the USA indicate that slightly more than half of Americans (54 per cent) are 'moderately mentally healthy' yet not flourishing – that is, they lack great enthusiasm for life and are not actively and productively engaged with the world.[2] This explains why the desire to be happier is felt not just by the clinically depressed, but by a wide range of us, from those of us who are not as happy as we'd like to be, who sense that we're not quite thriving, to those who may be doing quite well yet want more – more joy, more meaning in life, more stimulating relationships and jobs. Finally, some of us may have once known true happiness but feel powerless to bring that moment back.

This sense of languishing or having 'fallen in a hole' or being 'in a rut' can be daunting. We may feel that it would take a staggering amount of energy and stamina to pull ourselves up. But I have hopeful news. The 'work' to heave yourself out of the hole and onto higher ground can start out very small and will often yield immediate results. In one study, University of Pennsylvania professor Martin Seligman taught a single happiness-enhancing strategy to a group of severely depressed people – that is, those whose depression scores put them in the most extremely depressed category. Although these individuals had great difficulty even leaving their beds, they were instructed to log onto a website and engage in a simple exercise. The exercise involved recalling and writing down three good things that happened every day, for example, 'Rosalind called to say hello', 'I read a chapter of a book my therapist recommended', and 'The sun finally came out today'. Within fifteen days, their depression lifted from 'severely depressed' to 'mildly to moderately depressed' and 94 per cent of them experienced relief.[3]

So, you see, research suggests that the initial steps to becoming happier can be implemented straight away. The first step involves recognizing that our yearning to increase our happiness is not just wishful thinking. It is a vitally important goal, one that we all have a right to pursue and the wherewithal to achieve. Happiness isn't a knock of good fortune that we must await, like the end of the rainy season. Neither is it something that we must 'find', like a motorway exit or a lost wallet, if only we knew the secret path and if only we could acquire the right job or the right boyfriend. Interestingly, the notion that happiness must be found is so pervasive that even the familiar phrase 'pursuit of happiness' implies that happiness is an object that one has to chase or discover. I don't like that phrase. I prefer to think of the 'creation' or 'construction' of happiness, because research shows that it's in our power to fashion it for ourselves.

You will learn in these pages that achieving lasting happiness does not necessarily require (as a psychotherapist might tell you) digging deep into your childhood, psychoanalyzing your past traumatic experiences, or dissecting your habitual ways of relating to others. Nor is it essential to secure a bigger salary, to obtain a cure from illness or to recapture youth or beauty. In this book, I describe strategies that you can start doing right away and that will immediately boost your feelings of well-being, even if you are deeply despondent. To continue accruing happiness-boosting benefits, you will need to embark on a longer-term programme. The good news about a life-long plan to build and sustain personal happiness is that the effort to do so is greatest when the new behaviours and practices you'll learn don't yet feel 'natural', but, with time, the required effort diminishes, as such strategies become habitual and self-reinforcing. *The How of Happiness* describes an ongoing happiness-enhancing programme that you might choose to begin today and undertake for the rest of your life. The only person who has the power to make it happen is *you*.

A final note: If you've been diagnosed with depression, this happiness programme isn't meant to replace established treatments such as cognitive-behavioural therapy and antidepressant medication. But you should consider it a potent complement, which might help you feel better sooner, stronger and longer. See the final chapter, 'If you are depressed', for more.

Do you know what makes you happy?

At this point, you may be feeling sceptical about the happiness programme I'm describing. If permanently boosting our happiness is so attainable why, you might ask, are we so poor at it? Why do we try so often and fail? The prime reason, I suspect, is because we have been conditioned to believe that the wrong things will make us lastingly happy. Psychological scientists have amassed persuasive evidence that we are routinely off base about what will bring us pleasure and fulfilment and, as a result, we sometimes work to make things happen that don't actually make us happy.[4] Perhaps the most common error is that we assume that positive events – be they promotions at work, clean bills of health, hot dates or victories by our preferred political candidate or football team – will provide much more happiness than they really do. Take materialism as an example. Why is it so hard for us (even myself!) to believe that money really doesn't make us happy? Because the truth is that money *does* make us happy. But our misunderstanding, as one happiness researcher eloquently explains, is that, 'we think money will bring lots of happiness for a long time, and actually it brings a little happiness for a short time'.[5] Meanwhile, in our effortful pursuit of such dead ends to pleasure, we end up ignoring other, more effective routes to well-being.

Consider the cases of two people I interviewed who realized that the things most of us think create happiness – wealth, fame, beauty – don't really matter all that much.

Rock Star

I was introduced to Neil one summer during the filming of a documentary about the lives of very happy people.[6] Neil had wanted to be a rock star when he was young, and, against all odds, he actually achieved his dream. As the drummer for a successful folk-rock group, he made a fortune, appeared on *Saturday Night Live*, was nominated for several Grammy Awards, and, for a decade, travelled the continents, touring with the band. Then, his world abruptly collapsed. The band broke up, the touring stopped, he lost the big house, and his wife left him.

We spent an entire afternoon interviewing Neil at his new modest ranch-style home, with a big pile of dirt blocking the front. The single father and his two small children live on the outskirts of Winnipeg, Canada, in sparsely settled prairie country, miles away from the nearest shop or school. Even in July, the wind was brisk when we visited, setting the tall dry grasses blowing. It struck me as the kind of place that must be bitter cold and desolate during the long Manitoba winters. A trip for milk, let alone a day out, must be hard to manage.

Neil immediately struck me as a person completely comfortable and at peace with himself, genuine and at ease with his children, and fully engaged in his music. Did being a wealthy rock star make Neil very happy? 'I had it, the money and fame,' he said, 'and now I don't, but my happiness level is the same. There is no difference.'

Extreme Makeover

I met Denise on the set of a talk show where she came to tell her story. Denise lives in St Petersburg, Florida. She used to teach high school kids with learning disabilities and now stays at home with her three school-aged children. It's not easy to be a full-time mother of three kids. And, as she was turning forty, Denise felt that she had let herself go as she didn't wear make-up, stopped working out and looked tired all the time. Years spent under the scorching Florida sun had made her look wrinkly, she believed, and much older than her age. She put in an application for *Extreme Makeover* and, to her delight, made it on the show.

The surgery took twelve hours. Denise had an eye lift, an upper and lower forehead lift, and a full face lift. A bump was taken out of her nose, liposuction done under her chin, and laser resurfacing on her face. The cosmetic changes were so well-executed and seamless that the show's make-up artist, who spent at least half an hour working on Denise's face, was floored when I told her that Denise had been on *Extreme Makeover*. She hadn't noticed anything unusual about her reconstructed face!

After the surgical makeover, Denise felt that she had travelled back in time – she looked ten years younger. She received a lot of attention from family, friends, strangers, media. 'I think I was caught up with that,' she says. 'I had lived like a movie star and my confidence went overboard.' She considered leaving her husband and starting a new life.

A year later, Denise came to her senses and realized that giving up her marriage would have been a huge mistake. Did the plastic surgery make her happier? 'I do have to say it's nice to have fewer wrinkles,' Denise confesses. But it didn't make her happier in the long run. 'The makeover is nothing compared to *real* happiness.'

Neil and Denise may have once thought, 'If only I were rich . . . If only I were famous . . . If only I were beautiful,' I would be happy. And they would have been wrong. Intuitions such as theirs, combined with an avalanche of research evidence, have been formalized by my colleagues and myself into a theory of the causes of happiness. The story begins in an unlikely Mayan Riviera village.

Discovering the real keys to happiness

Positive psychology in Akumal

In January 2001, I travelled to a beautiful, serene resort in a small town in Mexico, two hours outside of Cancun, called Akumal. There, under a palapa and warm breezes, about a dozen or so researchers in the then-budding field of positive psychology gathered to share their latest findings and brainstorm new ideas. It was hard for me to concentrate at first, as I had left my twenty-month-old daughter behind with her dad in Los Angeles and, furthermore, had just found out that I was pregnant again. Nevertheless, several conversations that I had in Akumal ended up transforming the shape and direction of my work. One of those conversations was with fellow professors Ken Sheldon and David Schkade. I had e-mailed them before the trip and asked if we could meet to talk about writing an article that would categorize the different ways that people pursue happiness. Sitting together, however, we rapidly realized that almost no empirical research existed on this subject. Not only were researchers generally unaware of what strategies people use to become happier, but it became apparent to us that most psychologists were pessimistic about the very notion of permanently increasing happiness. Namely, two findings had caught the imagination of the academic community at that time: first, that happiness is heritable and extremely stable over the course of people's lives and, second, that people have a remarkable capacity to become inured to any positive changes in their lives. Consequently, the logic went, people cannot be made lastingly happier because any gains in happiness would be temporary and, in the long term, most cannot help but return to their original or 'baseline' levels of well-being.

The 40 per cent solution

Ken, David and I were sceptical of the conclusion that lasting happiness was impossible and determined to prove that it was wide of the mark. The result of our discussions over the next few years was a discovery about the causes of well-being. Together, we were essentially able to identify the most important factors determining happiness, represented in the following simple pie chart.[7]

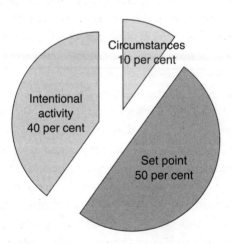

What determines happiness?

Imagine a cinema full of 100 people. These 100 individuals represent the full continuum of happiness – some are exceptionally happy, others less so, and others are terribly unhappy. The lower right slice of the pie shows that an astounding 50 per cent of the differences between people's happiness levels can be accounted for by their genetically determined 'set points'. This discovery comes from growing research done with identical and fraternal twins that suggests that each of us is born with a particular 'happiness set point' that originates from our biological mother or father or both – a baseline or potential for happiness to which we are bound to return, even after major setbacks or triumphs.[8] This means that if, with a magic wand, we could turn all 100 of the cinema-goers into genetic 'clones' (or identical twins) of one another, they *still* would differ in their happiness levels, but those differences would be reduced by 50 per cent.

The set point for happiness is similar to the set point for weight. Some people are blessed with a 'skinny disposition' – even when they're not trying, they easily maintain their weight.[9] By contrast, others have to work extraordinarily hard to keep their weight at a desirable level and, the moment they slack off even a bit, the pounds creep back on. The implication of this finding for happiness is that, like genes for intelligence or cholesterol, the magnitude of the set point we are born with – that is, whether it is high (a 6 on a 7-point scale) or low (a 2) or in-between (a 4) – governs to a large extent how happy we will be over the course of our lives.

Perhaps the most counterintuitive finding is that, as the chart shows, only about 10 per cent of the variance in our happiness levels is explained by differences in life circumstances or situations – that is, whether we are rich or poor, healthy or unhealthy, beautiful or plain, married or divorced, etc.[10] If, with a magic wand, we could put all 100 cinema-goers into the same set of circumstances (same house, same spouse, same place of birth, same face, same aches and pains), the differences in their happiness levels would be reduced by a measly additional 10 per cent.

A great deal of science backs up this conclusion. For example, a well-known study demonstrated that the richest Americans – those earning more than $10 million annually – report levels of personal happiness only slightly greater than the office staff and blue collar workers they employ.[11] And, although married people are happier than single ones, the effect of marriage on personal happiness is actually quite small – for example, in sixteen countries, 25 per cent of married people and 21 per cent of singles described themselves as 'very happy'.[12] This discovery that the circumstances of our lives (like income and marital status) have such little bearing on our well-being is astonishing to many of us, though Neil and Denise would probably not be surprised. It may be hard to believe that such things as riches, beauty and perfect health have only a short-term and limited influence on achieving happiness, but the evidence is formidable and I will offer several intriguing explanations for it later in this book. If we can accept as true that life circumstances are *not* the keys to happiness, we'll be greatly empowered to pursue happiness for ourselves.

Getting back to the pie chart – even if the 100 people in the cinema were all identical twins *and* they all had identical life situations, they *still* would differ in how happy they are. This finding suggests to me that even after we take into account our genetically determined personality (i.e., who we are) *and* the rich and complex circumstances of our lives (i.e., what we face), 40 per cent of the differences in our happiness levels are still left unexplained. What makes up this 40 per cent? There is one critical thing left: our behaviour. Thus, the key to happiness lies *not* in changing our genetic make-up (which is impossible) and *not* in changing our circumstances (i.e., seeking wealth or attractiveness or better colleagues, which is usually impractical), but in our daily 'intentional activities'. With this in mind, our pie chart illustrates the potential of the 40 per cent that is within our ability to control – 40 per cent for room to manoeuvre, for opportunities to increase or decrease our happiness levels through what we *do* in our daily lives and how we *think*.

This is terrific news. It means that all of us *could* be a great deal happier, if we scrutinize carefully what precise behaviours and thoughts very happy people naturally and habitually engage in. Our untapped potential for increasing our own happiness is precisely what much of my research has focused on – systematically observing, comparing and experimenting on very happy and unhappy people. Below is a sample of my observations, as well as

those of other researchers, of the thinking and behaviour patterns
of the happiest participants in our studies.

- They devote a great amount of time to their family and
  friends, nurturing and enjoying those relationships.
- They are comfortable expressing gratitude for all they have.
- They are often the first to offer a helping hand to
  co-workers and passers-by.
- They practise optimism when imagining their futures.
- They savour life's pleasures and try to live in the present
  moment.
- They make physical exercise a weekly – and sometimes
  daily – habit.
- They are deeply committed to life-long goals and
  ambitions (e.g., fighting fraud, building cabinets, or
  teaching their children their deeply held values).
- And, last but not least, the happiest people do have their
  share of stresses, crises and even tragedies. They may
  become just as distressed and emotional in such
  circumstances as you or I, but their secret weapon is the
  poise and strength they show in coping in the face of
  challenge.

As I discuss at greater length in Chapters 4 to 9, a now-massive
literature reveals what kinds of attributes, thoughts and behaviours
characterize the happiest people.[13] In my laboratory and that of
a few others, ways of harnessing the power of our own thoughts
and behaviours, that is, our intentional activities, have been
tested. We have conducted formal happiness-increasing 'intervention' studies devised to increase and maintain a person's
happiness level *over and above his or her set point*.[14] In Part II of this
book, I will introduce a dozen happiness-increasing strategies and
practices in detail, showing how they work in everyday life and
also describing the scientific evidence supporting them. The list
of things that very happy people do every day, sampled above,
may look intimidating, but that is because you do not, and should

not, try to be all those things. No one can do it all and the rare person can achieve the greater part. What you *can* do is select just one strategy (or a few) that will work for you. *You* are in control and can impact your life beginning today in a significant and meaningful way.

To fashion a successful set of strategies for your individualized happiness programme, a vital requirement is wise selection. As with any life-changing endeavour, some programmes will be more effective and more appropriate for particular individuals than for others. In Chapter 3, I will introduce an important self-diagnostic test, essentially a questionnaire that will help you identify which strategies will work best for you. Chapter 3 will assist you in *choosing* the four happiness-boosting strategies that fit your individual personality, your strengths, your goals and your current situation. Remember that the endeavour to become happier is about *you* – your interests, your values and your needs. Once you learn which activity will work best for you, you're more than halfway there.

The most rewarding 'work' you'll ever do

It may be obvious that to achieve anything substantial in life – learn a profession, master a sport, raise a child – a good deal of effort is required. But many of us find it difficult to apply the notion of effort to our emotional or mental lives. Without effort, we might 'get lucky', but, like a long forgotten New Year's resolution, the success will be short-lived.

Consider how much time and commitment many people devote to physical exercise, whether it's going to the gym, jogging, kickboxing or yoga. My research reveals that if you desire greater happiness, you need to go about it in a similar way. In other words, becoming lastingly happier demands making some permanent changes that require effort and commitment every day of your life. Pursuing happiness takes work, but, consider that this 'happiness work' may be the most rewarding work you'll ever do.

Why be happy?

Why should we put forth all this effort in order to be happier? In case anyone needed convincing, the scientific evidence reveals many compelling reasons to aspire to greater happiness and fulfilment. My collaborators Ed Diener, Laura King and I have documented a large and growing psychological literature showing that becoming happier doesn't just make you feel good.[15] It turns out that happiness brings with it multiple fringe benefits. Compared to their less happy peers, happier people are more sociable and energetic, more charitable and cooperative, and better liked by others. Not surprisingly then, happier people are more likely to get married and to stay married, and to have a richer network of friends and social support. Furthermore, contrary to Woody Allen's suggestion in *Annie Hall* that happy people are 'shallow and empty, and . . . have no ideas and nothing interesting to say,' they actually show more flexibility and ingenuity in their thinking and are more productive in their jobs. They are better leaders and negotiators and earn more money. They are more resilient in the face of hardship, have stronger immune systems and are physically healthier. Happy people even live longer.

Consider just two of the examples from above – money and marriage. Comedian Henny Youngman once quipped, 'What good is happiness? It can't buy money.' He was very funny, but he was wrong. One study has shown that those who were happy as first-year university undergraduates had higher salaries *sixteen years later* (in their mid-thirties) without an initial wealth advantage.[16] In another study, which also followed American undergraduates over time, women who expressed sincere joy in their college yearbook photos were relatively more likely to be married by age twenty-seven and more likely to have *satisfying* marriages at age fifty-two.[17]

Indeed, happiness is so important that an entire country – admittedly a very small country, the size of Switzerland – has made its goal to increase the well-being of its citizens. The King of Bhutan, the last Buddhist kingdom in the Himalayas, nestled between India and China, decided that the best way to foster economic development would be to boost his nation's Gross Domestic Happiness rather than GDP. Bhutan's emphasis on the happiness of its people above all else appears to have produced society-wide benefits. Although most people in this tiny country are subsistence farmers, they have what they need – food on the table and universal health care – and have refused to make money from commercial ventures that might compromise the health and beauty of their environment and their egalitarian existence.

In sum, across all the domains of life, happiness appears to have numerous positive by-products that few of us have taken the time to really understand. In becoming happier, we not only boost experiences of joy, contentment, love, pride and awe, but we also improve other aspects of our lives – our energy levels, our immune systems, our engagement with work and with other people, and our physical and mental health. In becoming happier, we also bolster our feelings of self-confidence and self-esteem, we come to truly believe that we are worthy human beings, deserving of respect. A final, and perhaps least appreciated, plus is that if we become happier, we benefit not only ourselves, but also our partners, families, communities and even society at large.

Chapter 2

How happy are you, and why?

Have you ever known someone who is deeply and genuinely happy? A person who truly has the ability to see the world through rose-coloured glasses? Someone who appears composed and untroubled even in the face of adversity? Perhaps it is a friend or a co-worker or even a member of your family. It's hard not to envy those people. How do they do it? Why aren't they bothered or distraught by the strains and ordeals of everyday life, like most of us?

It's especially frustrating and perplexing to be around such individuals when they're in the same difficult or troubling situation as we are, but seem happy in spite of it. Say, for example, that you both share a tormenting boss, a screamer who is never satisfied with your work. Or, you are both in the first year of law school and are loaded down with a crushing amount of reading and homework. Or, you are both new parents and overwhelmed with the sleep deprivation, anxiety and drudgery of caring for a newborn. Such situations drag you down, making you moody, nerve-racked and sometimes even terribly unhappy and low. But this happy person you know seems able to brush off the frustrations, the stresses, the hardships and the disappointments, to pick herself up each time and to put on a positive face. She sees challenge where you see only threat. She takes an uplifting, optimistic perspective when you feel distrustful and beaten down. She is galvanized to take action, while you are sluggish and passive.

Such individuals may be mind-boggling and intimidating and, yes, even off-putting at times. They can be demoralizing because they make us wonder about our own disposition. How can we be more like them? Can we ever be as happy as they are? I've asked myself that question too, and decided that the only way to find out is to do some research and study genuinely happy people systematically and intensively. By closely observing them, we can learn a great deal not just about them, but about ourselves. In my interviews and experiments with very happy people, I've even found a few who remain happy, or are able to recover their happiness fairly quickly, after a tragedy or major setback. Take the cases of Angela and Randy, for example.

Angela

Angela is thirty-four and one of the happiest people that I ever interviewed.[1] You wouldn't guess it, however, from all she's had to bear. When Angela was growing up in Southern California, her mother was emotionally and physically abusive to her, and her father did nothing to intervene. In addition to what she endured at home, she was overweight as a teenager and stigmatized at school. When Angela was in eleventh grade [about sixteen], her mother was diagnosed with breast cancer and the physical abuse ended. However, the emotional abuse only got worse, until Angela couldn't stand it any longer and moved out to marry a man she'd known for only three months. She and her new husband moved up north and lived there for four years. Soon after the birth of their daughter, Ella, they divorced and Angela moved back to California, where she still lives.

Angela is currently a single mother. Things are hard financially. Her ex-husband doesn't visit his daughter and pays no child support. To provide for her small family, Angela has taken a crack at several careers. During her last career change, she felt as though she had finally found her dream job (as a beauty therapist), but she was fired unexpectedly, her hopes and finances in ruins. She had to file for bankruptcy and go on welfare for a time. Right now, she is back in college full-time, working towards a degree in nursing.

Still, with all that has happened and all the challenges that have come to pass, Angela considers herself a very happy person. Her daughter Ella, to whom she is extremely close, brings her endless joy. They relish reading *Chronicles of Narnia* together, going to free concerts, and snuggling in bed watching videos. As Angela sees it, Ella doesn't always have what the other kids have, but she gets more love than she could possibly want. Angela also has an infectious sense of humour and, when she laughs about her troubles – the time on welfare, the day she lost her beloved job – it's impossible not to laugh along with her. She has made many friends, indeed, formed a whole community of like-minded people, and they are a pleasure and a support to her. She finds deep satisfaction in helping others heal from their own wounds and traumas, for, as she reasons, 'it's virtually impossible to face one's shadows alone'.

Randy

Like Angela, Randy endured a lot as a child. He lost two people close to him to suicide – his father at age twelve and his best friend at age seventeen. When he was in fifth grade [about ten years old in the US], his mother left his father and moved the family out of state and away from everyone he knew in order that she could live with her boyfriend, Roy. Although Randy's bond with his mother was, and still is, strong, Roy belittled Randy and their relationship was strained at best. Interestingly, much like Angela, Randy escaped his home life by marrying too soon and too young. His marriage was fraught with difficulty and finally ended when he discovered the extent of his wife's infidelities. Still, he was devastated initially by the break-up and felt that he had had more than his share of loss and death.

Today, Randy is one of those happy people who make everyone around them smile and laugh. He picked himself up after his divorce, moved to a new city, found work as a safety engineer, and eventually remarried. He is now forty-three, married for three years, and stepfather to three boys. How did he do it? Randy is an eternal optimist and claims that seeing the 'silver lining in the cloud' has always been his key to survival. For example, although some of his co-workers find their job frustrating and stressful, he says that it allows him 'to think outside the box'. Although a friend of his struggles with stepchildren, he is overjoyed by 'the opportunity to be a dad'. Indeed, one of his favourite activities is watching his sons play football. Although others might look back on their childhood with bitterness, he remembers the good times.

Where do you fit in?

Although they may appear special and unique, there are actually quite a few Randys and Angelas around. But, of course, there are many very unhappy individuals as well. All of us can identify people who are exactly the opposite, people who never seem to be happy, even during the good times, who are chronically sullen and sour, who accentuate the negative and focus on the down side of everything and who appear to be unable to find much joy in life.

Shannon

One such person I interviewed is Shannon. At twenty-seven, Shannon is studying for a certificate to teach English as a second language. She has a boyfriend, who's in school in Italy, and when he returns in two months, they plan on moving in together. Growing up, Shannon had an uneventful childhood, a stable and modest home, and several close friends. Her family did a lot of travelling all over the US. Shannon told me that when she was in eighth grade [year nine], her mother gave her a dog, Daisy, who is still alive today. Shannon considers the dog one of her best friends.

But despite the lack of tragedy or trauma in her life, Shannon seems to turn everything into a crisis. She found the transition from high school to college extremely stressful and often felt crushed and overwrought about the harder and less familiar workload. In the student residence, she shared a single room with a roommate, who was generally a nice person, but who nonetheless had irritating habits, like turning up the volume on the TV. Shannon was incredibly bothered by this and grew more and more distant and hostile towards her roommate. When Shannon was finally able to switch to a new roommate whom she liked and admired, she was ecstatic at first, but then became hurt that the other girl 'was never around'.

Today, Shannon is very active. She rock climbs and roller blades in the summer and snow boards and skis in the winter. She also told me that she enjoys teaching and feels there is mutual growth between herself and the children she currently tutors. So, on the surface, her life is quite good. She has a promising and enjoyable career ahead of her, a boyfriend, a stable family life, even a dog she loves. However, Shannon sees herself as a generally unhappy person. Although she is pleased with her academic achievements, she feels that she can't truly enjoy those achievements because of a lack of self-confidence. Indeed, she minimizes any success by explaining it away as due to luck or persistence. Furthermore, sometimes she is haunted by the feeling that she should have chosen a different career. Overall, Shannon feels very alone and believes her life to be unsteady and her relationships unreliable. She remembers her childhood fondly, as the only time she knew 'true happiness' and felt self-assured and carefree. Today, she depends a great deal on her boyfriend for positive feelings of self-worth, and experiences life as 'very lonely' when he's not around. She is prone to overspending and overeating at such times. When Shannon feels particularly insecure and hopeless, everything seems dark and she feels herself sinking into dejection and gloom.

The happiness continuum

Human happiness, like height or temperature or IQ, lies on a continuum – a numerical scale that ranges from very, very low to very, very high. Shannon represents the lower end of the happiness continuum. Randy and Angela are at the high end. All of us fit somewhere on that scale, and it is critical to find out exactly where that may be. No matter whether you are deeply depressed or are simply not as happy as you'd like to be, before you can begin the process of becoming happier, you need to determine your present personal happiness level, which will provide your first estimate of your happiness 'set point'.

From the Greek philosopher Aristotle to the father of psychoanalysis Sigmund Freud to *Peanuts* creator Charles Schulz, writers and thinkers have offered wide-ranging definitions of happiness. Aristotle wrote that happiness is 'an expression of the soul in considered actions', Freud voiced that it's a matter of *lieben und arbeiten* (to love and to work) and Schulz famously proclaimed that 'happiness is a warm puppy'. Most of us, however, are well aware of what happiness is and whether we are happy. To paraphrase the late US Supreme Court Justice Potter Stewart, happiness is like obscenity: we can't define it, but we know it when we see it.

I use the term 'happiness' to refer to the experience of joy, contentment or positive well-being, combined with a sense that one's life is good, meaningful and worthwhile. However, most of us don't need a definition of happiness, as we instinctively know whether we are happy or not. Academic researchers prefer the term 'subjective well-being' (or simply 'well-being') as it sounds more scientific and does not carry the weight of centuries of historical, literary and philosophical subtexts.[2] I will use the terms happiness and well-being interchangeably.[3]

SUBJECTIVE HAPPINESS SCALE

Instructions: For each of the following statements and/or questions, please circle the number from the scale that you feel is most appropriate in describing you. (Carefully take note of the labels, or 'anchors', for the 1-to-7 scales, as they differ for each of the four items.)

1 In general, I consider myself:

| 1 | 2 | 3 | 4 | 5 | 6 | 7 |

a very   not a very

happy   happy

happy   person

person

2 Compared to most of my peers, I consider myself:

| 1 | 2 | 3 | 4 | 5 | 6 | 7 |

more   less

happy   happy

happy

3 Some people are generally very happy. They enjoy life regardless of what is going on, getting the most out of everything. To what extent does this characterization describe you?

| 1 | 2 | 3 | 4 | 5 | 6 | 7 |

great   not at   a

all   deal

4 Some people are generally not very happy. Although they are not depressed, they never seem as happy as they might be. To what extent does this characterization describe you?

| 1 | 2 | 3 | 4 | 5 | 6 | 7 |

at   a great   not

deal   all

How to calculate your score:

Step 1

Total = Item 1:___ + Item 2:___ + Item 3:___ + Item 4:___ = _____

So, how do you measure the degree to which you are a happy or an unhappy person? Because no appropriate 'happiness thermometer' exists, researchers generally rely on self-reports. In much of my research with human participants, I have used a popular, simple four-item measure of overall happiness that I developed, called the Subjective Happiness Scale.[4] The title is fitting, as happiness is inherently subjective and must be defined from the perspective of the person. No one but you knows or should tell you how happy you truly are. So, reply to the four items above to determine your current happiness level, which you will need to know before you can estimate your set point. (More on that later.)

As you may have gathered, the highest happiness score that you could get is a 7 (if you give yourself a 7 on all four items) and the lowest is a 1 (if you rate yourself a 1 on all four items). I have administered this scale to many different groups of people, as have other researchers, and the average score runs from about 4.5 to 5.5, depending on the group. College students tend to score lower (averaging a bit below 5) than working adults and older, retired people (who both average a 5.6).[5]

Now you have determined the value of your current happiness score. If you're past college age and your happiness score is lower than 5.6 or so, then you're less happy than the average person. Put another way, more than 50 per cent of people in your age group rate themselves higher on the scale. If your score is greater than 5.6, then you're happier than the average person. Of course, what the 'average person' is for you will depend on your gender, your age, your occupation, ethnicity, etc. But what's important to remember is that *no matter what your score is*, you can become happier.

Could you be depressed?

Some of us are likely to be not just slightly unhappy, but clinically or subclinically depressed. If your happiness score is 4 or lower or if you've been feeling down for more than a couple of weeks, I encourage you to complete a depression scale. (If not, then you may choose to skip this subsection.) The depression scale takes less than ten minutes and those minutes may turn out to be invaluable. Alternatively, make an appointment to see your GP who will ask you to complete a similar questionnaire which will determine if you are depressed.

Below is a standard, commonly used (in the US) depression questionnaire called the Center for Epidemiological Studies Depression scale, or CES-D.[6] There are many measures of depression, but this one is recommended for use with the general (i.e., non-clinical or non-psychiatric) population.[7] Follow the instructions to complete the scale and determine your overall depression score.

The lowest score that you could possibly get is a 0 and the highest is a 60. Psychologists use the cut-off score of 16 to differentiate depressed persons from non-depressed ones. So, if your score is 16 or higher, then you would be classified as depressed. Exactly *how* depressed depends on how high your score is – depression can range from quite mild (a score of 16 to 20) to moderate (a score of 21 to 25) to severe (a score of 26 to 60).[8] Furthermore, unlike the happiness scale, the depression scale is acutely sensitive to your moods and to your general mental state, so that you would be expected to obtain different depression scores at different time periods, even as close as two weeks apart.

If you are currently depressed, or if you've ever been depressed, you are not alone. Studies show that 15 per cent of people in the US (and 21 per cent of women[9]) will become clinically depressed at some point during their lifetimes.[10] (In the UK it is estimated that one in four women and one in ten men will suffer depression during their lifetime.) Of the rest, half report experiencing mild depression occasionally, usually as a result of a major setback or crisis, be it a broken heart, the death of a loved one, a career failure or a financial loss. Furthermore, the age at which people experience their first depressive episode has fallen dramatically during the last several decades.[11] Incredibly, of all diseases, depression places the largest burden on society in the United States

CENTER FOR EPIDEMIOLOGICAL STUDIES
DEPRESSION SCALE

Instructions: This set of questions is related to how you *felt or behaved* in the past week. Using the scale below, please write the number which best describes how often you felt or behaved this way *during the past week*.

0	1	2	3
rarely or none of the time (less than 1 day)	some or a little of the time (1–2 days)	a moderate amount of the time (3–4 days)	most or all of the time (5–7 days)

1 You were bothered by things that usually don't bother you. **0**

2 You did not feel like eating; your appetite was poor. **0**

3 You felt that you could not shake off the blues even with help from your family and friends. **1**

4 You felt that you were just as good as other people. (X) **1**

5 You had trouble keeping your mind on what you were doing. **0**

6 You felt depressed. **2**

7 You felt that everything you did was an effort. **1**

8 You felt hopeful about the future. (X) **1**

9 You thought your life had been a failure. **1**

10 You felt fearful. **0**

11 Your sleep was restless. **0**

12 You were happy. (X) **2**

13 You talked less than usual. **1**

14 You felt lonely. **1**

15 People were unfriendly. **1**

16 You enjoyed life. (X) **3**

17 You had crying spells. **1**

18 You felt sad. **1**

19 You felt that people disliked you. **0**

20 You could not get 'going'. **2**

How to calculate your score:

Step 1: Your scores on Items 4, 8, 12 and 16 (the ones marked with an X) should be 'reverse-scored' – that is, if you gave yourself a 0, cross it out and change it to a 3; if you gave yourself a 1, change that to a 2; change a 2 to a 1; and change a 3 to a 0.

Step 2: Using the changed scores for those four items, now add your scores for *all* the 20 items.

Your total depression score is _20_ Date: _8/11/16_____

Your total depression score is _____ Date: _____

Your total depression score is _____ Date: _____

(and the fourth largest disease burden in the world in terms of reduced years of healthy life, after perinatal conditions, lower respiratory diseases like chronic obstructive pulmonary disease, and HIV/AIDS).[12] The World Health Organization predicts that, by the year 2020, depression will be the second-leading cause of mortality in the entire world, affecting 30 per cent of all adults.[13]

Many experts believe that depression has become an epidemic.[14] By some estimates, clinical depression is ten times more likely to torment us now than it did a century ago.[15] Several forces may be behind this development. First, our expectations about what our lives should be like are greater than ever before. We believe that we can do anything and are profoundly disappointed when reality doesn't meet or even come close to perfection. Second, our increasingly individualistic culture leaves us all alone to manage our everyday stresses and problems, compelling us to blame only ourselves for our shortcomings and failures. Increasing job insecurity also contributes to the many stressors of modern life. And, perhaps most important, may be the unravelling of the social fabric. Compared to previous generations, we feel far less belonging and commitment to our families and communities and are thus less buffered by social support and strong meaningful connections to others. So, all of these factors may combine to make more of us clinically depressed than ever before.

If you have scored as depressed, I encourage you to see a mental health professional – a GP, psychiatrist, clinical psychologist, or licensed counsellor with whom you can discuss your options for treatment, including psychotherapy and antidepressant medication. Moderate to severe depression, especially, requires urgent attention from a professional. If you are depressed, you will also likely greatly benefit from the happiness-increasing strategies described in Part II of this book. Additionally, if you scored in the depressed range, be sure to skip ahead and read the Postscript chapter ('If you are depressed') before continuing to learn about those strategies, as you will need to know how to adapt the happiness programme specially to your unique symptoms, feelings and needs.

Happiness myths

No matter where you fall on the happiness and depression scales, whether you are rarely happy, occasionally happy, or even fairly happy, you will learn how to apply the happiness-enhancing strategies that I will teach you to your own strengths and weaknesses, in order to make yourself permanently happier and more fulfilled. But, before you can start incorporating those strategies into your own life, I need to dispel a number of myths surrounding happiness.

One of the great obstacles to attaining happiness is that most of our beliefs about what will make us happy are in fact erroneous. Yet they have been drummed into us, socialized by peers and families and role models and reinforced by the stories and images ever-present in our culture. Many of the presumed sources of happiness seem so intuitive and so commonsensical that all of us – even happiness researchers! – are prone to fall under their spell. This is where science can shine a clear and vivid light. The three major myths about happiness that we tend to fall for are plainly illuminated by the happiness pie chart on page 20.

Myth No. 1: Happiness must be 'found'

The first myth is that happiness is something that we must *find*, that it's out there somewhere, a place just beyond our reach, a kind of Shangri-La. We could get there, yes, but only if the right things would come to pass – if we'd marry our true love, secure our dream job, purchase an elegant home. Don't be the person who is waiting for this, that or the other thing to happen before she can be happy. There's a cartoon in which a little boy on a tricycle says to a playmate holding a kite, 'I can't wait to grow up and be happy.'[16] If you're not happy today, then you won't be happy tomorrow unless you take things into your own hands and take action. To understand that 40 per cent of our happiness is determined by intentional activity is to appreciate the promise of the great impact that you can make on your own life through intentional strategies that you can implement to remake yourself as a happier person.

So, happiness is not out there for us to find and discover. And the reason that it's not *out* there is that it's *inside* of us. As banal and clichéd as this might sound, happiness, more than anything, is a state of mind, a way of perceiving and approaching ourselves and the world in which we reside. So, if you want to be happy tomorrow, the day after, and for the rest of your life, you can do it by choosing to change and manage your state of mind. These steps lie at the heart of this book.

Myth No. 2: Happiness lies in changing our circumstances

Another big fallacy is the notion that if only something about the circumstances of our lives would change, only then would we be happy. This kind of thinking is what I call 'I would be happy IF ___' or 'I will be happy WHEN ___'. This logic is shared by some of us who remember periods in our lives when we experienced real happiness but feel that we could never recapture the exact set of circumstances that had brought this real happiness about. Perhaps these were the college years (as they were for me, at least in hindsight), or when we fell in love for the first time, or when our children were young, or when we lived abroad. The reality is that the elements that determined our happiness in the past – and can make for future happiness – are with us right now and are right here waiting to be taken advantage of. As we can see from the pie chart, changes in our circumstances, no matter how positive and stunning – actually have little bearing on our well-being.

Myth No. 3: You either have it or you don't

One day, my brother, who's an electrical engineer, told me that he read an article about Buddhist monks who taught themselves to be happy through meditation. 'What a new concept!' he exclaimed. 'I never thought you could *teach* yourself to be happy. I thought you either have it or you don't.' This notion that we are born happy or unhappy is ubiquitous. Many of us, especially those of us who are not very happy, believe that our unhappiness is genetic and there's really nothing we can do about it. To the contrary, growing research demonstrates persuasively that we can overcome our genetic programming.

In the rest of the chapter, we'll consider each of these fallacies more deeply. Let's start by examining exactly what it is that scientists have learned about the ways that the circumstances of our lives do and do not influence us.

The limits of life circumstances

Life circumstances include, to quote Herman Melville, 'the wife, the heart, the bed, the table, the saddle, the fireside, the country'. Consider the incidental but stable facts about your life: your gender, age and ethnicity; where you grew up; which significant events shaped your childhood and adolescence (e.g., on the negative side parental divorce, car accident, stigma, bullying; on the positive side family harmony, winning an award, being popular); and which significant events have taken place in adulthood. Are you married, single, divorced, widowed or separated? What is your occupation, income and religious affiliation? What kind of living conditions and neighbourhood do you live in? Have you ever been diagnosed with a chronic or acute illness? Or, as Shakespeare might ask, have you suffered the slings and arrows of outrageous fortune?

As significant as our major life events are to each of us, studies suggest that they actually determine – as the pie chart shows us – a tiny percentage of our happiness. The 10 per cent figure on the pie chart represents an average from many past investigations, which reveal that all life circumstances and situations put together account for only about 10 per cent of how happy different people are. So, although you may find it very hard to believe, whether you drive to work in a Lexus hybrid or a battered truck, whether you're young, old or have had wrinkle-removing plastic surgery, whether you live in a frigid or balmy climate – your chances of being happy and becoming happier are pretty much the same.[17] How could this be?

Material wealth

Consider material wealth – your monthly income, nest egg, assets and possessions. For example, an American who is able to afford to buy this book and to have the leisure time to read it probably has an income above the US national median.[18] A compelling case can be made that the level of material comfort (or lack thereof in the US) they are experiencing today is equivalent to how the top 5 per cent lived half a century ago![19] I recently ran across a description of what life was like in the United States in 1940, while reading *No Ordinary Time*, Doris Kearns Goodwin's fine book about the Roosevelts.[20] Approximately one-third of all homes in 1940 did not have running water, an indoor toilet, or a bath/shower, and more than half had no central heating. If you were twenty-five years or older in 1940, you would have stood only a 40 per cent chance of having completed the eighth grade [year nine], a 25 per cent chance of having graduated high [secondary] school, and only a 5 per cent chance of having finished college.

When asked to rate their overall satisfaction with life, Americans in 1940 reported being 'very happy', with an average score of 7.5 out of 10.[21] However, times have changed. The typical house today has not only running water, two or more bathrooms and central heating, but is twice the size, with an average of two rooms per person, not to mention being equipped with microwave ovens, dishwashers, colour TVs, DVD players, iPods and personal computers. And real monthly personal income has more than doubled. So, what is the average score for Americans' happiness today? It's 7.2.[22]

Apparently, all that extra space and gadgets and appliances don't really make us happy, even if we think they will.[23] How many of us have ever said, 'If only I had [fill in blank here], I would be so happy!' I have said that many times myself, as a teenager before owning my first car, as a student before I could afford to live alone, and as a parent before each of my kids had their own bedroom. (They still don't.)

Very wealthy people have a great deal more than the average person, but the research shows that they are not much happier. Consider Michael Ovitz, former president of Walt Disney Company. In the *Los Angeles Times*, my favourite columnist Steve Lopez reported on Ovitz's plans to build a 28,059 sq ft mansion for himself and his wife. This home will have the world's largest basement (13,974 sq ft), a separate 4,997 sq ft office with guest quarters, a 2,407 sq ft covered tennis pavilion, a garage big enough to accommodate thirteen cars, a yoga room, and an art gallery.[24] I would bet that if Mr Ovitz were to complete the Subjective Happiness Scale and e-mail it to me, his overall score would not be any higher than my neighbour who teaches at a middle school and lives in a pleasant but tiny studio apartment.

Materialism and its costs.
As I write this, the high-end department store Macy's is unleashing its newest advertising campaign. Each of its full-page

full-colour advertisements feature a single beautiful model, dressed in a new cashmere sweater, holding a spanking new hand-bag, wearing tight jeans, with the tag line, 'What makes you happy?' If only one could acquire the sweater, handbag or jeans, the ad suggests, we would all be bursting with joy! Frank Lloyd Wright observed that 'many wealthy people are little more than the janitors of their possessions.'[25] You could become a janitor of your possessions, too, if your goals primarily revolved around material things. Indeed, not only does materialism not bring hap-piness, but it's been shown to be a strong predictor of *unhappiness*. Researchers examined the attitudes of 12,000 undergraduates at elite colleges and universities in 1976, when they were eighteen years old on average, and then measured their life satisfaction at age thirty-seven.[26] Those who had expressed materialistic aspir-ations as their primary goal as undergraduates were less satisfied with their lives two decades later. Furthermore, materialists are more likely than non-materialists to suffer from a variety of mental disorders![27]

One of the reasons for the failure of materialism to make us happier may be that, even when people finally attain their mon-etary goals, the achievement doesn't translate into an increase in happiness.[28] Also, materialism may distract people from relatively more meaningful and joyful aspects of their lives, such as nur-turing their relationships with family and friends, enjoying the present and contributing to their communities. Finally, materi-alistic people have been found to hold unrealistically high expectations of what material things can do for them.[29] One father confided to me that he believed that purchasing a forty-two-inch flat panel TV would improve his relationship with his eleven-year-old son. It didn't.

Few of us would admit that a widescreen television, a sub-zero refrigerator and a seven-foot-high SUV have noticeably improved our lives. (My husband, who is chopping vegetables while I write this, just shouted to say that he would be really, really happy, if only he had a kitchen island!) Yet most people still report that 'more money' would definitely enhance the quality of their lives.[30] For example, since 1967, an annual study called 'The American Freshman Survey' has probed the attitudes and plans of undergraduates all around the United States. In 2005, 263,710 students at 385 colleges and universities responded. A record high number of undergraduates, 71 per cent, said it's very important to be 'very well off financially', compared to 42 per cent in 1967.[31] Interestingly, only 52 per cent of current undergraduates admitted that it was very important or essential for them to 'develop a meaningful philosophy of life', compared to 86 per cent in 1967.

And, of course, the more those undergraduates attain, the more they'll want. Those with salaries of under $30,000 per year claim that $50,000 would thrill them, whereas those who earn more than $100,000 say they need $250,000 to be satisfied.[32] If they only knew how the wealthy truly felt. In a study of 792 well-off adults, more than half reported that wealth didn't bring them more happiness, and a third of those with assets greater than $10 million said that money brought more problems than it solved.[33] Indeed, although those with higher incomes report being somewhat more satisfied with their lives, studies of how they actually spend their days find that they don't spend time in any more enjoyable activities than their less prosperous peers and, in fact, are more likely to experience daily anxiety and anger.[34] A wise (and rich) person once said, 'I've never borrowed a significant amount of money in my life . . . [because] I never thought I would be way happier when I had 2X instead of X.'[35]

Beauty

Before I explain why having a huge amount of money isn't going to make most of you sustainably happy, I'd like to mention one other life circumstance that does not correlate with happiness, and that is physical attractiveness. Even I, as a seemingly objective scientist, have trouble believing that being very beautiful wouldn't make me happier. But would it?

The American Society for Aesthetic Plastic Surgery reports

that more and more of us are remaking our appearances every year. Just between 2003 and 2004 there was an increase of 44 per cent in the number of cosmetic procedures, including a record 2.8 million Botox injections, 1.1 million chemical peels, and hundreds of thousands of breast augmentations, eyelid surgeries, nose reshapings, and liposuction (and according to one research company in Britain we spend £50 million more on cosmetic surgery than we do on tea!).[36] Most people report being satisfied with their post-surgery physical appearance, but only for short periods of time.[37] The happiness boost is not likely to endure.

One explanation for why a cosmetic enhancement doesn't bring abiding happiness, and, in general, why being beautiful doesn't have a stronger effect on our well-being, is that we simply don't focus on our appearance when thinking about how happy we are. A fascinating study that investigated how people in the Midwest versus California were affected by their local weather backs up this argument. Researchers were interested in whether people who live in California are truly happier (as many believe) than those who live in the Midwest.[38] To this end, they asked college students at two California colleges and two Midwest ones to rate their satisfaction with their lives overall and their satisfaction with *the weather*. The former is a judgement of deep, overall well-being and the latter is a judgement of a more transient feeling. It turned out that *both* the Californians and the Midwesterners believed that people in California were happier. But they were not. There was absolutely no difference in the overall satisfaction of the two groups of students.

However, an enormous difference emerged in the students' ratings of their satisfaction with the weather. Midwesterners were much less happy with the summer weather they experienced and they were much, *much* less happy with their winter weather. Indeed, the Midwesterners were significantly less satisfied than Californians with a number of other aspects of their lives, such as personal safety, outdoor activities and the natural beauty of their surroundings. So, why weren't they less happy overall? Because, the researchers explained, people don't focus on such things as the weather or their personal safety, or any single aspect of their lives, for that matter, when they try to figure out how happy they are overall. While it's not fun to be cold and wet, being cold and wet doesn't make you believe that you're unhappy. I submit that the same phenomenon occurs with regard to physical attractiveness. If beautiful people were asked if they're happy with their looks, they'd say 'sure'. But if they were asked if they're happy overall, their looks would have a minimal, if any, effect on their judgement.

My assertion that there's no link between beauty and happiness implies that beautiful people are no happier than their plain-looking relatives, colleagues and friends. And that happens to be true. Ed Diener and his co-investigators did a series of very nice studies which, in my opinion, definitively resolve this issue.[39] Using a multi-method approach, dragging happy and unhappy undergraduate volunteers into the lab, Diener and others photographed and videotaped them, and then showed the photos and videos to a panel of judges who rated them on physical attractiveness. In some of the studies, Diener and colleagues instructed participants to come 'as they are', and in others they were asked to come 'unadorned', removing all cosmetics and jewellery and with their clothing and hair covered. The latter was accomplished by having the unwitting participant don a white shower cap (to cover all hair) and a white laboratory coat (to conceal clothing) or to insert her head in an oval cut-out of a big white piece of cardboard – like the ones in cheesy amusement parks that offer the chance to be photographed with the body of a muscleman or princess, but blank.

If you are thinking that this is an odd set-up for a laboratory study, it is. But it allowed Diener to study the happiness–attractiveness link. Are happier participants actually 'objectively' more attractive (as rated by judges who saw their photos or videos), or do they simply have higher opinions of their own handsomeness or beauty?

The results were quite revealing. Although the happiest participants tended to *believe* that they were quite attractive, the objective judges did not regard them as any nicer looking than their less happy peers. Interestingly, this finding was even more pronounced when the participants were 'unadorned', suggesting that happy people may be particularly skilled at enhancing their natural beauty.

So, the bottom line is that good looking people aren't any happier. Of course, this brings up the question of which comes first, the chicken or the egg, thinking you're beautiful or being happy. There's evidence that happy people are somewhat more likely to perceive *everything* about their lives, including their appearance, in more positive, optimistic ways.[40] But other people don't rate them as more physically striking – at least when viewed in a photograph or a ten-minute video, and especially not when their faces are sticking through a cardboard cut-out!

So, beauty is not associated with happiness. Becoming objectively more beautiful will not make most of you happier. Coming to *believe* that you are beautiful is another story, and research suggests that this may be one of many happiness boosters.

The curious and powerful phenomenon of hedonic adaptation

'When I am in New York, I want to be in Europe, and when I am in Europe, I want to be in New York.'

WOODY ALLEN

One of the great ironies of our quest to become happier is that so many of us focus on changing the circumstances of our lives in the misguided hope that those changes will deliver happiness. For example, in an attempt to allay unhappiness, a recent graduate may choose a high-paying job in a distant city, a middle-aged divorcee may undergo beautifying cosmetic surgery, or a retired couple may buy an apartment with a view. Unfortunately, all of these individuals will probably only become temporarily happier. An impressive body of research now shows that trying to be happy by changing our life situation ultimately will not work.

Why do life changes account for so little? Because of a very powerful force that psychologists call 'hedonic adaptation'.[41]

Human beings are remarkably adept at becoming rapidly accustomed to sensory or physiological changes. When you walk in from the bitter cold, the warmth of the crackling fire feels heavenly at first, but you quickly get used to it and may even become overheated. When a mild but conspicuous odour dwells in your apartment, you may completely fail to notice it until you have left for a while and returned. The same phenomenon, however, occurs with 'hedonic' shifts – that is, relocations, marriages, job changes – that make you happier for a time, but only a short time. To give a concrete example, I had laser eye surgery at age thirty-six, after a lifetime of near blindness, discomfort with contact lenses and loathing of glasses. The result was miraculous. For the first time in memory I could read street signs, tell the time when waking in the middle of the night and see my toes in the shower. The surgery made me wonderfully happy. Remarkably, however, after about two weeks, I was completely and perfectly adapted to my new 20/20 vision and it no longer provided the happiness boost it did on that memorable first day. Nearly everyone has stories like this about moving into a bigger house, securing a promotion or a pay raise, getting a make-over, or flying first class. And research psychologists have even tried to bottle this experience by investigating it systematically, for example by asking whether people show hedonic adaptation to such significant life events as marriage, sudden wealth or chronic illness. It turns out they do.

The altar, the lottery and a house in the suburbs

Any happy newlywed will wonder how it could be possible to adapt to the benefits of matrimony. Indeed, every married person reading this has undoubtedly grasped the enormous, life-changing impact of marriage. And, in fact, studies show that married people are significantly happier than their single peers.[42] Numerous anecdotal examples, including mine, prove the point:

getting married was one of the best things that I have ever done and I am absolutely convinced that I am happier now than before.

And yet, psychological researchers have evidence to prove me wrong. In a landmark study, residents of West Germany and East Germany, including citizens, immigrants and foreigners – 25,000 people in all – were surveyed every year for a total of fifteen years.[43] Over the course of the study, 1,761 individuals got married and stayed married. Using this spectacular data set, scientists showed that, alas, marriage has only a temporary effect on happiness. It appears that, after the wedding, husband and wife get a happiness boost for about two years, and then they simply return to their baseline in happiness, their set point. It seems wise not to share this bit of news with newlyweds.

Several lines of research suggest that a similar phenomenon occurs with the attainment of money and possessions. In a classic study conducted back in the 1970s, psychologists interviewed some lucky individuals who had won between $50,000 and $1 million (in 1970s dollars) in the Illinois State Lottery.[44] Strikingly, less than a year after receiving the potentially life-changing news of winning the lottery, they reported being no more happy than regular folks who had not experienced the sudden windfall. Indeed, the lottery winners mused that they now derived less enjoyment from day-to-day activities, such as watching television or going out to lunch, relative to the non-winners.

Why does hedonic adaptation occur? The two biggest culprits are rising aspirations (e.g., the bigger house you buy after your windfall feels natural after a while, you experience a sort of 'creeping normality', and begin to want an even bigger one) and social comparison (e.g., your new friends in the new neighbourhood are driving BMWs and you feel you should too). As a result, even as people amass more of what they want with every year that passes, their overall happiness tends to stay the same. As the Red Queen in *Alice in Wonderland* proclaimed, 'We're running faster and faster, but we seem to end up in exactly the same place.'

My cousin Dianna is a walking case study in hedonic adaptation. When she married her husband, he was still a graduate student and, for a year, they shared a single tiny dormitory room, lacking a kitchen, with their new baby and Dianna's mother. I remember thinking how insanely difficult this must have been: her husband labouring to finish his dissertation, the baby crying in the middle of the night, a mother-in-law sleeping a couple of feet away. Years later, the family, now with three beautiful girls, moved to a tidy suburban community north of San Diego, with a neighbourhood pool and an excellent state school. Their house is lovely and new – two storeys, four bedrooms, family room, enormous garden with playground set. A few months after they settled in, Dianna called to tell me about a house three doors down from them that had just gone on the market. It was identical to theirs, but it had an extra bedroom *and* an extra patio where one could mount a barbecue. She was obsessed with this house, ruminating about every possible way that it was superior to theirs. Could they afford to buy it? Maybe they could. Could they? Maybe somehow they could . . .

So, the bad news about hedonic adaptation is that it ultimately dampens your happiness and satisfaction after any positive event or uplift. But there is good news too. I would argue that human beings are actually lucky to have the ability to adapt quickly to changing circumstances, as it's extremely useful when bad things happen. Some studies of hedonic adaptation show, for example, that we have a phenomenal ability to recover much of our happiness after a debilitating illness or accident.

Do you think that having end-stage kidney disease would reduce your capacity for happiness? Imagine having to endure *nine hours* of haemodialysis per week during which you are attached to a machine filtering your blood. Imagine having to adhere to a strict diet, limiting meat, salt and even daily fluids. Most people are positive that this situation would make them quite unhappy. However, researchers put this belief to empirical test.[45] Two groups of people, healthy participants and dialysis patients, were asked to carry for a week a Palm Pilot that would beep them randomly every ninety minutes. After each beep, the participant was required to punch in the mood that he happened to be experiencing at that very moment (pleased? joyful? anxious? unhappy?). The average of a person's mood ratings gathered over the course of a week happens to be an excellent indicator of his general well-being, as such ratings are unlikely to be edited, filtered or otherwise biased. It turned out that the renal disease patients were just as happy as the healthy controls. It seems that they adapted quite well to their condition. But, the healthy participants truly believed that they would be less happy if they had to undergo regular dialysis, and even the patients themselves lacked insight into their own miraculous capacity for hedonic adaptation, as they were certain they'd be happier if they had not had to endure the disease.

Amazing as it may seem, people show a great deal of adaptation to disabilities like paralysis and blindness, and other conditions that involve losing an important capacity or function. Consider a multiple sclerosis patient whose disease, as it developed, transformed from something frightening to something manageable. Although, with time, Ernest could no longer drive, run, walk or even stand, these things 'lost much of their importance . . . [they] are no longer within the sphere of possibility and are therefore not missed as though they were possible.' He explained his change in perspective this way:

> Gradual changes have taken place in my outlooks, in my likes and dislikes, in what I feel to be a natural part of my life and in what I had always regarded as a necessity for happiness . . . Probably had I known in 1956 what would be the symptoms that have appeared by now, I would have been anxious about and discouraged by the prospect of the future. Now that I actually find myself here, however, it seems that things are not nearly so bad as I would have thought then.[46]

Summing up

We cannot and will not adapt to everything. But the evidence for hedonic adaptation, especially with regard to positive events, is very strong. Human beings adapt to favourable changes in wealth, housing and possessions, to being beautiful or being surrounded by beauty, to good health and even to marriage. The only exception that I would argue is the effects of having children. As a mother of two, I can attest that the first time you cuddle your child, it feels wonderful. The thousandth time, it feels – oh, maybe 95 per cent as wonderful.

The happiness set point

I hope that you have now accepted the fact that the specifics of your life circumstances, unless they are truly dire, are really not the crux of your unhappiness. If you're unhappy with your job, or your friends, or your marriage, or your salary, or your looks, the first step you should take towards reaching greater lasting happiness is to put those things aside in your mind for now. Hard as it is, try not to reflect on them. Keep reminding yourself that these things are really not what is preventing you from getting happier. It will take a great deal of discipline and self-control, and you may lapse, but it's important to unlearn this commonly held but false belief.

One of my guilty pastimes is reading newspaper advice columns. Some months ago, a woman wrote in to my local paper, complaining about every job that she's ever had. At her first job, she was plagued by spiteful, gossipy co-workers, at her second it was an overbearing boss, at her third, it was utter monotony, and so on. So, she appealed for help in finding a job she likes. The wise advice columnist's blunt reply to her letter was something like this: 'It's not the colleagues or the boss or the nature of the work – it's something that *you're* doing!'

If the cause of your unhappiness is really not your circumstances, then surely it must be that you were just born this way. This is also a fallacy – the myth of 'you either have it or you don't'. Challenging the veracity of this belief is trickier because, you see, it is partly true. As the pie chart illustrates, your genetically determined predisposition for happiness (or unhappiness) accounts for 50 per cent of the differences between you and everyone else. Notably, a susceptibility to clinical depression has also been found to be partly rooted in our genetic make-up. Before we get depressed about being born depressed, however, I'd like to highlight one vital implication of these findings, that those of us who wish we were a great deal happier should be a little less hard on ourselves. We are, after all, dealing with a stacked deck to some extent. So, another critical step in clearing the way to committing to becoming happier is to appreciate the fact that 50 per cent is a long way from 100 per cent, and that it leaves ample room for improvement. So, how exactly do we know that the happiness set point accounts for 50 per cent?

Helen and Audrey

The strongest evidence for the set point comes from a series of fascinating studies done with identical and fraternal twins. The reason that studying twins reveals so much about the genetics of happiness is that twins share specifically known portions of their genetic material – identical twins share 100 per cent and fraternal twins (like regular siblings) share 50 per cent. So, by measuring the degree to which twins are similar in their happiness levels, we can infer how much of their happiness is probably rooted in their genes.

One of the most famous twin studies, the Happiness Twins study, was carried out by behaviour geneticists David Lykken, Auke Tellegen and their colleagues at the University of Minnesota. Using data from the Minnesota Twin Registry, they have been following a large number of mostly Caucasian twins born in Minnesota.[47] Let's consider two participants from their study, Helen and Audrey, who are thirty years old and identical twins, born in St Paul.[48] Suppose our task was to guess how happy Audrey is, and we are given the following information about her life during the past ten years. A lot has happened – she graduated from Carleton College in Northfield, Minnesota and launched a career in graphic design, she had a long-term relationship that didn't work out, then started another one with the man who is now her husband of two years. The couple recently moved to Chicago and live together in a two-bedroom apartment. She's not religious, but she considers herself a spiritual person.

If we wanted to predict how happy Audrey is from examining her life over the last ten years, we wouldn't do very well. The correlation between happiness and income (or occupation or religiosity or marital status) is very small. In the Happiness Twins study, for example, income accounted for less than 2 per cent of the variance in well-being, and marital status accounted for less than 1 per cent. However, if we tried to guess how happy Audrey is by considering the happiness level of her twin sister Helen, who still lives in St Paul, we'd be much more accurate. In fact, if we considered Helen's happiness level ten years ago, at age twenty, that level would be very close to Audrey's happiness today. In other words, the average happiness of your identical twin (even if assessed ten years earlier) is a much more powerful clue to your happiness today than *all of the facts and events* of your life!

However, to be completely sure of their striking findings of the comparable levels of the happiness of identical twins, researchers had to compare the happiness of fraternal twins as well. Recall that fraternal twins are one-half as genetically similar to one another than identical twins. Interestingly, the researchers found that, if Helen and Audrey had been fraternal twins, and thus no more alike than any two sisters, you could *not* guess Audrey's happiness from knowing Helen's. Whether or not your fraternal twin (or any other sibling) is happy or unhappy implies nothing about how happy or unhappy you might be. This fact – that identical twins (but not fraternal ones) share similar happiness levels – suggests that happiness is largely genetically determined. Indeed, the present-day consensus among researchers, based on a growing number of twin studies, is that the heritability of happiness is approximately 50 per cent, hence the '50 per cent' slice of the pie on my pie chart.

Separated at birth

There's a significant problem with such twin studies, however. To make conclusions from them, the researchers must assume that both types of twins – identical and fraternal – experience similar family environments. But is this really true? Unlike identical twins, fraternal twins of the same sex often look and behave quite differently. Thus, their parents, teachers and friends are likely to treat them differently, and the twins themselves are likely to emphasize their uniqueness. So the environment and upbringing of fraternal twins is not really as closely shared as that of identical twins.

Fortunately, this problem can be addressed by doing a different kind of study altogether. Researchers can compare twins who were raised together with twins who were separated in infancy and raised apart. This is a tough-to-find sample, but one researcher managed to assemble a set of such twins who had already reached middle age and asked them to complete measures of well-being.[49] Their findings have been deemed a classic in psychology. The identical twins were extremely similar to one another in their happiness scores and, remarkably, the similarity was no less if the twins were raised apart! Thus, the happier one identical twin was, the happier was the other – no matter whether the twins grew up under the same roof or in different parts of the country. Interestingly, however, regardless of whether they were raised together or apart, the happiness levels of the fraternal twins were completely uncorrelated. So, like any siblings, fraternal twins do not resemble each other in their average levels of happiness. Again, these findings are fascinating, underscoring the conclusion that happiness is, to a large extent, influenced by genetic factors – that each one of us inherits a preprogrammed set point, but 40 per cent is still available to us to mould.

I've probably come across the twins data a dozen times, yet they freshly surprise me each time I see them. I picture two little identical twin boys separated at birth and growing up to be teens and then men, with different parents and siblings, in different homes, schools and cities. I imagine them meeting each other for the first time in their thirties or forties and being floored by how similar they are. The Minnesota Twin Registry has documented many such meetings, the most famous of which is that of two men, both named James, who encountered each other for the first time at age thirty-nine.[50] The day they met, they were both six feet tall and weighed exactly 180 pounds. Each smoked Salems, drank Miller Lite and habitually bit his fingernails. When they discussed their life histories, some incredible coincidences emerged. Both had married women named Linda, had divorced them, and then remarried women named Betty. Each James enjoyed leaving love notes to his wife throughout the house (though perhaps both Lindas didn't appreciate it enough). Their first-born sons were also named James – one James Alan and the other James Allen – and both men had named their dogs Toy. Each James had owned a light-blue Chevrolet and had driven it to the same beach in Florida (Pas Grille Beach) for family holidays. I would bet anything that they were equally happy (or unhappy).

Do genes predestine us to be happy or unhappy?

No matter which way we look at it, the empirical data from the Happiness Twins study led to the conclusion that the genetic basis for happiness is strong – very strong. Even if major life changes, like a new relationship or a car accident, might push our happiness level up or down, we tend to revert back to this genetically determined set point. Evidence for this phenomenon comes from studies that follow people over time as they react to good and bad things happening in their lives. For example, one study tracked Australian citizens every two years from 1981 to 1987 and found that positive and negative life events (e.g., 'made lots of new friends', 'got married', 'experienced serious problems with children', or 'became unemployed') influenced their feelings of happiness and satisfaction as we would expect. But, after the events passed, their feelings returned to their original genetically determined baselines.[51] Another study conducted in the US with undergraduates showed essentially the same thing – the big and small events experienced by these students boosted or deflated their well-being, but only for a period of about three months.[52] So, although you may be made temporarily ecstatic or miserable by what comes to pass, it seems that you can't help but eventually return to your set point. And, as far as anyone knows, this set point cannot be changed. But, just because your happiness set point cannot be changed, this doesn't mean that your happiness level cannot be changed.

In *The African Queen*, Katharine Hepburn declares to Humphrey Bogart, 'Nature, Mr Allnutt, is what we are put in this world to rise above!' We can rise above our happiness set points, just like we can rise above our set points for weight or cholesterol. Although, on the face of it, the set point data appear to suggest that we are all subject to our genetic programming, in actuality they do not. Our genes do not *determine* our life experience and behaviour. Indeed, our 'hard wiring' can be dramatically influenced by our experience and our behaviour. This is illustrated, as I describe in detail later, by the notion that there's a great deal of room to improve our happiness by the things we *do*, our intentional activities. Even the most heritable traits like height, which has a heritability level of .90 (relative to about .50 for happiness), can be radically modified by environmental and behavioural changes. For example, since the 1950s, the average height of Europeans has been growing at a rate of 2 centimetres per decade, in part due to better overall nutrition.[53]

Or take the case of a rare condition known as phenylketonuria. PKU stems from a mutation in a single gene on chromosome 12 and, without treatment, leads to brain damage resulting in mental retardation and premature death.[54] PKU is said to have a heritability of 1, because it is *entirely* genetically determined. But this doesn't mean that an infant born with the gene that causes PKU is doomed to its lethal effects. If the parents ensure that the infant's diet is free of an amino acid called phenylalanine, which is found in such common foods as eggs, milk, bananas and NutraSweet, the brain damage may be entirely prevented. It's important to note that the infant's genetic endowment doesn't change, she will always carry the mutant gene, but the expression of her genetic endowment *can* change.

I make much the same case for happiness. If you are born with a low set point for happiness, the genes coding for that set point will always be a part of you. However, for those genes to be fully expressed, they must encounter the appropriate, fitting environment, much like a seed requires a particular soil to grow. In fact, there is a powerful study that shows just what a dramatic effect one particular environmental factor can have on whether or not people who have a 'depression gene' actually succumb to depression. That environmental factor is severe stress.

The case of the 'Depression Gene'

When I was an undergraduate, I was a research assistant for a psychology professor named Paul Andreassen. Paul was a good friend of another professor, Avshalom Caspi, who dropped by our lab on a regular basis. At the time, I was in awe of research, of professors, indeed of anything having to do with Harvard, and I remember Avshalom as a dark striking figure with long hair and an Israeli accent. Little did I know that years later and a continent away, along with his future wife and collaborator, Terri Moffitt, he would conduct a truly groundbreaking study.[55] Caspi, Moffitt and their colleagues at King's College in London were interested in the relationship between stress and depression. Why do stressful life experiences, like being evicted from one's apartment or losing a pregnancy, trigger depression in some people, but not others?

It turns out that depression is associated with a particular gene, called the 5-HTTLPR, which comes in two forms – the long and the short. The short allele is undesirable to have, because it rids the brain of a substance needed to fend off depressive symptoms.[56] So Caspi tracked the presence of this so-called 'bad' gene in a sample of 847 infants born in New Zealand and learned that more than half carried it. At the time of the study, those infants were already twenty-six years old; thus, the researchers were able to identify the number of stressful or negative life events the participants had experienced during the past five years (since age twenty-one), as well as evidence of depression during the past year (at age twenty-six). A quarter (26 per cent) reported having experienced three or more adverse life events and 17 per cent had had a major depressive episode.

Not surprisingly, overall, the more stress and trauma the New Zealanders had experienced during their last five years, the more likely they were to become depressed. The critical finding, however, was that the stressful experiences led to depression *only* among those participants who carried the 'bad' short allele of the 5-HTTLPR gene. Interestingly, the same result was found for stress suffered in childhood. Those participants who were maltreated between ages three and eleven were more likely to become depressed at age twenty-six, but, again, *only* if they carried the ill-fated short allele.

So, our genes play an important role in depression, as they do in happiness, but they need to be 'expressed' or turned on or off. The findings of the New Zealand study, which was voted by the editorial board of *Science* magazine as the second biggest finding of that year (the biggest was on the origins of life!), suggest that the short allele variant of the 5-HTTLPR gene is activated by an environmental trigger – namely, stress. Similarly, the long 'good' allele appears to protect us from responding to a stressful experience by becoming depressed, by making us resilient. So, the fact that many of us may carry genes for a particular vulnerability (be it PKU or cardiovascular disease or depression or happiness) does not mean that we will express that vulnerability in our lives. If the New Zealanders with the short 'bad' allele of the 5-HTTLPR gene were able to avoid highly stressful situations or to engage a psychotherapist or supportive confidante when they anticipated stress, their genetic propensity for depression may never have been triggered. Furthermore, new research has shown that individuals who are unfortunate enough to possess the 'bad' gene, yet who are fortunate to have had either a supportive family environment or several present-day positive life experiences, do *not* become depressed.[57] So, in order to express or not express themselves, genes need a particular environment (e.g., a happy marriage or job lay-off) or a particular behaviour (e.g., seeking out social support). This means that, no matter what your genetic predisposition, whether or not that predisposition is expressed is in your hands.

What electrodes can teach us

A better understanding of the happiness set point comes from perhaps the most exciting laboratory right now in the area of well-being – that of Richard Davidson at the University of Wisconsin-Madison. Like the behaviour geneticists, Davidson argues that each of us has a natural set point, which he defines as a baseline of activity in the prefrontal cortex (front part) of the brain. In a fascinating discovery, he noticed that happy people show greater activity in one side of their brain than the other, and unhappy people show the reverse pattern.

Davidson uses a procedure called electroencephalography (EEG) to measure a person's brain activity.[58] He finds that happy people, those who smile more and who report themselves as enthusiastic, alert and engaged in life, show a curious asymmetry in their brain activity – they have more activity in their left prefrontal cortex than the right.[59] Although no researcher would claim that the left side of the front region of the brain is the 'happiness centre', clearly this region is associated with positive emotion. Even newborns who are given something nice to suck display increased activation in the left side of their brains, and so do adults who are shown funny film clips. The right prefrontal region, by contrast, is activated during unpleasant states and negative emotions.

So, what does it mean to any of us that the left side of a happy person's brain lights up more than the right side? Perhaps only something as seemingly ineffable as the fact that happiness appears to be hardwired in the neural circuitry. Thus, although Davidson's work doesn't offer proof for the notion of a happiness set point, it certainly supports it. If the set point is genetically determined, it's presumably rooted in our neurobiology.

Implications for you

Some of us simply possess a higher set point for happiness, a more cheerful disposition, a higher potential for well-being. Perhaps 'the sun shines more brightly for some persons than others.'[60] Having a high set point may feel like more of our days are sunny ones. It may mean never having to work very hard at being happy. But this is not the situation facing most of us. So, let's start with the premise that we may have a disappointingly low set point and then ask ourselves first, precisely how low is that set point and, second, what can we do about it?

To address the first question, it's impossible to know exactly what our set point is unless we evaluate it over time. So, you need to record the date that you first completed the Subjective Happiness Scale (see p. 33). Your score on that scale is your *pre-liminary estimate* of your set point. The reason it's preliminary is that it's somewhat sensitive to what's happening around you. For example, your score could have been influenced by a recent event, by your stress level that day and even by the weather. So, you will need to fill out the Subjective Happiness Scale again, ideally at least two weeks after initially taking it but *before* you begin the happiness building programme described in this book. If you intend to begin straight away, then retake the scale the day before you start; the *average* of your two scores (or three scores, if you take it three times, and so on) will serve as the estimate of your set point. The more often you take the Subjective Happiness

Scale, and the farther apart in time you take it, the more reliable the estimate of your set point.

So, what can you do if your happiness set point is lower than you like? (Although the average is around 5, your own hoped-for yardstick may be a lot higher or a lot lower.) To begin with, I must stress that if you desire to become lastingly happier, the answer is not to try to change your set point. By definition, the set point is constant. Analogously, if you were born with brown eyes, your eyes will forever remain truly brown. However, your life experiences are under your control and their potential for influencing your happiness lies in the activities and strategies that make up the large 40 per cent of our happiness 'pie'. Through these activities, you can change your happiness *level*, if not your set point, much like you can change your eye colour (through tinted contact lenses), if not the innate colour of your eyes.

The promise of intentional activity

'Happiness consists in activity. It is a running stream, not a stagnant pool.'

JOHN MASON GOOD

Many are familiar with the Serenity Prayer, written by German philosopher Reinhold Niebuhr and widely adopted for use in twelve-step programmes: 'God, grant me the serenity to accept the things I cannot change, the courage to change the things I can, and the wisdom to know the difference.' But how can you know the difference?

It should be obvious by now where the secret to happiness does not lie. The fountain of happiness lies not in changing our genetically determined set point. And we are unlikely to find lasting happiness by changing our life circumstances. Although we may achieve a temporary boost in well-being it is unlikely to be long-lasting. The primary reason, as I have argued, is that people readily and rapidly adapt to positive circumstantial changes. Furthermore, circumstantial changes may prove unsuccessful in making us permanently happier because they can be very costly, often impractical and sometimes even impossible. Does everyone have the money, resources or time to change their living situation, their job, their spouse, their physical appearance?

So is it possible to attain greater happiness and sustain it? To be sure, most of us do become happier at some point during our lives. Indeed, contrary to popular belief, people actually get happier with age. A twenty-two-year study of about 2,000 healthy veterans of World War II and the Korean War revealed that life satisfaction increased over the course of these men's lives, peaked at age sixty-five, and didn't start significantly declining until age seventy-five (see below).[61]

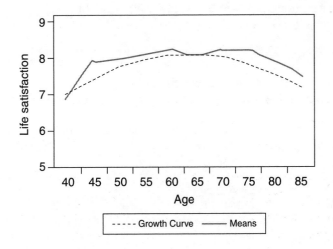

This is heartening news. But what precisely can we do to hasten or bolster such increases in happiness? The answer lies in the pie-chart theory of happiness and the 40 per cent that comprises our intentional activities and strategies. If we observe genuinely happy people, we will find that they do not just sit around being contented. They make things happen. They pursue new understandings, seek new achievements and control their thoughts and feelings. In sum, our intentional, effortful activities have a powerful effect on how happy we are, over and above the effects of our set point and the circumstances in which we find ourselves. If an unhappy person wants to experience interest, enthusiasm, contentment, peace and joy, he or she can make it happen by learning the habits of a happy person.

Let's return, for a moment, to the massive German study, in which researchers followed 1,761 people over the course of fifteen years, starting when they were single, then after they became married and stayed married. On average, as this remarkable study found, people were no happier during their years after marriage than during their years before marriage, and the average 'marriage boost' in happiness only lasted for two years. Notably, however, there was significant variability in people's responses to tying the knot.

Markus and Roland: Thwarting adaptation

Consider Markus and Roland, two somewhat unusual participants who both happened to wed their girlfriends while the study was going on. Markus's happiness increased more than average when he got hitched, and, eight years later, he is *still* happier being married (just declining a tiny bit from his high point) than he was when he was single. Roland, on the other hand, actually ended up *less* happy during the first two years of marriage, and has become even less happy in the six years since.

What is unique about these two men? Well, Markus didn't want the effects of marriage to 'wear off'; he didn't want to adapt to the rewards of marriage and take it for granted. So, he decided to dedicate himself to being the best husband he could be and not take his wife and their relationship for granted. He consciously remembers to say 'I love you', to bring her flowers, to initiate plans, trips and hobbies, to take an interest in his wife's challenges, successes and feelings. In contrast, Roland was disappointed at the outset that matrimony did not live up to his idealistic expectations and, since then, has failed to observe the slow but steady deterioration of his relationship.

The lesson from Markus and Roland is that, while it's true that we tend to adapt to positive changes in our lives, it's in our power to apply effort to try to inhibit or slow down the adaptation process. Markus tried to inhibit adaptation to his marriage by actively and creatively behaving in ways that preserved his and his wife's love and affection for each other, a strategy that we can learn from as an example of a conscious goal that we can undertake and commit to practise. For example, I have argued that moving to a new location – however magnificent it may be initially – eventually leads to a dampening of enthusiasm. This will undoubtedly occur, but only if we passively accept our situation. But it doesn't have to be that way. When I moved to California from New England, I recall waking up every morning and saying to myself, 'What a beautiful day!' But, just like Steve Martin's parody of the weatherman in *LA Story* announcing every day that 'it's going to be sunny . . . again!' this recognition of beauty eventually grew old. So, like most people around me, I became accustomed to the splendour of my surroundings and the serenity and blueness of my skies, no longer deriving the extra boost in happiness they initially afforded me. But, in the last few years, still living in California, I have been taking my own research advice to heart. Most mornings, I go running on a path overlooking the Pacific Ocean and I make a conscious decision to take a moment and more attentively look at the beach and the mountains in the distance, to breathe extra deeply the salty air. The other day, some Swedish tourists asked me in the middle of a run to take a photograph of them in front of the ocean view. Instead of being annoying, the interruption made me thankful to these tourists for unknowingly deepening my appreciation for the singular, special and lovely place where I live.

Judith: Choosing to be happy

Judith was born and raised in Indiana, but has been living in Edmonton, Alberta, for over thirty years. I interviewed her outdoors, at one of her favourite neighbourhood restaurants. She is sixty years old, once divorced and with a grown daughter. Once upon a time in life, Judith was deeply unhappy. She grew up in a dysfunctional, abusive family. Her mother used to beat her with anything she could get her hands on – a paddle, a hairbrush – and wouldn't stop until the object broke. As an adult, Judith illustrated perfectly the 'toxic triangle' of food, alcohol and depression that Susan Nolen-Hoeksema describes in her book, *Eating, Drinking, Overthinking*.[62] She had a major weight problem, turned to alcohol, and was clinically depressed and insecure.

Today, Judith admits to being 'an incredibly happy person'. She has a fulfilling job, volunteers widely, and cares for a fourteen-year-old foster boy. She decided to return to college at age fifty-two. She is spiritual and she is forgiving, now referring to her troubled mother as 'poor thing'.

'I chose to be happy,' Judith says. 'I learned to simply change my mind. What a concept.' Indeed, she purely exemplifies the value of focusing on the 40 per cent of our happiness that we have the power to control. 'The beginning for me was to look into the mirror and say (in Barbra Streisand's accent): "Hellooo, gorgeous!" I kept saying it until I didn't burst into laughter every time I said it.' This may seem easy, or trivial, but it's not when you appear ugly and worthless to yourself. 'I also worked very hard,' Judith told me, 'to stop the negative thoughts (I called them the "bad" thoughts) by simply saying in my mind, "STOP!!" and then I would say to myself, "you are okay right now."'

Judith was probably born with a low set point for happiness, and, starting early in life, she was saddled with difficult life circumstances and damaging experiences. Even today, there are trying times. Recently, a dear friend of hers committed suicide and she failed to get her job contract renewed. But Judith has risen above both her circumstances and her nature by striving for a life-transforming goal: to change how she thought about herself and the world around her, to build her self-esteem and nurture optimistic thinking – by choosing to be happy.

Conclusion

The media are constantly telling us about the latest new-fangled strategy shown to 'really' work in boosting health and well-being. These strategies keep changing, each one evidently better than the previous, such that every new pronouncement becomes harder to believe. If the new kind of yoga or meditation or marital therapy technique were as effective as the reports claim, then wouldn't everyone be doing it and benefiting from it? Well, no. Any major life-changing endeavour must be accompanied by considerable sustained effort, and I would speculate that the majority of people do not or cannot continue putting in that kind of effort. What's more, all new happiness-enhancing or health-boosting strategies have something in common, and that is that each one bestows on the person a specific *goal*, something to do and to look forward to. And, as I describe later on, having goals in and of themselves is strongly associated with happiness and life satisfaction. That's why, at least for a time, any new happiness strategy does work!

In a nutshell, the fountain of happiness can be found in how you behave, what you think and what goals you set every day of your life. 'There is no happiness without action.'[63] If feelings of passivity and futility overcome you whenever you face up to your happiness set point or to your circumstances, you must know that a genuine and abiding happiness is indeed within your reach, lying within the 40 per cent of the happiness pie chart that's yours to guide.

Chapter 3

How to find happiness activities that fit your interests, your values and your needs

'Different men seek after happiness in different ways and by different means, and so make for themselves different modes of life . . .'

Aristotle

If 40 per cent of our happiness is rooted in intentional activity, then precisely which activities or strategies can help you reach your desired level of well-being? Many of us persist in searching for 'the one' true secret path to happiness (or to career success or to spiritual fulfilment and so on) like the one diet that will work when all others have failed. In truth, there is no one magic strategy that will help every person become happier. All of us have unique needs, interests, values, resources and inclinations that undoubtedly predispose us to put effort into and benefit from some strategies more than others. For example, an extrovert may be more likely to stick with an activity that brings her into regular contact with other people, and a very nurturing person may benefit more from an activity that grants him opportunities to take care of others. Furthermore, some people are best served by working on an area of specific weakness (whether it's pessimism or overthinking – see Chapter 4 for more on this – or problems with friendship), and others profit from engaging in a happiness strategy that meshes with their personal ideal of happiness (be it positive thinking or gratifying relationships or fulfilling work). This general 'matching' notion is supported by much recent research.[1]

It is also fairly intuitive. If you want to become physically fit or chuck an addiction, there are many programmes and strategies you can try, and you would be prudent to choose one that fits your goals, resources and lifestyle best. Interestingly, although the importance of good fit is widely recognized, even obvious, in the domains of diet and fitness, it is rarely considered in regard to a person's emotional life. Yet fit is absolutely critical. So much so that I'll go out on a limb here and say that if there's any 'secret' to becoming happier, the secret is in establishing which happiness strategies suit you best. Once you have done so, half the battle is won – the way to greater happiness is in your hands.

Three ways that strategies can 'fit'

When it comes to determining which happiness strategies will work best for a particular individual, I believe in taking an idiographic or personalized approach. The goal is 'person–activity fit'. When you choose wisely, you will feel motivated to try a particular happiness activity, persist at it and experience its rewards. It goes without saying that a person needs to make an honest effort into trying a new strategy in order to achieve any benefit. However, even the most ardently pursued activities won't bring happiness for every single individual. One of the chief reasons that many of us fail in our efforts to become happier is unfortunate choosing – either picking a strategy or approach that is inherently fruitless (like pursuing wealth, approval or beauty, as discussed in the previous chapter) or picking one that is not well suited to us. A good person–activity fit can be achieved in a number of ways. These ways, described below, can work independently or in concert. Let's consider all the options.

Fit with the source of your unhappiness

The first approach is to contemplate what underlies your own unhappiness. Leo Tolstoy famously opened *Anna Karenina* by declaring that 'Happy families are all alike; every unhappy family is unhappy in its own way.' As a psychologist who studies individuals, not families, I prefer the following restatement, which has its own truth: 'Happy people are all alike; every unhappy person is unhappy in his or her own way.' The research bears this out – there are many varieties and sources of unhappiness. Each individual is unhappy for a unique constellation of reasons. Some of us feel apathetic and powerless over our lives, whereas others are convinced that the future is bleak. The crux for some is an inability to obtain much pleasure from daily activities. For others, it's being too shy to join in social events, or being traumatized and unsettled by a past experience. This means that particular happiness-enhancing activities may uniquely address our specific problems or areas of weakness. The pessimist may benefit from cultivating optimism, the pleasure-lacking individual from savouring, the traumatized person from learning coping skills, and so on.

Fit with your strengths

Person–activity fit, however, does not have to be based on repairing your specific weaknesses. Alternatively, you can start by identifying your strengths, talents or goals. For example, an achievement-oriented person may do well at pursuing significant life goals or taking up competitive sports as a way to boost his happiness. And a creative person may choose to express gratitude or forgiveness through painting or writing. Indeed, different people can attain happiness in different ways, so it makes sense that some of us should focus on a particular set of happiness-increasing activities, while others should focus on an entirely different set of activities.

Fit with your lifestyle

Think about the extent to which the activities you choose can be adapted to your needs and lifestyle. For example, if your life is stressful and hectic, then you can choose activities (like counting blessings) that don't take any extra time out of your day. If you are satisfied with your relationships, but not with your work, then you can choose activities (like increasing flow or striving for new goals) that can help you enjoy your job more and pursue novel opportunities. If you're not spiritual or religious, then you can pass on the religion strategy. If you're a lifelong practitioner of concentrative meditation, then you can opt out of the happiness activity that involves meditating. Much like a diet that you can individualize to fit your food preferences, you can tailor the happiness strategies to fit your personality and your way of life. There are probably as many ways to achieve happiness as there are to lose it.

Corniness, again

Finally, I have to raise the issue of corniness again. It's possible that you will read over the list of the dozen happiness activities and observe that some of these activities, or perhaps many of them, appear cringey or undoable to you. You may even react with distaste: 'This is not for me!' I myself have had this experience. It's not uncommon and it doesn't mean that you are destined never to become happier. The reality is that some of us have an aversion to advice that seems overly sentimental or simplistic. We can't picture ourselves 'counting blessings' or 'savouring life's joys' or 'learning to forgive', as these suggestions smack of mawkishness and even naïveté. Such reactions are authentic and I can't dispute them. Fortunately, if this describes your reaction, you have a choice. Other activities are available that may be a better fit for your interests, needs and values. However, even the corniest-sounding exercise can grow on you and end up being practised sincerely and from the heart. Chris Peterson, professor at the University of Michigan and one of the founders of positive psychology, admitted once that he couldn't bring himself to write 'gratitude letters', which he regularly assigned to his own students. When he finally forced himself to do it, he wound up masking any embarrassing sentiments with humour and ended up feeling insincere. Needless to say, the exercise did not succeed in boosting his happiness. So, he tried again, and this time, he says, 'I spoke from the heart'.

'Person–activity fit' diagnostic

Learning that there are several ways to make a strategy fit makes it all seem very complicated. How do you go about selecting the set of activities that are the optimal fit for you? Which *type* of fit is best? Fortunately, the answer is quite simple and straight-forward. I have developed a self-diagnostic test that conveniently incorporates all the different ways of measuring fit, whether it is fit with your weaknesses, with your strengths and goals, or with your needs and lifestyle. This test of person–activity fit uses a systematic, empirically based approach to determine which set of happiness activities (out of twelve) will be most valuable for you to try. Set aside fifteen to thirty minutes to complete it in a quiet setting, as the test requires effort and concentration, and be sure to rate all twelve of the activities presented. How you answer this diagnostic is crucial to everything else that you will learn in this book. But, having said that, it's not a 'test' in the sense that there are right or wrong responses but rather an opportunity to define yourself, so the only prerequisite is to be honest and true.

'PERSON–ACTIVITY FIT' DIAGNOSTIC
(adapted from Sheldon)

Instructions: Consider each of the following twelve happiness activities. Reflect on what it would be like to do it *every week* for an extended period of time. Then rate each activity by writing the appropriate number (1 to 7) in the blank space next to the terms Natural, Enjoy, Value, Guilty and Situation.

People do things for many different reasons. Please rate why you might keep doing this activity in terms of each of the following reasons. Use this scale:

1	2	3	4	5	6	7
not at all			somewhat			very much

Natural: I'll keep doing this activity because it will feel 'natural' to me and I'll be able to stick with it.

Enjoy: I'll keep doing this activity because I will enjoy doing it; I'll find it to be interesting and challenging.

Value: I'll keep doing this activity because I will value and identify with doing it; I'll do it freely even when it's not enjoyable.

Guilty: I'll keep doing this activity because I would feel ashamed, guilty or anxious if I don't do it; I'll force myself.

Situation: I'll keep doing this activity because somebody else will want me to, or because my situation will force me to.

(1) Expressing gratitude: Counting your blessings for what you have (either to a close other or privately, through contemplation or diary-writing), or conveying your gratitude and appreciation to one or more individuals whom you've never properly thanked.

_____Natural _____Enjoy _____Value _____Guilty _____Situation

(2) Cultivating optimism: Keeping a journal in which you imagine and write about the best possible future for yourself, or practise looking at the bright side of every situation.

_____Natural _____Enjoy _____Value _____Guilty _____Situation

(3) Avoiding overthinking and social comparison: Using strategies (such as distraction) to cut down on how often you dwell on your problems and compare yourself to others.

_____Natural _____Enjoy _____Value _____Guilty _____Situation

(4) Practising acts of kindness: Doing good things for others, whether friends or strangers, either directly or anonymously, either spontaneously or planned.

_____Natural _____Enjoy _____Value _____Guilty _____Situation

(5) Nurturing relationships: Picking a relationship in need of strengthening, and investing time and energy in healing, cultivating, affirming and enjoying it.

_____Natural _____Enjoy _____Value _____Guilty _____Situation

(6) Developing strategies for coping: Practising ways to endure or surmount a recent stress, hardship or trauma.

_____Natural _____Enjoy _____Value _____Guilty _____Situation

(7) Learning to forgive: Keeping a journal or writing a letter in which you work on letting go of anger and resentment towards one or more individuals who have hurt or wronged you.

_____Natural _____Enjoy _____Value _____Guilty _____Situation

(8) Doing more activities that truly engage you: Increasing the number of experiences at home and work in which you 'lose' yourself, which are challenging and absorbing (i.e., 'flow' experiences).

_____Natural _____Enjoy _____Value _____Guilty _____Situation

(9) Savouring life's joys: Paying close attention, taking delight and replaying life's momentary pleasures and wonders – through thinking, writing, drawing or sharing with another.

_____Natural _____Enjoy _____Value _____Guilty _____Situation

(10) Committing to your goals: Picking one, two or three significant goals that are meaningful to you and devoting time and effort to pursuing them.

_____Natural _____Enjoy _____Value _____Guilty _____Situation

(11) Practising religion and spirituality: Becoming more involved in your church, temple or mosque, or reading and pondering spiritually themed books.

_____Natural _____Enjoy _____Value _____Guilty _____Situation

(12) Taking care of your body: Engaging in physical activity, meditating, and smiling and laughing.

_____Natural _____Enjoy _____Value _____Guilty _____Situation

How to calculate your 'fit' score and determine your set of best-fitting activities:

Step 1: For *each* of the twelve activities, subtract the average of the GUILTY and SITUATION ratings from the average of the NATURAL, ENJOY and VALUE ratings. In other words, for each of the twelve activities:

Fit score = (Natural + Enjoy + Value) ÷ 3 − (Guilty + Situation) ÷ 2

Step 2: Write down the four activities with the highest Fit scores:

1) _____   3) _____

2) _____   4) _____

Date: _____

As you can see, the 'Person–Activity Fit' Diagnostic yields a 'short-list' of four happiness activities for you to undertake as you begin the happiness-increasing programme described here. Some of you will be surprised by your short-list and thus will have learned something valuable about yourself. Others will find their short-list to be exactly what they expected. In any case, depending on your level of energy and motivation, you may choose initially to engage in only one of the four activities, or up to two or three simultaneously. Feel free to jump ahead after this chapter and only read about the activities in Part II of this book that suit you best. With time, as you make progress, you can add more activities or even advance to trying out those that yielded somewhat lower fit scores. The six chapters making up Part II will give you the 'goods' on each of the twelve happiness activities, describing in detail how precisely to implement them and why.

The rationale behind the 'Person–Activity Fit' Diagnostic is that a particular happiness-increasing strategy will match you better if it feels natural to you and you are truly motivated to pursue it − that is, you want to do it because you value doing it and because you find it enjoyable and *not* because you feel forced or pressured into doing it, either out of guilt or a desire to please. The 'fit score' is in large part a measure of what Ken Sheldon and his co-authors call 'self-concordant motivation', that is, a commitment to pursue a goal that's grounded in one's genuine interests and deeply held fundamental values.[2] Research suggests that if you have this kind of motivation in striving for greater happiness, you will continue putting effort into the endeavour and, ultimately, be more likely to succeed.[3] In other words, where there is a good fit, you will try harder and 'feel right' about what you're doing.

The results of a recent study by one of my graduate students confirm these benefits of person-activity fit.[4] We randomly assigned participants to carry out a single happiness strategy (in this case, either practising gratitude or optimism) over a two-month period; they also completed the 'Person–Activity Fit' Diagnostic. As we anticipated, those participants who were lucky to be assigned the activity that fitted them were more likely 1) to report finding its practice 'natural' and 'enjoyable' after the fact, 2) to continue engaging in the activity even after the study was over, and 3) to derive greater happiness as a result of practising it.[5] So, there you have it – the significance of fit!

P.S. More options

There are several reasons I present precisely twelve activities in this book. First, I chose only evidence-based happiness-increasing strategies whose practice is supported by scientific research. Second, I sought to include a wide variety of activities, so that every individual could find a unique set that is right for him or her. This is why there are twelve and no fewer.

Nonetheless, there's a risk that even an activity with a high fit score may not at first work for you. In that case, you need to keep persisting at it, or attempt a different activity, or try a combination. Research has shown that, when it comes to changing something fundamental about themselves, people often need to make multiple attempts. For example, one study recruited hundreds of individuals who were successful at losing weight and maintaining the weight loss for at least five years.[6] Most recounted trying several different diets and forms of exercise to lose the weight, and it took four to five tries (and sometimes more) for them to finally succeed. This is another reason why it is worthwhile to choose from a range of strategies.

Don't be constrained, however, by your list of four best-fitting activities. I have found that people who find a particular well-fitting activity tend to find several other complementary activities to fit as well.[7] That is, certain happiness strategies complement other strategies. So, in Part II, after the description of each one of the twelve happiness activities, I suggest two others, based on research evidence from my lab, that you might find valuable to try even if you did not establish them as one of your four primary activities. For example, the very first strategy I describe is expressing gratitude. If this activity has yielded a high fit score for you, you should give it your best shot. If you feel yourself becoming happier, do continue to express gratitude on a regular basis. At this point, however, you may also add one or more activities to undertake from your set of four best-fitting ones. And if gratitude appeals to you and seems to be especially effective, there are two others that you might consider trying: 1) practising kindness and 2) learning to forgive. To this end, skip ahead to the kindness or forgiveness sections if you wish.

For your convenience, I've created a grid in the Appendix that shows which happiness-increasing strategies go together. Again, use this grid to help you find additional helpful happiness activities besides your list of four best-fitting ones, but generally it's a good idea to first exhaust that list of four.

Final words

Aiming for greater happiness is no small endeavour, requiring effort and commitment. Taking these first steps may be a bit daunting, but it is also empowering, because the control in how you undertake this path (or whether you choose to do so) resides entirely in you. The 'Person–Activity Fit' Diagnostic has this power. Selecting an appropriate activity to undertake vastly increases the chances that you will succeed. On the other hand, if the wrong strategy is chosen, it is likely to fail and you may give up altogether. The Fit Diagnostic has been developed to help prevent you from feeling frustrated and to optimize the way you determine the four happiness-enhancing strategies that fit your current values, goals and needs and will be most effective for *you*. Again, I encourage you to start with that set of strategies. Jump ahead now to your best-fitting activity. Alternatively, many people may benefit from opting to read about them all. Finally, it's critical to your success to read about *how* and *why* such happiness-enhancing activities work. This important material is presented in 'The five "hows" behind sustainable happiness' (Chapter 10).

PART II

In Part II, you will learn about and embark on one or more of the happiness activities that best 'fit' you, as determined by the 'Person–Activity Fit' Diagnostic from the last chapter. Before beginning your endeavour, however, it's important to determine your initial happiness score by completing the happiness scale below. You will revisit this scale, the Oxford Happiness Inventory, on a regular basis in order to track your progress. Your initial and future scores on the Oxford scale, I should note, reflect your happiness level, not your happiness set point established at birth. Your happiness level, by contrast, can shift up or down depending on what you do and how you think – in other words, by the activities embodied by the 40 per cent of the happiness pie chart.

THE OXFORD HAPPINESS INVENTORY[1]

Instructions: Overleaf, there are groups of statements about personal happiness. Please read all three statements in each group and then pick out the one statement that best describes the way you have been feeling *in the past week, including today*. Circle the letter (a, b or c) beside the statement that you have picked.

1
a. I do not feel happy
b. I feel fairly happy
c. I am very happy

2
a. I am not particularly optimistic about the future
b. I feel optimistic about the future
c. I feel I have so much to look forward to

3
a. I am not really satisfied with anything in my life
b. I am satisfied with some things in my life
c. I am satisfied with many things in my life

4
a. I feel that I am not especially in control of my life
b. I feel at least partially in control of my life
c. I feel that I am in control most of the time

5
a. I don't feel that life is particularly rewarding
b. I feel that life is rewarding
c. I feel that life is very rewarding

6
a. I don't feel particularly pleased with the way I am
b. I am pleased with the way I am
c. I am very pleased with the way I am

7
a. I never have a good influence over events in my life
b. I occasionally have a good influence on events
c. I often have a good influence on events

8
a. I get by in life
b. Life is good
c. Life is very good

9
a. I am not very interested in other people
b. I am moderately interested in other people
c. I am very interested in other people

10
a. I do not find it easy to make decisions
b. I find it fairly easy to make decisions
c. I find it easy to make decisions

11
a. I find it difficult to get started to do things
b. I find it moderately easy to start doing things
c. I find it easy to do things

12
a. I rarely wake up feeling rested
b. I sometimes wake up feeling rested
c. I usually wake up feeling rested

13
a. I don't feel at all energetic
b. I feel fairly energetic
c. I feel very energetic

14
a. I don't think things have a particular 'sparkle'
b. I find beauty in some things
c. I find beauty in most things

15
a. I don't feel mentally alert
b. I feel quite mentally alert
c. I feel very mentally alert

16
a. I don't feel particularly healthy
b. *(circled)* I feel moderately healthy
c. I feel very healthy

17
a. I do not have particularly warm feelings towards others
b. *(circled)* I have some warm feelings towards others
c. I have very warm feelings towards others

18
a. I do not have particularly happy memories of the past
b. *(circled)* I have some happy memories of the past
c. Most past events seem to have been happy

19
a. *(circled)* I am never in a state of joy or elation
b. I sometimes experience joy and elation
c. I often experience joy and elation

20
a. There is a gap between what I would like to do and what I have done
b. *(circled)* I have done some of the things I wanted
c. I have done many of the things I wanted

21
a. I can't organize my time very well
b. *(circled)* I organize my time fairly well
c. I organize my time very well

22
a. *(circled)* I do not have fun with other people
b. I sometimes have fun with other people
c. I often have fun with other people

23
a. I do not have a cheerful effect on others
b. *(circled)* I sometimes have a cheerful effect on others
c. I often have a cheerful effect on others

24
a. *(circled)* I do not have any particular meaning or purpose in my life
b. I have a sense of meaning and purpose
c. I have a great sense of meaning and purpose

25
a. *(circled)* I do not have particular feelings of commitment and involvement
b. I sometimes become committed and involved
c. I often become committed and involved

26
a. I do not think the world is a good place
b. *(circled)* I do think the world is a fairly good place
c. I do think the world is a very good place

27
a. *(circled)* I rarely laugh
b. I laugh fairly often
c. I laugh a lot

28
a. I don't think I look attractive
b. I think I look fairly attractive
c. *(circled)* I think I look attractive

29
a. *(circled)* I do not find things amusing
b. I find some things amusing
c. I find most things amusing

How to calculate your score:

For each item, a = 0, b = 1, and c = 2. *Add* your scores for all the 29 items.

Your total happiness score is __*22*__ Date: ___*8|12|15*___

Your total happiness score is _____ Date: _____

Your total happiness score is _____ Date: _____

Your total happiness score is _____ Date: _____

Your total happiness score is _____ Date: _____

Your total happiness score is _____ Date: _____

The lowest possible score on the Oxford Happiness Inventory is a 0 (if you circled 'a' for all twenty-nine items), and the highest possible score is a fifty-eight (if you circled 'c' for all twenty-nine items). The average is around a thirty-eight.[2]

Keep a record of your happiness score and the date you complete the scale. As you engage in the happiness activities, you will want to complete the scale on a regular basis – for example, on the first day of each month or after a particular goal is met. Either way, you will be able to observe how your happiness changes – and increases – as you continue the happiness programme.

Chapter 4

Practising gratitude and positive thinking

It is a truism that how you *think* about yourself, your world and other people is more important to your happiness than the objective circumstances of your life. 'The mind is its own place, and in itself / Can make a Heaven of Hell, a Hell of Heaven,' John Milton wrote in *Paradise Lost*. The three happiness-increasing activities in this chapter all aim to transform the way we think about our lives – making a Heaven of Hell, finding something to be glad about, and not sweating the small stuff.

Philosophers, writers and great-grandmothers of times past have long extolled the virtues of the three happiness activities I describe here – expressing gratitude, cultivating optimism and avoiding overthinking and social comparison. Such exhortations as 'try to be more optimistic', 'don't dwell too much', and 'you'd feel better if you were more appreciative' have been around for generations. So, what makes them important for us today? Why should you spend your valuable time and energy in learning them, in turning them into habits? Furthermore, how do we know, first, that these habits are even learnable (as opposed to inborn); and, second, that even if you could train yourself to do them, you'd be happier? The answers to these questions are found within these pages. I have selected for this book only those activities (from among many) that have been shown to be successful through science rather than conjecture. What's more, I describe why these strategies work and how precisely they should be implemented to maximize their effectiveness using evidence from the latest research. In every grandmotherly bit of advice lies a kernel of truth. I've chosen the biggest kernels, established what the data show, and sought to determine for whom these truths might work best and how and why. Apply these activities to your own life and you will harness the promise of the 40 per cent solution.

Happiness Activity No. 1: Expressing gratitude

The expression of gratitude is a kind of meta-strategy for achieving happiness. Gratitude is many things to many people. It is wonder, it is appreciation, it is looking at the bright side of a setback, it is fathoming abundance, it is thanking someone in your life, it is thanking God, it is literally 'counting blessings'. It is savouring, it is not taking things for granted, it is coping, it is present-oriented. Gratitude is an antidote to negative emotions, a neutralizer of envy, avarice, hostility, worry and irritation. The average person, however, probably associates gratitude with saying 'thank you' for a gift or benefit received. I invite you to consider a much broader definition of gratitude.

The world's most prominent researcher and writer about gratitude, Robert Emmons, defines it as 'a felt sense of wonder, thankfulness, and appreciation for life'.[1] So, you could strive to feel grateful by noticing how fortunate your circumstances are (and how much worse they could be), by calling an old mentor and thanking him for guiding you through one of life's crossroads, by relishing moments with your child, or by recalling all the good things in your life at present. By definition, the practice of gratitude involves a focus on the present moment, on appreciating your life as it is today and what has made it so.

Expressing gratitude is a lot more than saying 'thank you'. Emerging research has recently started to draw attention to its multiple benefits. People who are consistently grateful have been found to be relatively happier, more energetic and more hopeful, and to report experiencing more frequent positive emotions. They also tend to be more helpful and empathic, more spiritual and religious, more forgiving, and less materialistic than others who are less predisposed to gratefulness. Furthermore, the more a person is inclined to gratitude, the less likely he or she is to be depressed, anxious, lonely, envious or neurotic.[2] All of these research findings, however, are correlational, meaning that we cannot know conclusively whether being grateful actually *causes* all those good things (or inhibits bad things), or whether possessing traits like hopefulness, helpfulness and religiosity simply makes people feel grateful. Fortunately, several experimental studies have now been done that solicit expressions of gratitude from unsuspecting individuals and then record the consequences.

In the very first such set of studies, one group of participants was asked to write down five things for which they were thankful, namely, to 'count their blessings', and to do so once a week for ten weeks in a row.[3] Other groups of participants took part in the control groups – instead of focusing on gratitude every week, these individuals were asked either to think about their five daily hassles or five major events that had occurred. The findings were exciting. Relative to the control groups, those participants from whom expressions of gratitude were solicited tended to feel more optimistic and more satisfied with their lives. Even their health received a boost – they reported fewer physical symptoms (such as headaches, acne, coughing or nausea) and more time spent exercising.

Other studies have prevailed on both students and adults with chronic illness to try the 'count your blessings' strategy, with similar results. These studies have shown that, on the days that individuals strive to express their gratitude, they experience more positive emotions (that is, feelings like interest, excitement, joy and pride) and are more likely to report helping someone, to feel connected with others and even to catch more hours of quality sleep.

These investigations show for the first time that expressions of gratitude are causally linked to the mental and physical health rewards that we have seen. However, the goal of this research has been to determine the extent of gratitude's *real-time* influence on positive affect and health, that is, whether you feel happier on a day that you are trying to be more grateful. My laboratory, by contrast, is interested in the question of how people can become happier over time. When my graduate students and I were deciding what to do for our very first happiness 'intervention' (an experiment aimed to make people happier), testing the strategy of counting one's blessings seemed like the obvious choice. So, building on these findings, we conducted a new experiment, in which we measured participants' happiness levels, then implemented our gratitude intervention, and, once it was over, measured their happiness levels again immediately. The gratitude intervention was very similar to the one I just described. We directed our participants to keep a sort of gratitude journal – that is, to write down and contemplate five things for which they were grateful. Their exact instructions were as follows:

> There are many things in our lives, both large and small, that we might be grateful about. Think back over the events of the past week and write down on the lines below up to five things that happened for which you are grateful or thankful.

Five blank lines followed, headed by 'This week I am grateful for:'

The participants engaged in this happiness exercise over the course of six weeks. Half of them were instructed to do it once a week (every Sunday night) and half to do it three times a week (every Tuesday, Thursday and Sunday). The things that our participants recorded covered quite a wide range – from 'mum', 'a healthy body', and 'having a Valentine' to 'getting tested on only three chapters for my midterm' and 'AOL instant messenger'.

As we expected, our simple exercise was effective in producing higher levels of thankfulness and appreciation. More important, those participants who counted their blessings on a regular basis became happier as a result. Compared to a control group (i.e., people who did not practise any kind of exercise), the gratitude group reported significantly bigger increases in their happiness levels from before to after the intervention. But, interestingly, this effect was only observed for those who expressed gratitude every Sunday night. The participants who counted their blessings three times a week didn't obtain any benefit from it. This finding might seem puzzling at first, but we believe there is an explanation: the average person made to express his or her gratitude every Tuesday, Thursday and Sunday appeared to have become bored with the practice, perhaps finding it a chore, whereas the person made to express gratitude only once a week probably continued to find it fresh and meaningful over time. We'll return to this specific finding later, as it has important implications for how to carry out the gratitude activity – or any happiness-increasing activity for that matter – with success.

Eight ways that gratitude boosts happiness

It may sound corny, but the research clearly demonstrates that you would be happier if you cultivated an 'attitude of gratitude'.[4] However, instead of following this advice blindly, it's important to understand why and how expressing gratitude works to make you happier. Indeed, there are no fewer than eight reasons why I advise people to practise it.

First, grateful thinking promotes the savouring of positive life experiences. By relishing and taking pleasure in some of the gifts of your life, you will be able to extract the maximum possible satisfaction and enjoyment from your current circumstances. When my first child was only a few months old, an older woman approached me while I was struggling with the pushchair. 'Your baby is so beautiful,' she said. 'Appreciate this age – it goes by so fast!' At the time, I was feeling overwhelmed and sleep deprived and, to be honest, didn't much appreciate her glib intrusion, but it had a powerful effect. Taking time to feel grateful for this small child allowed me to step outside the dreariness of my long days caring for her and to savour the magic of the small moment I shared with my daughter.

Second, expressing gratitude bolsters self-worth and self-esteem. When you realize how much people have done for you or how much you have accomplished, you feel more confident and efficacious. Unfortunately, for many people, it comes more naturally to focus on failures and disappointments, or on other people's slights and hurts. Gratefulness can help you unlearn this habit. Instead of automatically thinking 'Woe is me' in response to any setback, the practice of gratitude encourages you instead to consider what you value about your current life, or how you are thankful that things aren't worse.

Third, gratitude helps people cope with stress and trauma. That is, the ability to appreciate your life circumstances may be an adaptive coping method by which you positively reinterpret stressful or negative life experiences.[5] Indeed, traumatic memories are less likely to surface, and are less intense when they do, in those who are regularly grateful.[6] Interestingly, people instinctively express gratitude when confronted with adversity. For example, in the days immediately after the September 11, 2001 terrorist attacks on the US, gratitude was found to be the second most commonly experienced emotion (after sympathy).[7]

Expressing gratefulness during personal adversity like loss or chronic illness, as hard as that might be, can help you adjust, move on and perhaps begin anew. Although it may be challenging to celebrate your blessings at moments when they seem least apparent to you, it may be the most important thing that you can do. In one of my recent courses, I had a severely disabled older student named Brian. He has some but not much mobility in his hands and is able to control a wheelchair by pressing on a lever located near his shoulder, with his bent right hand. One day the class was going around the room and talking about their happiest moments in life. This is what Brian said: 'My happiest moment is kind of a perverse one. It was the day that I came home from the hospital, after my accident. I felt *defiant*. I said, "Ha! I'm still alive! I beat you!" I don't know who exactly I beat. But I felt grateful that I was home. It seemed like a little thing, but being home from the hospital after four months was so good.' Echoing this perspective, sixty-seven-year-old Inger, who had been given a short time to live, described her illness this way: 'When you can hear the minutes ticking and you know the buzzer is going to go off in any minute and your time will be up, you see things so clearly. You just know without a doubt where your values are and why you're alive, and you're so grateful for each moment.'[8] Inger and Brian have a remarkable capacity for gratitude, a capacity that undoubtedly serves them well in both sickness and health.

Fourth, the expression of gratitude encourages moral behaviour. For example, as I mentioned earlier, grateful people are more likely to help others (e.g., you become aware of kind and caring acts and feel compelled to reciprocate) and less likely to be materialistic (e.g., you appreciate what you have and become less fixated on acquiring more stuff). To wit, an Auschwitz survivor was once described this way: 'His life was rooted in gratitude. He was generous, because the memory of having nothing was never far from his mind.'[9] In one study, people induced to be grateful for a specific kind act were more likely to be helpful towards their benefactor, as well as towards a stranger, even when the helping involved doing an unpleasant, tedious chore.[10]

Fifth, gratitude can help build social bonds, strengthening existing relationships and nurturing new ones.[11] Keeping a gratitude journal, for example, can produce feelings of greater connectedness with others. Indeed, several studies have shown that people who feel gratitude towards particular individuals (even when they never directly express it) experience closer and 'higher quality' relationships with them.[12] As Robert Emmons argues, when you become truly aware of the value of your friends and family members, you are likely to treat them better, which may produce an 'upward spiral' – a sort of positive feedback loop – in which strong relationships give you something to be grateful for, which in turn fortifies those very same relationships, and so on. In addition, a grateful person is a more positive person, and positive people are better liked by others and more likely to win friends.[13]

Sixth, expressing gratitude tends to inhibit invidious comparisons with others. If you are genuinely thankful and appreciative for what you have (e.g., family, health, home), you are less likely to pay close attention or envy what the Joneses have.

Seventh, the practice of gratitude is incompatible with negative emotions and may actually diminish or deter such feelings as anger, bitterness and greed.[14] As one psychiatrist has argued, 'gratitude . . . dissolves negative feelings: anger and jealousy melt in its embrace, fear and defensiveness shrink.'[15] Indeed, it's hard to feel guilty or resentful or infuriated when you're feeling grateful. My friend's sister is one of the few working mums I know who feels not an ounce of guilt. The reason is that she is a prodigy at asking friends and family for help and thanking them so profusely and sincerely afterwards that they feel like rock stars.

Last but not least, gratitude helps us to thwart hedonic adaptation. If you recall, hedonic adaptation is illustrated by our remarkable capacity to rapidly adjust to any new circumstance or event. This is extremely adaptive when the new event is an unpleasant one, but not when a new event is positive. So, when you gain something good in your life – a romantic partner, a genial officemate, recovery from illness, a brand new car – there is an immediate boost in happiness and contentment. Unfortunately, because of hedonic adaptation, that boost is usually short lived. As I've argued earlier, adaptation to all things positive is essentially the enemy of happiness, and one of the keys to becoming happier lies in combating its effects, which gratitude does quite nicely. By preventing people from taking the good things in their lives for granted – from adapting to their positive life circumstances – the practice of gratitude can directly counteract the effects of hedonic adaptation.

How to practise gratitude

If you learned in Chapter 3 that gratitude is one of the happiness activities that 'fit' you best, then you already have a leg up as you're already motivated and willing to put in the effort and commitment it takes to become more grateful. How exactly you accomplish this is up to you – what's needed is simply to select at least *one* activity from the array of possibilities below.

Gratitude journal

If you enjoy writing, if you are good at it, or it feels natural to you, then a promising way to practise this strategy is with a 'gratitude journal', much like the one used by my gratitude intervention participants. Choose a time of day when you have several minutes to 'step outside' your life and thoughtfully reflect. It may be first thing in the morning, or during lunch, or while commuting, or before bedtime. Ponder the three to five things for which you are currently grateful, from the mundane (your dryer is fixed, your flowers are finally in bloom, or your husband remembered to go to the shop) to the magnificent (your child's first steps or the beauty of the sky at night). One way to do this is to focus on all the things that you know to be true, for example, something you're good at, what you like about where you live, goals you have achieved, and your advantages and opportunities.[16] Don't forget specific individuals who care for you, have made contributions or sacrifices for you, or somehow touched your life. The results of my laboratory's gratitude intervention suggested that, on average, doing this once a week is most likely to boost happiness, and that's my recommendation to the majority of people. However, 'on average' means that some individuals, and those may include you, may benefit most from doing this strategy on an entirely different timetable – perhaps even daily or three times a week or twice a month. You need to determine the ideal timing tailored to your lifestyle and disposition. (See Chapter 10 for more about timing.)

Paths to gratitude

Furthermore, the particular *means* by which you go about counting your blessings will depend on your individual personality, goals and needs. Instead of writing, some of you may choose a fixed time to simply contemplate each of your objects of gratitude and perhaps also to reflect on why you are grateful and how your life has been enriched. Others may choose to identify just one thing each day that you usually take for granted and which ordinarily goes unappreciated. Alternatively, some may want to acknowledge one ungrateful thought per day (e.g., 'my sister forgot my birthday') and substitute a grateful one (e.g., 'but she's always been there for me').[17]

Friends and family can also help foster your appreciation. One idea is to procure a 'gratitude partner' with whom you can share your 'blessings' list and who prompts and encourages you if you lose motivation or simply forget. Chapter 10 describes the power and potential of social support in greater detail. Another idea is to introduce a visitor to the things, people and places that you love. Show off your comic book collection, your favourite park or your favourite niece. Doing this will help you see the ordinary details of your life through another person's eyes, affording you a fresh perspective and making you appreciate them as though you're experiencing them for the very first time.

Keep the strategy fresh

Another important recommendation is to keep the gratitude strategy fresh by varying it or not over-practising it. My research suggests that variety, the spice of life, is extremely important.[18] (Again, consult Chapter 10 to find out more.) For example, if you count your blessings every single day in the exact same way, you may become bored with the routine and may cease to extract much meaning from it. However, you might instead pause to express gratitude only after particular triggers, for example, after enduring a hardship or when you are most needful of a 'boost'. Or, you may choose to write in a journal some weeks, talk to a friend other weeks and express gratitude through art (photography, collage, watercolour) during other weeks. On the other hand, you may purposefully want to vary the domains of your life on which to focus, for example, alternately counting your blessings with respect to your supportive relationships or work life or past events or your physical surroundings or even for life itself. These techniques will help make the expression of gratitude a meaningful practice, such that it continues to bolster happiness instead of hitting a plateau.

Express gratitude directly to another

Finally, the expression of gratitude may be particularly effective when done directly by phone, letter or face-to-face to another person. If there's someone in particular whom you owe a debt of gratitude, express your appreciation in concrete terms. Perhaps it's your mum, favourite uncle or an old friend; perhaps it's an old coach, teacher or supervisor. Write him or her a letter now, and, if possible, visit and read the letter out loud in person either on a special day (birthday, anniversary or holiday) or a random one. Describe in detail what they did for you and exactly how it affected your life; mention how you often remember their efforts. Furthermore, some people find it uplifting to write a gratitude letter to someone they don't know personally, but who's influenced their lives (such as an author or politician) or has made their lives easier (such as their postie or bus driver).

A person close to me shared this letter that he had sent to his high school English teacher more than thirty years after being in her class. I'd like to think that this chapter on gratitude (which he had freshly read) inspired him to write it:

The main thing I want to tell you is that you were, without question, the most influential teacher I encountered at Deer Park High School, and that I am extremely grateful for the interest you took in me. You seemed to think I had something on the ball, and trust me on this, that was a minority opinion among the school faculty. Your estimation of my abilities, inflated as it may have been, translated into a certain degree of self-confidence that served me well, I think, in the years that followed.

Perhaps more importantly, you treated me – a pretty unsophisticated seventeen or eighteen year old – as an adult, and there is nothing on earth more empowering, to a teenager, than that. Even allowing for the fact that the 1970s were very different times than these, I sometimes find myself thinking 'What was she thinking?'

Martin Seligman and his colleagues tested the well-being benefits of expressing gratitude in this way.[19] They investigated a
simple and quick 'gratitude visit' exercise, which was completed
over the course of just one week. People from all walks of life
logged onto the researchers' website and received their instructions there. In the 'gratitude visit' condition, participants were
given one week to write and then deliver a letter of gratitude in
person to someone who had been especially kind and caring to
them but whom they had never properly thanked. In other conditions, participants were offered alternative self-guided
happiness exercises. Those participants who did the gratitude visit
showed the largest boosts in the entire study – that is, straight
away they were much happier and much less depressed – and
these boosts were maintained one week after the visit and even
one month after. These findings reveal just how powerful it is to
express your gratitude directly to an important person in your life.
It's an activity that you can assign yourself to do on a regular basis,
perhaps intermixing the writing of gratitude letters (directed at
the same or different individuals) with keeping a weekly gratitude
journal.

There will be times, however, when you will choose to write
the letter but not to send it. Indeed, in a recent study from my
laboratory, we found that simply writing a gratitude letter and not
sending or otherwise delivering it was enough to produce substantial boosts in happiness.[20] Participants were asked to identify
several individuals who had been especially kind to them over the
past several years. Those who spent fifteen minutes once a week
(over the course of eight weeks) writing letters of gratitude to
these individuals became much happier during and after the
study. Notably, the happiness boost was especially pronounced if
the study participants were especially motivated to become happier, if the 'gratitude letter' activity fit their goals and preferences,
and if they put extra effort into the writing task.

For one of the homework assignments in my Psychology of
Happiness class, I regularly ask my undergraduate students to
compose a gratitude letter. Every year, it's been one of the most

potent and moving exercises that they do. Last year, Nicole, one of the best students in the class, described for me the experience of writing a gratitude letter to her mum:

> I felt overwhelmed with a sense of happiness. I noticed I was typing very quickly, probably because it was very easy for me to express gratitude that was long overdue. As I was typing, I could feel my heart beating faster and faster . . . Towards the end of the letter, as I reread what I had already written, I began to get teary eyed and even a little bit choked up. I think my expressing my gratitude to my mum overwhelmed me to such a point that tears streamed down my face.

Nicole then recalled the effects the letter had on her:

> Later that week (three days after I initially wrote the gratitude letter), I was sitting in front of my computer writing a paper and I was extremely frustrated. Since I was not having much success with my paper, I felt compelled to open up my gratitude letter. I reread it and even made a few changes. Instantly, I noticed that I had a smile on my face. It was almost strange how fast my mood had shifted. I had not even looked at the letter with the intention of elevating my mood, but rather I was merely bored of my research paper, so I thought I'd just do something else. Similar to my reactions the day I actually wrote the letter, after reading it, I felt much happier and less stressed for the rest of the evening. Overall, I found that the effects of writing such a letter to be quite amazing in that the letter not only elevated my mood, but the changes were lasting.

In sum, there are multiple ways to practise the strategy of gratitude and it would be wise to choose what works best for you. Select at least one option from this section and give it a go. When the strategy loses its freshness or meaningfulness, don't hesitate to make a change in *how*, *when* and *how often* you express yourself.

Spontaneous gratitude: A postscript

I am reluctant to reveal this, but, although I wholeheartedly recognize its many rewards, expressing gratitude turns out to be one of the strategies that suits me least. It's no big deal; each of us will wind up with a list of happiness activities that fit and a longer list of activities that don't fit, which is unavoidable. The important fact is that, as much of a platitude as 'counting blessings' is sometimes, as the scientific evidence shows persuasively, it is also incredibly effective. The anecdotal evidence is also hard to disregard – I know many (now happy) individuals who report that becoming grateful changed their lives.

So, having said this, something that happened during the writing of this chapter took me by surprise. One day, after spending long hours reading through the research on gratitude, I spontaneously wrote an e-mail to all my colleagues publicly thanking our department chair for something he had done. He wrote me back immediately saying how much he appreciated my note. It felt great. And it only hit me later what had occurred – reading about gratitude must have rubbed off and I had unwittingly written a gratitude letter that day!

COMPLEMENTARY ACTIVITIES

If you benefit from this activity, you may also want to try:

1) Practising acts of kindness (Happiness Activity No. 4, p. 125)

2) Learning to forgive (Happiness Activity No. 7, p. 172)

Happiness Activity No. 2: Cultivating optimism

Looking at the bright side, finding the silver lining in a cloud, noticing what's right (rather than what's wrong), giving yourself the benefit of the doubt, feeling good about your future and the future of the world, or simply trusting that you can get through the day are all optimism strategies. Cultivating optimism has a lot in common with cultivating gratitude. Both strategies involve the habit of striving to make out the positive side of your situation. Building optimism, however, is not only about celebrating the present and the past, but anticipating a bright future.

Before continuing, I want to dispel some myths about optimism. Learning to be optimistic doesn't mean coming to believe that you live in the 'best of all possible worlds' (as Candide would have it) or that your past, present and future are pristine and without complications. Indeed, consider the distinction between 'big optimism' and 'little optimism'.[21] The difference involves how specific or small are one's positive expectations – for example, 'My flight tomorrow will arrive on time' (little optimism) versus 'We are on the threshold of a glorious age' (big optimism). Both are adaptive, but in different ways. Little optimism predisposes people to behave in constructive, healthy ways in specific situations (e.g., completing the next project at the office), whereas big optimism produces an overall feeling of vigour; it makes you feel resilient, strong and energetic. I will add another form of optimism, which you could call 'very small optimism'. This is just the feeling that you will make it through this day, this month, this year, that there may be ups and downs, but everything will turn out all right in the end. Although, for some of you, practising optimistic thinking may mean posting optimistic quotes on your website or your walls or chanting daily affirmations of the order of 'I'm good enough, I'm smart enough, and doggone it, people like me!,[22] for others, the exercise of optimism may look very different. If optimism befits your lifestyle and personality, it can be practised with maturity, level-headedness, grace and even humour.

Like gratitude, optimism means different things to different people. For example, optimism is most widely assumed to mean expecting a desirable future, that good things will be abundant and bad things scarce.[23] Obviously, what one person perceives as desirable or good (e.g., marrying Peter or enrolling in college or following the Grateful Dead) is another person's nightmare. In addition, a person can be optimistic in one context (e.g., about recovering from knee surgery), but pessimistic in another (e.g., about reconciling with an old friend).

Psychologists who study optimism have offered somewhat different definitions. Some researchers characterize it as a global expectation about a positive future – that is, a belief that one's goals can be accomplished (somehow).[24] Others diagnose optimism (versus pessimism) in the ways that people tend to explain their outcomes.[25] When faced with a negative or unpleasant event, we invariably ask 'why?' So, for example, a person who has tried and failed to sell her car would be called optimistic if she attributes her failure to causes that are external, transient and specific ('wintertime is a buyer's market'), as opposed to causes that are internal, long-lasting and pervasive ('I'm terrible at persuading people'). It turns out that such explanations are quite important, as they influence our reactions to our circumstances and make it more or less likely whether we'll succeed, fall prey to depression or succumb to illness. Finally, other researchers focus not on the target of our optimism (e.g., 'I will secure that job'), but on how we believe we'll get there. This approach is concerned with people's determination to attain a particular goal and their beliefs regarding specific steps needed to reach that goal.[26] So, optimism is not only thoughts like 'I will get there', but also about exactly how it will be accomplished.

Your best possible selves

My friend Laura King, a professor at the University of Missouri-Columbia, pioneered the first-ever systematic intervention (or experimental study) of optimism.[27] It's actually quite simple. She asked participants to visit her laboratory for four consecutive days. On each day, they were instructed to spend twenty minutes writing a narrative description of their 'best possible future selves'. Basically, this is a mental exercise in which you visualize the best possible future for yourself in multiple domains of life. For example, a twenty-nine-year-old woman might imagine that in ten years, she'll be married to her soul mate, have two healthy children, be working in the field of advertising, and play the violin in an amateur chamber music ensemble. This is essentially her fantasy of what her life might be like if all her dreams were realized. Then again, perhaps the term 'fantasy' is poorly chosen as it implies that this vision of her life is only a fanciful, farfetched daydream. To the contrary, this exercise involves considering your most important, deeply held goals and picturing that they will be achieved. Laura King found that people who wrote about their visions for twenty minutes per day over several days, relative to those who wrote about other topics, were more likely to show immediate increases in positive moods, to be happier several weeks later, and even to report fewer physical ailments several months hence.

The 'Best Possible Selves' exercise turned out to be a potent intervention and we decided to apply it in our own laboratory. So, Ken Sheldon and I instructed participants to do the same exercise, except we had them complete just one writing session in the lab and then urged them to continue the writing sessions at home – as often and for as long as they wished – over the course of four weeks. Precisely, the participants were told:

> You have been randomly assigned to think about your best possible self now and during the next few weeks. 'Think about your best possible self' means that you imagine yourself in the future, after everything has gone as well as it possibly could. You have worked hard and succeeded at accomplishing all of your life goals. Think of this as the realization of your life dreams, and of your own best potentials.[28]

As we expected, participants who engaged in the Best Possible Selves exercise caught a significant lift in mood relative to a control group who simply wrote about the details of their daily lives. Additionally, as described in Chapter 3, the biggest boosts in happy mood were observed among those participants who felt that the exercise 'fit' them best (i.e., who found it interesting, challenging and meaningful) and who practised it with sustained effort. This constitutes yet more direct empirical evidence that if you want to reap long-term emotional benefits from a happiness activity, you need to devote persistent effort. Of course, if you identify with and enjoy what you are doing, you'll be more energized and committed. Our participants were clearly willing to adopt our recommendation to continue carrying out the Best Possible Selves activity at home and seemed to have turned it into a personal goal of their own. That should be your aim as well when it's time for you to select a happiness-enhancing activity to pursue.

Why did the Best Possible Selves strategy work so well? Our participants who tried it apparently found it motivating, relevant to their current lives and easy to relate to. They appeared to enjoy visualizing *reaching* their future goals. But the exercise wasn't just about imagining a model future for them, it was also about building a best possible self *today* that can make that future come true. Committing their Best Possible Selves to writing enabled them to recognize that it's in their power to transform themselves and to work towards valued goals, that their dreams today and tomorrow don't hinge on their spouse or on money or on some stroke of luck.

Another advantage of the Best Possible Selves exercise is the fact that it's conducted through writing.[29] Because writing is highly structured, systematic and rule-bound, it prompts you to organize, integrate and analyse your thoughts in a way that would be difficult, if not impossible, to do if you were just fantasizing in your head. So, writing about your goals helps you put your thoughts together in a coherent manner, allowing you to find meaning in your life experiences. Writing about your dreams also gives you an opportunity to learn about yourself, to better understand your priorities, your emotions and your motives, your identity, who you really are and what's in your heart. In other words, the Best Possible Selves exercise can help you see the 'big picture' of your life anew and where you're going. This new understanding may provide you with a feeling of control (e.g., 'I now see a way to make my dream come true') and help you recognize and reduce conflict between your goals and the obstacles that might stand in your way (e.g., 'How can I honour my family's wishes but also strike out on my own?'). And all of those things will ultimately make you happier.

One young woman, Molly, did this exercise and wrote to me how it made her understand what her goals really were and realize that they were not unattainable:

> Before beginning the exercise, I felt nervous since I'm not certain as to exactly what I want to do or where I want to be in the future. I was nervous that I wouldn't have anything to write about. During the [writing] sessions . . . the time went by as though it was nothing, it felt very relaxing to allow myself to express my goals. After the writing sessions I felt really good, really happy with myself. The more I thought about the goals, the more I realized that they weren't unattainable and far out of my reach, in actuality they were within my reach – they didn't seem so far away . . . [The exercise] made me realize that I could be doing more to reach these goals, and with a little effort now I could achieve this best possible life. I had never really contemplated them seriously, so now I feel like I have more of an idea of what is important to me, what I can achieve, and how far I have to go to get these things. I had never realized so much that what I want is a stable life (love, family, friends, occupation, living situation). I hope to be with a complementary partner, successful in my work, continue to maintain the relationships I have today with my friends and family, and to try my hardest to live in a city that makes me happy, with lots of things to do and close to the ocean. I think that would make me ultimately happy, and I do not think that these goals are unreachable.

Molly demonstrates several benefits of the Best Possible Selves strategy. She gained insight into her goals and needs, recognized what might make her happy, and became more confident in how to get what she wants. She is now more likely to effortfully strive to achieve her dreams and, I hope, to be a happier person.

Why does optimistic thinking boost happiness?

The Best Possible Selves strategy is one of several effective ways to tap into optimistic thinking. All such strategies share the benefits of an optimistic outlook. Let's now consider the many advantages of becoming more optimistic. After all, if you are willing to put a great deal of energy into something, you should be assured that it will work.

First, if you're optimistic about the future – for example, you're confident that you'll be able to achieve your life-long goals – you will invest effort in reaching those goals. For this reason, optimistic thoughts can be self-fulfilling. If you perceive an outcome as attainable you will persist at the plan even when you hit inevitable obstacles or when progress is slow. Indeed, researchers have shown that optimists are more likely to persevere and to engage fully even in the face of difficulty.[30] They also set a greater number of goals and more difficult goals for themselves.[31] So, optimism motivates us and leads us to take the initiative. Optimists don't easily give up. This is likely to be one major reason why optimists are more successful across a wide variety of arenas – professional, academic, athletic, social and even in health. And, of course, persistence, social skill, vigour, health and career success are all things that contribute to our happiness.

Another important way that optimistic thinking enhances happiness is that it prompts us to engage in active and effective coping.[32] There's a great deal of evidence that optimists routinely maintain relatively high levels of well-being and mental health during times of stress.[33] For example, optimistic women are less likely to become depressed following childbirth than women who are less optimistic, and optimistic undergraduates are less likely to experience distress three months after starting at college. Furthermore, optimists are more likely to make plans and take direct action when faced with adversity. They are good copers.

Even during the worst of times, such as after receiving a grave diagnosis, they don't deny the situation, but instead are likely to accept the reality of their condition and make efforts to make the best of it and even grow from it. This seems almost too good to be true (are they for real?), but research bears it out. Perhaps due to these strengths, research has found that people who have frequent optimistic thoughts are physically healthier.

Finally, you may not be surprised to learn that optimistic thinking promotes positive moods, vitality and high morale. Studies also show that optimists are relatively more likely to report a sense of mastery and high self-regard and less likely to show depression and anxiety. It feels good to believe that your prospects are bright. If you have something to look forward to you will feel energized, motivated and enthusiastic. You will feel good about yourself and feel able to control your destiny. You will even be better liked by others.[34] In short, you will reap the benefits of an excellent happiness–enhancing strategy.

How to practise optimism

If cultivating optimism is a well-fitting strategy for you, you can begin to practise it today with one of the ideas below.

'Best Possible Selves' diary

There are many ways to practise optimism, but the one that has been empirically shown to enhance well-being is the original 'Best Possible Selves' diary method. To try it out, sit in a quiet place and take twenty to thirty minutes to think about what you expect your life to be one, five or ten years from now. Visualize a future for yourself in which everything has turned out the way you've wanted. You have tried your best, worked hard and achieved all of your goals. Now describe in writing what you imagine.

This writing exercise in a sense puts your optimistic 'muscles' into practice. Even if thinking about the brightest future for yourself doesn't come naturally at first, it may get there with time and training. Amazing things can come about as a result of writing. William Faulkner reportedly once said, 'I never know what I think about something until I read what I've written on it.' You may discover new insights into yourself as you write about your future and your goals. Keeping a journal may even be a way of cultivating patience and persistence.

Goals and subgoals diary

A twist on the 'Best Possible Selves' diary is that, as part of developing hopeful thinking, identify your long-range goals and break them up into subgoals.[35] So, for example, during the first session of your journal writing, you could describe how five years from now you'll be the owner of your own business. In future sessions, you could write about the steps you'll take to reach that point. (Remember that there may be many such steps or paths, not just one.) If a discouraging or pessimistic thought comes to mind ('How could I ever get the money?'), pinpoint it and try to generate alternative scenarios or possible resolutions. One technique is to recall times in the past when you've been successful at something, recognize the strengths and resources that you already have (and will continue to develop), allowing that to motivate and invigorate you.

Identify 'barrier thoughts'

Another strategy to increase optimistic thinking involves identifying automatic pessimistic thoughts. For example, you might put a penny in a jar every time you have a pessimistic thought. Then, try to replace that thought with a more charitable or favourable point of view. For example, spontaneous thoughts such as 'I feel so stupid for giving the wrong advice to my office mate; he'll never ask me again to collaborate on a project' or 'Ever since my relationship ended, I feel unlovable and unappealing' are called 'barrier thoughts' because they serve as a barrier to optimism. Write your barrier thoughts down and then consider ways to reinterpret the situation. In the process, ask yourself questions like:

- What else could this situation or experience mean?
- Can anything good come from it?
- Does it present any opportunities for me?
- What lessons can I learn and apply to the future?
- Did I develop any strengths as a result?[36]

Be sure to practise this exercise when you're in a neutral or positive mood and consider writing down your answers. This approach should prevent your reflections from devolving into circular, negatively biased ruminations (see Happiness Activity No. 3).

A successful twelve-week optimism training programme for fifth and sixth graders in the US [years six and seven] has already used a very similar technique.[37] The children were taught to be more optimistic by learning to identify pessimistic explanations (e.g., 'My friend didn't call me today; he must hate me'), to dispute them ('What evidence do I have that this is really true?') and then to generate more optimistic alternatives (e.g., 'Maybe he's too busy').[38] Notably, the children who participated in this programme were less depressed than a control group for an entire two years after the programme ended, and their reduction in depression turned out in some measure to be due to their learned optimism.

Making optimism a habit

Essentially, all optimism strategies involve the exercise of construing the world with a more positive and charitable perspective, and many entail considering the silver lining in the cloud – identifying the door that opens as a result of one that has closed. It takes hard work and a great deal of practice to accomplish effectively, but if you can persist at these strategies until they become habitual, the benefits could be immense. Some optimists may be born that way, but scores of optimists are made with practice.

So, although it might seem that your naturally optimistic peers are in a far-flung category from you, there's really no trick to their way of thinking. All that is required to become an optimist is to have the goal and to practise it. The more you rehearse optimistic thoughts, the more 'natural' and 'ingrained' they will become. With time, they will be a part of you and you will have made yourself into an altogether different person. The positive spins and the silver linings will come about automatically and habitually, such that you would only need to 'practise' optimistic thinking effortfully and intentionally during times of stress, insecurity or heartbreak.

A recipe for self-deception?

Some of you may still be sceptical. Making oneself 'think positive' or 'look on the bright side' sometimes smacks of naïveté or, worse, of foolishness. Perhaps you're a person who values 'seeing things as they really are' above all else. According to this view, reframing negative events in a positive and optimistic way or anticipating a sunny future would actually be wrong, or at the very least unrealistic. To this reaction, I prefer the rejoinder by my graduate school adviser Lee Ross:

> [Optimism] is not about providing a recipe for self-deception. The world can be a horrible, cruel place and at the same time it can be wonderful and abundant. These are both truths. There is not a halfway point – there is only choosing which truth to put in your personal foreground.

Being optimistic involves a choice about how you see the world. It doesn't mean denying the negative or avoiding all unfavourable information. It also doesn't mean constantly trying to control situations that cannot be controlled. Indeed, research shows that optimists are *more* not less vigilant of risks and threats[39] (they don't have their blinkers on), and optimists are very much aware that positive outcomes are dependent on their efforts (they don't wait around for good things to happen). Like anything in life, however, you should aim for moderation in optimistic thinking. Optimism expert Martin Seligman recommends a 'flexible optimism' to be marshalled when the situation calls for it, but not when 'clear sight or owning up is called for'.[40]

COMPLEMENTARY ACTIVITIES

If you benefit from this activity, you may also want to try:

1) Savouring life's joys (Happiness Activity No. 9, p. 196)

2) Learning to forgive (Happiness Activity No. 7, p. 172)

Happiness Activity No. 3: Avoiding overthinking and social comparison

'Finish each day and be done with it. You have done what you could; some blunders and absurdities have crept in; forget them as soon as you can. Tomorrow is a new day; you shall begin it serenely and with too high a spirit to be encumbered with your old nonsense.'

RALPH WALDO EMERSON

During all the years that I've been studying happiness, I've also been keenly interested in a phenomenon that psychologists call 'self-focused rumination'. My friend and collaborator Susan Nolen-Hoeksema has spent two decades investigating this phenomenon, which she calls 'overthinking', which is exactly what it is. Overthinking is thinking too much – needlessly, passively, endlessly and excessively pondering the meanings, causes and consequences of your character, your feelings and your problems: 'Why am I so unhappy?' 'What will happen to me if I continue to procrastinate at work?' 'I'm so dismayed by how thin my hair has become', 'What did he really mean by that remark?' and so on.

Many of us believe that, when we feel down, we should try to focus inwardly and evaluate our feelings and our situation in order to attain self-insight and find solutions that might ultimately resolve our problems and relieve unhappiness. Susan Nolen-Hoeksema, myself and others have compiled a great deal of evidence challenging this assumption. Numerous studies over the past two decades have shown that, to the contrary, overthinking ushers in a host of adverse consequences. It sustains or worsens sadness, fosters negatively biased thinking, impairs a person's ability to solve problems, saps motivation and interferes with concentration and initiative.[41] And, notably, although people have a strong sense that they are gaining insight into themselves and their problems during their ruminations, this is rarely the case. What they do gain is a distorted, pessimistic perspective on their lives.

I received recently an e-mail from one of three sisters, Theresa, who described herself as a chronic overthinker: 'I'm the youngest of three girls and the most likely to ruminate, [making] myself unhappy by pondering and yearning and wondering and just feeling stuck.' If Theresa is feeling unhappy about trying to drum up clients for her tax preparation business, obsessing over the 'whys', 'hows' and 'what ifs' of her problems will not only fail to deliver any insight or make her feel better, but it might make things even worse. The combination of rumination and negative mood is toxic. Research shows that people who ruminate while sad or distraught are likely to feel besieged, powerless, self-critical, pessimistic and generally negatively biased. The more she overthinks her problems, the more likely that Theresa will have thoughts like, 'I'm not assertive enough for this business', 'I'll never get another client', 'This is just like that summer I couldn't find a job', 'Maybe I should just quit', or 'My finances will be in ruins'. She may also have trouble concentrating at work and be less able to resolve minor dilemmas or obstacles that might come her way or she may perceive making calls or even doing routine tasks as an unbearable hurdle. Ultimately, Theresa's distorted predictions and beliefs could create a self-fulfilling prophecy – she really *will* now have even more trouble attracting new clients. Ruminators can make less than appealing social partners, so her friends and co-workers might start avoiding her. All these factors together could lead Theresa to lose confidence in herself and even to spiral into clinical anxiety or depression.

The evidence that overthinking is bad for you is now vast and overwhelming. If you are someone who is plagued by ruminations, you are unlikely to become happier before you can break that habit. Indeed, I will go so far as to say that if you are an overthinker, one of the secrets to your happiness is the ability to allay obsessive overthinking and to reinterpret and redirect your negative thoughts into more neutral or optimistic ones. I have found that truly happy people have the capacity to distract and absorb themselves in activities that divert their energies and attention away from dark or anxious ruminations.[42] Daily life is replete with minor upsets, hassles and reversals. In most people's experience, other unavoidables include illness, rejection, failure and sometimes devastating trauma. However, those who react strongly to life's ups and downs and have great difficulty shaking off unfavourable information are the unhappiest people in my studies. Even slightly difficult, unpleasant or disagreeable events can make such people feel bad about themselves. Becoming happier means learning how to disengage from overthinking about both major and minor negative experiences, learning to stop searching for all the leaks and cracks – at least for a time – and not let them affect how you feel about yourself and your life as a whole.

My friend Leda was going through a very tough time taking care of her mother, who was terminally ill. Leda once described to me taking a daily break from the endless nursing by paying a visit to the local farmer's market. She loves outdoor markets and this one was especially lively, thronged and brimming with beautiful produce, warm breads, fresh fish and many other goods. Leda said she was absolutely joyful during her free hour and a half. She could have easily slid into worry and despair, grieving the imminent loss of the dearest person in the world to her, feeling sorry for herself, obsessing over medical bills, or depressed that she didn't have a social life. Of course, she had bad moments. Of course, there were times when scrutinizing the medical bills was necessary. But, even during a trying time, she was able to absorb herself in an attention-grabbing activity, stay busy and feel joy.

Overthinking in the laboratory

A notable feature of overthinking is that it draws on a person's mental resources. Have you ever tried to read an article or a book immediately after an unpleasant encounter or after hearing bad news? You may notice yourself reading the same sentence over and over again. You may have trouble concentrating at school, during work, in the midst of conversations and even when trying to have fun. My students and I decided to conduct a series of studies to test this phenomenon in the laboratory. We found, indeed, that some of our participants tend to ruminate about bad experiences and that this overthinking harms their concentration, and ultimately their performance, at demanding everyday activities like reading and writing.[43] Not surprisingly, those who show this pattern are the ones who report being the most unhappy.

We also found evidence that, in the face of an unpleasant event (e.g., a teacher's criticism, a social snub, an ambiguous health symptom), some people – but not all – find themselves pondering negative aspects of themselves. They may be distressed or anxious, chewing over what's happened and wondering about its implications. In some studies, we expose our participants to negative feedback, for example, informing them that they've done very poorly on a test of verbal ability. Immediately afterwards, we offer them a sort of 'puzzle' task, in which they are asked to complete words. For example, how would you fill in the missing letters to complete the following words? Don't spend more than fifteen seconds thinking about each word.

- D U __ __
- __ __ S E R
- I __ __ __ T
- E M __ __ __ __ __ __ __

Interestingly, relative to individuals who had learned they had 'succeeded', those participants told earlier that they had presumably 'failed' (an experience likely to trigger ruminative thoughts) were likely to complete the words as DUMB, LOSER, IDIOT and EMBARRASS, revealing what was on their minds – namely, negative, self-evaluative thoughts. However, it was only the participants who identified themselves as fairly unhappy who did this. Our happiest participants, by contrast, were able to shake off the ruminations. If you are the type of person who is 'jolted by every pebble in the road', persistent rumination is likely to take a significant toll on you. You need to imitate the behaviour of the happy person and work to break free of overthinking.

Social comparison

Social comparisons are ubiquitous. In our daily lives, we can't help but notice whether our friends, co-workers, family members and even fictional characters in the movies are brighter, richer, healthier, wittier or more attractive. Every time we ask, 'How was your day?', every time we flip through a magazine, every time we chat about our relationships with others, we are inviting social comparisons. Researchers have shown that such comparisons can be useful.[44] Sometimes they inspire us to strive for an ambitious goal or to improve a weakness. Watching a piano prodigy play a beautiful sonata can motivate the amateur to work harder. At other times, social comparisons can make us feel better about our own plight. In the neonatal intensive care unit, the parent of a low birth weight infant may be comforted by noticing that other parents' babies are even more fragile.

Much of the time, however, observations of how other people are doing or about what they have can be pernicious. 'Upward' comparisons (e.g., 'He's paid a higher salary', 'She's thinner') may lead to feelings of inferiority, distress and loss of self-esteem, while 'downward' comparisons (e.g., 'He got laid off', 'Her cancer's spread') may lead to feelings of guilt, the need to cope with others' envy and resentment, and fears of suffering the same (or worse) fate. The more social comparisons you make, the more likely you are to encounter unfavourable comparisons; and the more sensitive you are to social comparisons, the more likely you are to suffer their negative consequences. Indeed, social comparisons are particularly invidious because no matter how successful, wealthy or fortunate we become, there's always someone who can outdo us. I heard an anecdote on the radio once that brought this home to me. A woman was recounting her father's sage advice in response to her complaints that other people had more than her: 'My father used to say to me, "Look at these two mansions on Mission Street – they're both stunning, multi-million dollar homes. But the mansion on the left side of the street has an ocean view, and the one across from it does not. Do you think that the people who live in the second mansion are envious?"'

You can't be envious and happy at the same time. People who pay too much attention to social comparisons find themselves chronically vulnerable, threatened and insecure. Interestingly, the phenomenon of comparing ourselves to others was the first topic I ever investigated as a research scientist. During my very first year in graduate school at Stanford, my adviser Lee Ross and I decided to seek out people who had been singled out by their acquaintances and friends as being 'exceptionally happy' or 'exceptionally unhappy' and to interview both groups at length. Our initial hypothesis (quite naïve in hindsight) was that the happy people would be more likely to compare themselves to others who are inferior (thus making themselves feel better off), whereas unhappy people would be inclined to compare themselves to others who are superior (thus, rendering themselves unhappy). However, when we asked the participants our carefully prepared questions about social comparison, the happy folks didn't know what we were talking about! Of course, they understood what it meant to compare themselves to others – everyday observations, social interactions, and the media inundate us with information about others' successes and failures, opinions, personalities, lifestyles and relationships – yet faced with such readily available and inescapable opportunities for social comparison, the happy people we interviewed didn't seem to care. Instead, they appeared to use their own internal standards to judge themselves rather than letting others' performances influence their feelings about themselves (not falling prey to thoughts like, 'Ella is so much more knowledgeable than I am; therefore, I must be mediocre'). Intrigued by these preliminary findings, Lee and I resolved to confirm them in more controlled laboratory studies. Indeed, over the next few years, we found that the happiest people take pleasure in other people's successes and show concern in the face of others' failures. A completely different portrait, however, has emerged of a typical unhappy person – namely, as someone who is deflated rather than delighted about his peers' accomplishments and triumphs, and who is relieved rather than sympathetic in the face of his peers' failures and undoings.

Social comparison under the microscope

The social comparison studies were fun to do. For example, on one occasion, we brought happy and unhappy people into the lab and told them they'd be solving 'anagram puzzles' alongside a peer.[45] If you had been the participant in this study, you and your peer would have been asked to take a seat in side–by–side chairs, with the experimenter (often myself) sitting by a table in front. At the beginning of the session, I would have handed each of you a card with three anagrams on it and your task would have been to unscramble them (e.g., A-S-S-B-I, Y-O-N-S-W, and N-O-X-T-I).[46]

Every time you or your peer would have finished a card, you would have handed it back to me and then I would have given you a new one. The set-up was created to make it incredibly apparent to you at what rate the *other* person was going because you couldn't help but notice the exchange of cards. In addition, the cards were numbered consecutively, so if you had been handed card No. 1 followed by card No. 5, then you would have

grasped immediately that while you had been frantically working on card No. 1, the other participant had already solved cards
No. 2, No. 3, and No. 4. So you would have known you were
behind. In addition, we asked that participants use exercise books
as rough paper, which required turning the page every time a
new anagram was begun. The swooshing of pages again would
have highlighted the discrepancy between your speed and that of
the other participant, an effect familiar to anyone who's ever
taken a test.

Here's the clincher. Your supposed 'peer', unbeknownst to
you, would not actually have been another participant but a con-
federate working for me, whom I'd have instructed to solve the
anagrams (or pretend to solve them) either a great deal faster or
a great deal slower than you. How would that experience have
made you feel?

The results of this study were dramatic. After the anagram-
solving task was over, happy participants felt more upbeat than
they had been earlier and thought better of their ability, *regardless*
of whether they had witnessed someone perform much better or
much worse than them. The self-assessments of unhappy people,
by contrast, were keenly sensitive to the experience of witnessing another person's superior performance. Unhappy people
thought *less* of themselves – for example, judging their anagram-
solving ability as quite a bit worse – and reported feeling more
sad, frustrated and anxious after sitting next to someone who out-
performed them.

Since then, my students and I have conducted many more
studies showing essentially the same result – that the happier the
person, the less attention she pays to how others around her are
doing. Once again, the research tenders an example of what we
can learn from the habits of a happy person. Indeed, the practice
of incessantly comparing ourselves to others is part and parcel of
the wider-ranging habit of overthinking.

How to shake off ruminations and social comparisons

Rumination can be very compelling. When you're in the tangle of it, it pulls and pushes you. You feel that you absolutely need to continue, that you need to figure things out. But, as we have learned, when a person is distraught or stressed or nervous or insecure, no insight is gained from overthinking. To the contrary, rumination only makes things worse. Susan Nolen-Hoeksema advises chronic overthinkers to try the following three-step approach to battle their persistent ruminations – break free, move to higher ground and avoid future traps.[47] These steps are described below. If this is a well-fitting activity for you, choose at least one strategy to try from each of the sections that follow.

Cut loose

First, you need to free yourself from the clutch of your rumina-tions – in other words, to immediately stop overthinking and stop focusing on comparisons with others. There are no fewer than five effective strategies to accomplish this and, as always, you should pick the ones that feel most natural and most meaningful to you. The first strategy to arrest overthinking is simple and underrated, yet incredibly powerful: distract, distract, distract. The distracting activity you select must be engrossing enough so that you don't have the opportunity to lapse back into ruminations. Good bets are activities that make you feel happy, curious, peace-ful, amused or proud. So, when you catch yourself thinking, 'Why did I get so few lines in the community play?' or 'I'll never get a promotion if Howard doesn't give me more responsibilities', or 'She has so much more free time than I do', you should re-direct your full attention somewhere else – read or watch something that's funny or suspenseful, listen to a song that's trans-porting, meet a friend for tea, do a physical activity that gets your heart rate up. It doesn't matter what you do, as long as it absorbs you, compels you and it isn't potentially harmful. Sometimes, all it takes to stop ruminating is to get up and leave the scene of the crime.

It's worth noting that although distraction seems like an almost too-simple short-term solution or quick fix, the positive emotions that it begets can 'de-bias' your thinking (opening up a new, more objective and more positive perspective on your troubles) and hone resources and skills (like creativity, sociability and problem-solving skills) that will be useful in the future.[48] Even a transient lift in mood can make you feel energized, more motivated to interact with people, and more creative in how you approach your problems.

The second strategy is the 'Stop!' technique, in which you think, say or even shout to yourself 'Stop!' or 'No!' when you find yourself resuming overthinking. (A hairdresser once told me she imagines a red stop sign as she's doing this.) Use your intellectual powers to think about something else, like your shopping list or what you will say when you call the plumber or the steps you need to take in planning your next holiday. This technique is valuable in many situations, including moments when your thoughts wander even during a distracting pastime. I remember once finding myself ruminating whenever I would go running and I would force myself to stop and redirect my attention to something else. This feat involved what seemed at the time like terrific powers of mental control, but it worked.

The third is a strategy I learned from an agony aunt a long time ago. She advised an obsessive reader to set aside thirty minutes every day to do nothing but ruminate. Accordingly, if you find the negative thoughts pushing and pulling, you can truthfully tell yourself, 'I can stop now, because I'll have the opportunity to think about this later.' Ideally, that thirty-minute period should be at a time of the day when you're not anxious or sad. More often than not, when the appointed time arrives, you'll find it difficult and unnatural to force yourself to overthink and the issues you had set aside to contemplate will seem less consequential than before.

The fourth strategy is to talk to a sympathetic and trusted person about your thoughts and troubles. Much of the time, a simple tête-à-tête will bring an immediate reprieve to your feelings of negativity. You may find yourself feeling that your problems aren't as overwhelming as you initially thought they were. Or you might recognize the futility of being envious of a fellow mum's apparent parenting virtuosity and realize that in fact she is just as flawed as you are. However, a couple of caveats are in order. One is to choose your confidant(e) carefully – he or she must be able to think objectively, not make you feel even worse *or* end up ruminating out loud with you. The other is not to abuse your opportunity. If you bring up your negative thoughts and worries ad infinitum, you may wear people out so much that they avoid you.

The final strategy involves writing. Whether in a handsome journal, computer file or on a scrap of paper, writing out your ruminations can help you organize them, make sense of them and observe patterns that you haven't perceived before. Writing is also a way to unburden yourself of your negative thoughts, allowing you to move past them.

Act to solve problems
Second, you need to gain a new perspective on yourself and on your life in general. Essentially, this step jumpstarts you into trying to solve the very real, concrete problems that might inspire your overthinking. So, for example, even if you're feeling weighed down by your problems and responsibilities and are indecisive about what to do, take a small step now. Perhaps this entails making an appointment with a marriage counsellor (even if you're pessimistic about the outcome), or starting the first day of a financial planning programme, or doing research on the internet about possible new jobs, or writing an e-mail to someone who's slighted you. It could be writing a list of every possible solution to a particular problem – for example, ways to improve your relationship with your boss, to help your daughter's sleeping problems, to make extra money during the summer – and then implementing one of those solutions. If you're hesitant, think of a person whom you highly respect and admire and ask yourself which solution he or she would choose. Don't wait for something to happen or for someone else to step in and help

you – act right away. Even small steps will improve your mood and self-regard.

Dodge overthinking triggers
Third, you need to learn how to avoid future overthinking traps. For example, write a list of situations (places, times and people) that appear to trigger your overthinking. If at all possible, avoid those situations or modify them just enough to thwart their ability to trigger an episode of overthinking. This is not that different from what a smoker must do when quitting – avoiding locations, times of the day and specific people that set off his desire to smoke. Another technique is to strengthen your identity and work towards building your sense of self-worth. This is a biggie, but you can begin by taking small active steps, like learning or undertaking something new (e.g., cooking, hiking, gardening, painting, dog training). (Don't take on anything too grand.) This will enhance your self-confidence ('I'm much better at taking photos than I thought') and provide an alternative source of self-esteem by expanding your identity ('I've always thought of myself as a bookworm, but now I feel so good when I go to dance class. It brightens the days when my teaching job isn't going well').

    Finally, if this is up your alley, learn how to meditate. The skills involved in this relaxation technique can help you distance yourself from your worries and ruminations and impart a positive sense of well-being. See Chapter 9 for detailed instructions or read one of the many books on the topic. Many people who meditate habitually claim that they find themselves feeling less burdened, worried and stressed for the rest of the day.

Take in the big picture
To add to these recommendations, I challenge those of you who have chosen to commit to avoiding overthinking and social comparisons to try a couple of techniques proposed in *Don't Sweat the Small Stuff*.[49] Whenever a rumination or social comparison prevails upon you ('How will I ever get through this week?' 'Teddy has been so distant and short-tempered lately', 'Once again, our

manager took more notice of Cecilia's presentation than of mine', 'Could that light-headed feeling be another flu coming on?' 'Was I the only one not invited to the party?') ask yourself the following question: will this matter in a year? Your answer will afford you a big picture view of your troubles and diminish your worries. It's remarkable how quickly things that seem so momentous and pressing this very moment emerge as fairly trivial and insignificant. Sometimes when I'm facing a horrendous week or am upset over a perceived slight, I remind myself that I won't remember it (much less care about it) one month, six months or a year from now. (The more extreme version of this strategy is to use the 'deathbed criterion': will it matter when you're on your deathbed?)

Another valuable approach is to distance yourself from rumination even further by contemplating your particular problem in the context of space and time. If you're an astronomy enthusiast, visualize yourself (and the strains, worries and tribulations facing you) as a microscopic dot on Earth, which is a tiny part of the Milky Way, which makes up an infinitesimal speck of the universe. This may seem like a silly exercise, but in doing it, the recognition will undoubtedly dawn on you that your problems are trifling. When my son went through an astronomy phase, I was taken aback about how serene and unruffled I felt every time I read him a book about galaxies, stars or planets. How can I stress over my carpooling situation when the farthest galaxy is thirteen billion light years away? When the universe is expanding! It seemed magical that this knowledge would have this impact, but it did. An alternative exercise is to reflect on how 150 years from now, no one who is alive today will still be living. This also sharply brings home the point that few things in life are so significant that they are worth overthinking.

Finally, if you resolve that the trouble you're enduring now is indeed significant and *will* matter in a year, then consider what the experience can teach you. Focusing on the lessons you can learn from a stress, irritant or ordeal will help soften its blow. The lessons that those realities impart could be patience, perseverance, loyalty or courage. Or perhaps you're learning open-mindedness, forgiveness, generosity or self-control. Psychologists call this 'post-traumatic growth'[50] and it's one of the vital tools used by happy, resilient people in facing the inevitable perils and hardships of life.

COMPLEMENTARY ACTIVITIES

If you benefit from this activity, you may also want to try:

1) Developing strategies for coping (Happiness Activity No. 6, p. 154)

2) Committing to your goals (Happiness Activity No. 10, p. 213)

Chapter 5

Investing in social connections

~

'If I am not for myself, who will be for me? If I am only for
myself, what am I?
And if not now, when?'

TALMUD

~

The centrality of social connections to our health and well-being
cannot be overstressed. 'Relationships constitute the single most
important factor responsible for the survival of homo sapiens,'
writes one social psychologist.[1] I don't think this is an overstate-
ment. One of the strongest findings in the literature on happiness
is that happy people have better relationships than their less happy
peers.[2] It's no surprise then that investing in social relationships
is a potent strategy on the path to becoming happier. This chapter describes two happiness activities that have social connections
in common – practising kindness and nurturing relationships.

Happiness Activity No. 4: Practising acts of kindness

The moral dimension of being kind, generous and giving is
undisputed. The Bible exhorts us 'to be generous and willing to
share' (1 Timothy 6:18), and a principled, moral person helps
those who are in need and, when necessary, sacrifices his own
well-being for another. Indeed, the German philosopher
Schopenhauer wrote that 'Compassion is the basis of all morality.' So, from a very early age, we are inculcated with the idea that
kindness and compassion are important virtues. Of course, we are
taught to develop and apply these virtues for their own sakes

because, by definition, it is the right, good and ethical thing to do. What scientific research has recently contributed to this age-long principle is evidence that practising acts of kindness is not only good for the recipient, but also good for the doer. It may be ironic, but being kind and good, even when it's unpleasant or when one expects or receives nothing in return, may also be in the doer's self-interest. This is because being generous and willing to share makes people happy.

The milk of human kindness is . . . happiness

To be sure, the notion that doing acts of kindness can make a person feel good is not exactly novel. Writers, philosophers and religious thinkers have appreciated this truth for centuries. 'If you want to be happy, practise compassion', is a common refrain of the spiritual leader of Tibetan Buddhism, the fourteenth Dalai Lama. 'True happiness consists in making others happy,' according to a Hindu proverb. And Scottish-born essayist Thomas Carlyle quipped, 'Without kindness, there can be no true joy.' Nice thoughts, but their veracity had until recently not been tested systematically, using the scientific method. My laboratory was the first, to my knowledge, to accomplish this. Previous research had only reported correlations (but not causation) between happiness and helping. So, for example, we know that happier people are more likely to describe themselves as doing frequent altruistic acts (e.g., shopping for a sick friend or stopping to help a stranger), to spend a greater percentage of their time helping others and to perform behaviours at the office that go beyond the call of duty (e.g., helping a colleague with work problems despite their own heavy workloads).[3] These findings are illuminating, but they have little to say about whether doing all those things (helping a stranger or a colleague) actually *makes* people happy.

To address this very question, my collaborators and I conducted a happiness 'intervention' or experiment in which we recruited participants into two groups and asked them to perform five acts of kindness per week over the course of six weeks.[4] The first group was instructed to do these acts anytime throughout the week, but the second group was instructed to do the five acts on one single day each week. These were our exact instructions:

> In our daily lives, we all perform acts of kindness for others. These acts may be large or small and the person for whom the act is performed may or may not be aware of the act. Examples include feeding a stranger's parking meter, donating blood, helping a friend with homework, visiting an elderly relative, or writing a thank-you letter. Over the next week, you are to perform *five* acts of kindness. The acts do not need to be for the same person, the person may or may not be aware of the act, and the act may or may not be similar to the acts listed above. Do not perform any acts that may place yourself or others in danger.

Every Sunday night, our participants turned in their 'kindness reports', in which they described the acts of kindness they had done each week, to whom and when. Examples of the types of kind acts that they performed ranged widely from very small, simple helpful behaviours to fairly big ones: 'bought a friend a sundae', 'washed someone else's dishes', 'donated blood', 'stayed with a friend on her first night at a new place', 'visited a nursing home', 'helped a stranger with computer problems', 'let my sister borrow my car for the weekend', 'gave a homeless man 20 dollars' and (my personal favourite) 'told a professor "thank you" for his hard work'.

The results were a bit surprising. As expected, being generous and considerate made people happy – that is, the participants who committed acts of kindness over the course of the study experienced a significant elevation in their happiness. But, interestingly, this boost was only reported by those who showed their weekly generosity all in one single day. So, although both groups who committed kind acts described themselves as being much more helpful after the intervention than before, the group that was instructed to distribute their five weekly acts of kindness over the course of the week didn't become any happier. Why did this happen? My hunch is that, because many of the kind acts that the participants performed were small ones, spreading them over seven days each week might have diminished their conspicuousness, their prominence and their power, or made them less distinguishable from the participants' habitual kind behaviour. After all, most of us do minor thoughtful and helpful things on a regular basis and we may not even be aware of it.

So we see evidence in this study for the notion that optimal *timing* is critical for a happiness activity to be effective. In the section on gratitude (in Chapter 4), I noted that when we asked people to 'count their blessings' on a regular basis, only those who did it once a week (versus three times a week) were rewarded with an increase in well-being. So, you need to determine precisely how, when and how often to commit to a happiness-enhancing practice in order to maximize its success. The results of our kindness intervention suggest that doing more than is your custom (at least when it comes to kindness) is ideal.

Our study was the first to show that a strategy to increase kind behaviours is an effective way to elevate happiness. Since then, we have been conducting longer and more intensive investigations, working out how and why this and other strategies work. For example, we did another study in which we asked people to commit acts of kindness though this time we checked in on them a month after the intervention had ended, to determine whether their happiness levels were preserved.[5] Furthermore, some of our participants had the opportunity to vary the kindnesses that they performed, whereas others did not. At the beginning of the study, everyone was asked to make a list of acts of kindness that they would 'like to do more in the future' and that are 'easily repeatable on a daily basis'. For example, they might choose to do an extra household chore, send e-cards to family members, help someone carry or pick up something, give their pet a special treat, or make breakfast for their boyfriend. Those in the 'high variety' condition could mix and match any three acts they wanted to do each week, but those in the 'low variety' condition had to perform the same three acts every week for ten weeks in a row.[6]

This second kindness study confirmed for us, once again, that doing acts of kindness on a regular basis makes people happy for an extended period. But the extent to which people vary what they do makes an enormous difference. Indeed, those participants who had to repeat their three kind acts over and over again actually dropped in happiness by the middle of the study before bouncing back to their original levels. These individuals probably found their exercise to be just another item on their to-do list – that is, a tedious experience that detracts rather than adds to happiness. If an activity is meant to enhance well-being, it needs to remain fresh and meaningful. Of course, when you embark on your own happiness-increasing programme, you will do so by your own free will, not because an experimenter in a white lab coat is prompting you. Indeed, when you select an activity that 'fits' you, you are choosing, by definition, to do something that you value and that you believe you will enjoy. This is empowering in and of itself. The singular act of choosing an activity can make you feel brighter and gladder even before you commit your first act of kindness (or gratitude or whatever else). Nevertheless, this study alerts us to be mindful of not falling into a rut when practising our chosen strategy. Spicing up your happiness strategies will be worth the effort. (See Chapter 10 to hear more.)

Why does doing kind deeds make people happy? Let us count the ways

Plentiful evidence for the reasons (or 'mechanisms') for why helping brings happiness comes from psychological theory and research. Being kind and generous leads you to perceive others more positively and more charitably (e.g., 'the homeless veteran may be too ill to work' or 'my brother really tries at maths, but it doesn't come easily to him') and fosters a heightened sense of interdependence and cooperation in your social community (e.g., 'it takes a village to raise a child' or 'we must all pitch in to improve the environment'). Acting kindly often relieves guilt, distress or discomfort over others' difficulties and suffering and encourages a sense of awareness and appreciation for your own good fortune. In other words, helping others makes you feel advantaged and thankful by comparison. Indeed, providing assistance or comfort to other people can deliver a welcome distraction from your own troubles and ruminations, as it shifts the focus from you to somebody else.

A considerable benefit of kindness is its impact on self-perception. When you commit acts of kindness, you may begin to view yourself as an altruistic and compassionate person. This new identity can promote a sense of confidence, optimism and usefulness. That is, helping others or volunteering for a worthy cause highlights your abilities, resources and expertise and gives you a feeling of control over your life.[7] You may learn new skills or discover hidden talents, for example, by honing your teaching aptitude or social skills, through uncovering a flair with children, or by learning the workings of a hospital. This in itself can confer a sense of efficacy and accomplishment. Some researchers argue that acts of kindness can even promote a sense of meaningfulness and value in one's life.[8]

Finally, and this is probably the most important factor, kindness can jumpstart a cascade of positive social consequences. Helping others leads people to like you, to appreciate you, to offer gratitude. It also may lead people to reciprocate in *your* times of need.[9] So, helping others can satisfy a basic human need for connecting with others, winning you smiles, thankfulness and valued friendship. My laboratory actually obtained evidence for this dynamic in our second kindness intervention. We measured not only how helpful our participants were and how much their happiness increased over ten weeks, but also the extent to which they perceived gratitude in those they helped. And, indeed, we found that a chief reason why being kind to others made our participants happier is that it led them to recognize how much the recipients appreciated their kind acts.

So, there are multiple ways that kindness can make us happier. Surveys of volunteers, for example, show that volunteering is associated with diminished depressive symptoms and enhanced feelings of happiness, self-worth, mastery and personal control – a 'helper's high'.[10] Although these studies can't disentangle causal direction (i.e., 'Does volunteering make people feel good about themselves, or are people who feel good about themselves more likely to volunteer in the first place?'), studies that follow volunteers over time strongly suggest that it's the munificent behaviour of the volunteers that enhances happiness and not the other way around.

Consider an unusual study that followed five women volunteers over a three-year period.[11] These five women, all of whom had multiple sclerosis (MS), were chosen to act as peer supporters for sixty-seven other MS patients. They were trained in active and compassionate listening techniques and instructed to call each patient for fifteen minutes once a month. The results showed that, over the three years, the peer supporters experienced increased satisfaction, self-efficacy and feelings of mastery. They reported engaging in more social activities and enduring less depression. Indeed, when interviewed, these five women described having undergone dramatic change in their lives as a result of their volunteering experience. For example, their role as peer supporters appeared to shift their focus away from themselves and their problems and towards others. They recounted acquiring improved, non-judgemental listening skills and becoming more open and tolerant of other people. They also reported a stronger sense of self-esteem and self-acceptance, for example, confidence in their ability to cope with life's ups and downs and in managing their own disease. One woman stated, 'There's no cure for MS, but I really feel that I'm able to handle whatever comes my way.'

Remarkably, the positive changes experienced by the five women peer supporters were larger than the benefits shown by the patients they supported. For example, the volunteers witnessed a boost in their global life satisfaction that was seven times greater than that shown by the patients! Furthermore, the benefits experienced by the peer supporters grew as time went on – an incredible finding, given that the benefits incurred by most happiness interventions (no matter how powerful) tend to diminish over time.

This was a small study, with only five participants,[12] but it nicely illustrates the multiple rewards of helping. Although volunteering or 'community service' is a unique type of helping activity, involving sustained commitment within an institutional framework, it has many of the same features and the benefits as other, more spontaneous or mundane types of helping behaviour.

How to practise kindness

I have some very altruistic friends. One who especially comes to mind is always there for other people, always saying yes, forever sensitive to a situation when he's needed. I don't know how he does it, how kindness has become so habitual to this man, but many of us need to consciously and intentionally practise what comes so easily to him. Then again, the advantage for the rest of us is that doing something over and above what we are used to will give us an extra lift, a special boost in positive well-being.

I have come across numerous books, magazine articles and web sites advocating doing acts of kindness,[13] and I always get the sense, perhaps unfounded, that they patronize the reader a bit. If you decide to become a more generous, compassionate and giving person, you will know what you should do. Ever babysat for a harried parent when you weren't asked? Ever travelled to see a friend in need? Donated your money or your time? Smiled at someone who needs a smile even when it's the hardest thing to do at that very moment? Needless to say, the options for helping are unlimited. You need only to open your mind to the possibilities for kindness – if you look with fresh eyes, they are all around you.

Furthermore, no particular talent, measure of time, or amount of money is required. The deed need not be grand or complicated. And, if you're ever at a loss about *what* act of kindness, generosity or charity to carry out, you need look no further than your home, your work place or your community. Sometimes people go to great lengths seeking a special cause to which to dedicate themselves, when that special cause could be your spouse, child, co-worker or old friend. An acquaintance with a newborn at home related to me a story about her husband. He was a musician – a cello player – and had learned about a community service music programme that involved visiting nursing homes once a month and entertaining the residents there. Despite a gruelling work schedule that left him with little time to see his wife and baby daughter, he started taking out several hours per month to do this. He was very earnest and well-meaning about the new endeavour. But his wife was beside herself. 'How can he play for strangers, when he doesn't have time to entertain his own little girl?' she complained to me. Choose your acts of kindness with care, as any change in your behaviour can have unintended consequences, good or bad. Above all, you don't have to be a Mother Teresa or the Dalai Lama – the acts can be small and brief.

Timing is everything
So, the first step in practising the kindness strategy is to select which acts you intend to do and how often and how much. The results of my intervention studies suggest that this is an important decision point. If you do too little, you won't obtain much benefit in happiness. If you do too much, you may end up feeling overburdened, angry or fatigued. My suggestion is to follow the model of the one group in my first kindness intervention that was rewarded with the biggest increases in happiness – namely, pick one day per week (say, a Monday) and on that day (and on no others) commit one new and special large act of kindness or,

alternatively, three to five little ones. I say 'new and special' because you probably already dole out numerous small and large kindnesses every day, and the kindness strategy calls for doing something extra, something that pulls you out of your usual routine. So, if you always let cars pull out ahead of you or you already volunteer at a hospital once a week, then, of course, don't make those your new and special acts of kindness. Resolve to do something else.

Variety is the spice of life

A second implication stemming from my kindness studies is to mix up, spice up, *vary* what you do. Putting change into a parking meter or doing an extra chore gives you a lift the first few times you do it, but after a time, you will adapt to the new habit and it will no longer grant the same amount of happiness. (This doesn't mean that you should necessarily stop doing it, only that you'll be obliged to add another act of kindness to your routine.) Major commitments that involve regular contact with other people – e.g., tutoring a school child, visiting a sick neighbour, fundraising for a cause – may not lend themselves to the same degree of adaptation and may continue delivering benefits to you (and others!) in terms of happiness, self-esteem and other resources and skills.

Continually varying your acts of kindness takes effort and creativity. Here are some ideas. First, if you're short of money or other resources, give the gift of time: offer to make a needed repair, weed a garden, take a child to the playground, or look over someone's taxes. Second, surprise someone with a home-cooked meal, an outing, a gift, a letter or a phone call. Third, each week, try to do more of something that doesn't come naturally. For me, it's being courteous to telemarketers. For another person, it may be offering a sincere smile and hello (or thank you) to a passer-by or the cashier at your supermarket. Or, fully listening (with eye contact) to a friend's concerns. Fourth, work to develop your compassion – that is, the willingness and ability to sympathize with others' plights and points of view. It may be a cliché, but it's very difficult to really put yourself in another person's shoes and see the world from their perspective. Imagine what it would be like to be unable to pay your bills, to be laid off, to care for a disabled child, to be illiterate, or to be too weak to change a light bulb. Offering assistance each week to such a person can help enhance your gratitude and develop and reinforce your compassion. Fifth, at least once a week, do a kind deed about which you tell no one and don't expect anything in return. Resolve not to sit around and wonder why other people aren't as considerate as you. This resolution will fortify your conviction that you are not being generous solely for approval and admiration and this will deepen your sense of value, meaning and self-worth.[14]

Chain of kindness

Standing at the cash register at Whole Foods recently, I overheard a twenty-something guy in front of me tell the cashier, with great embarrassment, that he was $1.15 short of his shopping bill. I don't remember ever doing this before, but I immediately offered him the $1.15. He was at first a bit taken aback and then incredibly and genuinely grateful. He thanked me earnestly and at length. The experience was unexpectedly exhilarating and wonderful (even to me, who does research on kindness!). A dollar is so trivial, I thought, and here was someone who indisputably appreciated and valued what I did. He had a wide and self-conscious smile on his face, yet as he hurried out I saw him helping a woman in a wheelchair to lift her groceries.

In designing your unique kindness strategy, remember that acts of kindness often have such ripple effects. The recipient may be cheered, surprised or comforted, and your thoughtful act may trigger him or her to return the favour to other individuals, who may, in turn, be more generous the next day, and so on. In other words, one benevolent act can set a series of kind acts in motion. Another way that acts of kindness can have positive social consequences is that, as recent research shows, simply *witnessing* or hearing about a kindness leads people to feel 'elevated' and increases their desire to perform good deeds.[15] After observing the heroic acts of kindness by New York City firefighters, emergency personnel and others in the aftermath of 9/11, TV viewers left their couches and went on to donate blood at two to five times the normal rate.[16]

A final caveat

All the recommendations outlined here are aimed to maximize how much happiness you receive as a result of committing to a kindness strategy. Sometimes this involves doing less or stopping what you're doing. I want to underscore that most people act compassionately and generously not primarily for their own benefit but for that of others. Thus, they may continue volunteering or repairing or teaching or listening or cleaning or donating because it's their moral duty. So, take my suggestions with a grain of salt. At times, you'll be called to help others at the expense of your own well-being. As long as this is not a persistent pattern in your life, and a key cause underlying your unhappiness, you should consider saying yes.

When kindness is pernicious

The platitude that being kind to others can bring you happiness has several important qualifications. The first is that certain categories of helping behaviour are actually detrimental to physical and mental health. The one researchers know the most about is full-time care-giving for a chronically ill or disabled loved one. Studies show, for instance, that care-givers of spouses with Alzheimer's disease show depression levels *three times* greater than the average person.[17] Care-givers of spouses with spinal cord injuries report severe physical and emotional stress, burn-out, fatigue, anger and resentment. Furthermore, these care-givers are even more depressed than their disabled partners.[18] The care-giving job is relentless and often accompanied by grieving for the loss of companionship and/or the impending loss of life. Of course, this doesn't mean that care-giving should be forsaken, but that benefactors need to recognize the detriments, so that they can prepare for them and cope as best they can. Indeed, any helping behaviour that is burdensome, interferes with your daily goals and functioning or causes bitterness would surely backfire as a path to happiness, though it may remain the appropriate, honourable or right thing to do.

Another caveat is that a kind act needs to be done freely and autonomously to bring the maximum improvement in well-being. If you are forced to help someone, you may still feel yourself a generous and decent person and you may still garner the appreciation and gratitude of the one you helped, but these benefits could be outweighed by the resentment you might feel or the sense of being taken advantage of.

Finally, other people may not always welcome your kindness. Helping someone can put them in an uncomfortable position, making them feel needy, disadvantaged and beholden. Consequently, instead of gratitude and appreciation, the response from the recipient may be something closer to hostility and resentment. Your attitude and approach can diffuse or minimize such potential feelings. When you undertake your weekly acts of kindness, don't behave self-righteously or condescendingly. Don't puff up your abilities and resources or talk down to the person you are helping. And, unless the situation is critical, don't help those who don't want your help.

Postscript: Kindness versus wealth

As I recounted in Chapter 2, there is now overwhelming evidence that money doesn't make people happy or, more precisely, that it doesn't make people as happy (and for as long) as they suppose. So, what if I told you that becoming a more generous, compassionate and charitable person would make you happier than earning a higher income – would you believe me? I actually won't allege this, because there are no data that directly compare kindness and wealth. But there is plenty of anecdotal evidence. The most persuasive, in my mind, comes from the example of Bill Gates, who announced that he would give up his day-to-day duties as chairman of Microsoft in 2008 to devote more energy to philanthropy. He is the richest man in the world, according to Forbes, yet he spends a great deal of time and effort *giving his money away* – more than half of his fortune, to be exact. Since 2000, for example, the Bill and Melinda Gates Foundation has donated $6 billion – more than most nations – to improve health in developing countries, including hundreds of millions of dollars for vaccinations for children and for medical research, and $2.5 billion for education for the poor. It is entirely possible that one of his donations will make more of a difference in the world than anything he has ever done as chairman of Microsoft. Why does he do it? I can't say, except to speculate that it makes him as happy to give money away as to make it. 'It's fun, and it is also an enormous responsibility,' is how Gates explains his philanthropy. 'But having my job at Microsoft is also fun and a huge responsibility. That is true for being a parent. Many of the most important things in life are like that. Why else would you want to get up in the morning?'[19]

Another fascinating example is that of Sherry Lansing, the first woman to run a major Hollywood studio. She gave up power, fame and riches (as head of Paramount Pictures) to pursue philanthropy full time. According to news reports, her associates and friends were stunned. But it appears that she may be far wiser than they are in appreciating what truly makes for lasting happiness. She's been busy starting a non-profit foundation that targets cancer research and education, advocating on behalf of stem cell research and fundraising for human rights causes. Presumably, Lansing finds this more gratifying than a seven-figure salary.

COMPLEMENTARY ACTIVITIES

If you benefit from this activity, you may also want to try:

1) Savouring life's joys (Happiness Activity No. 9, p. 196)

2) Increasing 'flow' experiences (Happiness Activity No. 8, p. 185)

Happiness Activity No. 5: Nurturing social relationships

One of the themes of this book is that in order to become happier, we must learn to imitate the habits of very happy people. Happy people are exceptionally good at their friendships, family and intimate relationships. The happier a person is, the more likely he or she is to have a large circle of friends or companions, a romantic partner and ample social support. The happier the person, the more likely she is to be married and to have a fulfilling and long-lasting marriage. The happier the person, the more likely she is to be satisfied with her family life and social activities, to consider her partner her 'great love', and to receive emotional and tangible support from friends, supervisors and co-workers.[20]

The causal relationship between social relationships and happiness is clearly bidirectional. This means that romantic partners and friends make people happy, but it also means that happy people are more likely to acquire lovers and friends. This conclusion, which my colleagues and I have put forth on the basis of numerous studies, is actually rather optimistic. It implies that if you begin today to improve and cultivate your relationships, you will reap the gift of positive emotions. In turn, the enhanced feelings of happiness will help you attract more and higher-quality relationships, which will make you even happier, and so on, in a continuous positive feedback loop. In other words, by applying this happiness-increasing strategy, you will embark on what psychologists call an 'upward spiral'.

What's great about relationships

Why are social connections so important to well-being? Because good social relationships serve many vital needs.

Lessons from Darwin

An article called 'The Need to Belong'[21] has become a classic in social psychology and I can now appreciate why. In it, the authors lay out a persuasive case that humans are powerfully motivated by a pervasive drive to seek out and maintain strong, stable and positive interpersonal relationships. We strongly resist the break-up or dissolution of relationships and friendships, and, without a sense of belongingness, we suffer numerous negative consequences for our physical and mental health. This is not surprising, as most scientists would agree that a desire to form and preserve social bonds has an evolutionary basis. Human beings would not have been able to survive or reproduce without such a motivation. Social groups hunted together, shared food and fought off common enemies. Adults who 'pair bonded' bore children, protected them from predators and from the elements and raised them to maturity. 'No man [or woman] is an island,' proclaimed John Donne, and 'The Need to Belong' has shown us the reasons why.

Social support

One of the most important functions of a social bond is the provision of social support in times of stress, distress and trauma. I know first-hand (and the research confirms) that there may be no better coping mechanism than confiding or sharing a problem with a friend or intimate. Social support can be tangible (e.g., driving us to the hospital), emotional (e.g., listening, reassuring and helping us generate solutions or alternative perspectives on problems) and informational (e.g., providing financial advice). Indeed, people with strong social support are healthier and live longer.[22] An intriguing analysis of three communities of very long-living people – Sardinians in Italy, Okinawans in Japan and Seventh Day Adventists in Loma Linda, California – revealed that they all had five things in common. At the top of that list were 'put family first' and 'keep socially engaged'.[23]

All you need is love

My four-year-old used to insist that we teach him a new word at bedtime. One night, I tried something new. 'Your word tonight is "love",' I said. 'I knooooow what looove means! I love *you*, mummy.' 'But what does it mean that you love me?' He thought about this. 'It means I want to kiss you a lot. And I want to live with you forever.' In ten years he might regret having said that, but I think that definition of love is perfect. From the time of their conception to the moment of their death, human beings are embedded in relationships with others. It is within interpersonal relationships that most of us experience for the first time the emotion of love – the most wildly happiness-inducing emotion there is – and find meaning and purpose in our lives. Of course, as everybody knows, love has its ups and downs, but, nonetheless, most identify it as one of the chief things that makes them happy.[24]

Less hedonic adaptation

As the pie chart theory vividly portrays, all of our life circumstances combined (health, wealth, age, job title, ethnicity, residence, life events, etc.) only have a small influence on our happiness. This is primarily because we so rapidly adapt to any circumstantial life change. For example, as we acquire income and consumer goods that we desire (e.g., gadgets, computers, cars, homes or swimming pools) our aspirations simply rise to the same degree, thereby trapping us in a hedonic treadmill. In one study that surveyed people over a thirty-six-year period, respondents were asked how much income was needed by a family of four to 'get along'.[25] The higher the person's income, the more they estimated was required for a family of four. And, remarkably, the estimate for 'get along' income increased almost exactly to the same degree as did actual income, suggesting that the more you have, the more you think you 'need'.

But what about our friendships, family and intimate relationships? Do we adapt to them as easily and quickly as we adapt to material goods? The answer turns out to be 'no'. One economist has shown, for example, that people's desires for a happy marriage, for children and for 'quality' children (as bizarre as that term sounds) do not change as they successfully attain those things.[26] In other words, there is something special and unique about relationships and we would do well to strengthen, nourish and enjoy them.

Strategies for investing in relationships

Because at least 90 per cent of adults eventually marry, most of my recommendations in this section refer to strengthening intimate (or 'romantic') relationships, such as marriages. However, you'll recognize that many of the suggestions apply to other kinds of close relationships, such as with close friends and family members. Pick one strategy from the array below and start doing it *today*.

John Gottman is a marriage researcher who has psychologically dissected hundreds of married couples. His book, *The Seven Principles For Making Marriage Work*, is, in my opinion, the best marital advice manual on the market *by far*.[27] I have talked it up to dozens of acquaintances and friends, indeed to anyone who currently is, has been, or wishes to be in a committed romantic relationship. Even if your relationship is already solid, there is always room to strengthen and enjoy it even more. In his research, Gottman videotapes married couples and systematically observes how they behave and talk with one another. He then follows them over time to see what happens in their relationship. Based on these observations, he is able to predict with 91 per cent accuracy which couples will stay together and which will divorce. This level of predictive accuracy, I should add, is unprecedented in the field of psychology.

Make time
So, what are the secrets of the successful marriages? The first is that the partners talk – a lot. The successful couples spend five hours more per week being together and talking.[28] So, the first recommendation is to commit to extra time each week with your partner, perhaps starting with one hour and working your way up towards more. Spend five minutes every day expressing appreciation or gratitude for particular behaviours (even if it's simply to

say 'thank you for taking care of the bills this month'). Furthermore, before you part in the morning, find out *one thing* that each of you is going to do that day. When you meet again in the evening, have a 'reunion conversation' in a low-stress set-ting and *listen*. Coming from a household with two full-time jobs and two small kids, I fully appreciate that this is easier said than done. Be creative. If you're in a situation similar to mine, then return from work fifteen minutes before your kids do (or your babysitter leaves) or allow them to watch a fifteen-minute video or play a video game immediately when you come home. (The potential adverse effects of the media are far outweighed, in my expert opinion, by the benefits of a better marriage.) If children aren't the issue, then create a routine to reunite – taking a walk together, sitting on the sofa, having a drink in the kitchen, what-ever works. It doesn't have to be the moment you step in the door. My husband used to be notorious for his – dare I say it? – rigidity in needing time to put his stuff away, potter around and glance at the paper before he could even think about saying 'How was your day?' The immediacy of babies' demands changed that.

There are several other ways to reserve time together. First, make every effort (including creatively reshuffling work or hiring a sitter or carpooling) to schedule several hours together once a week and make it a dedicated ritual. It could be Thursday night or Friday lunch or Sunday morning. During this time, you can talk or do something side by side in silence, go for a walk, enjoy each other's company. Ideally, share an experience together like taking a drive somewhere to look at a view or a historic build-ing, cooking together, reading poetry out loud, going out to dinner or to a sporting event.

Second, create a media-free zone in your home and reserve it for conversations only. If you're the kind of couple who truly shares listening to music or watching television (laughing, dis-cussing, mocking), then by all means continue. But, for most, television-watching and web-surfing rob us of our intimacy and time together. It's remarkable how many couples insist that their harried lives leave them with utterly no time to spend with one another, yet if you ask them how many hours a week they watch TV, you'll be surprised.

Regarding whether it's right to take time away from work (if it's even possible) or children (if you have them) to dedicate to your relationship, this is a no-brainer. A massive literature shows that people who are lonely or in unhappy relationships suffer severe ill effects, including depression, anxiety, jealousy, stress and impaired health. Needless to say, your job and your children will suffer if your marriage or partnership is tense, hostile or unhappy.

Express admiration, appreciation and affection
One of the key conclusions of two decades of research on marriages is that happy relationships are characterized by a ratio of positive to negative affect of five to one.[29] This means that for every negative statement or behaviour – criticizing, nagging, lecturing – there are five positive ones. Make your weekly goal to raise your positive affect ratio. You can do this, first, by increasing the number of times you show affection to your partner either verbally (e.g., saying or e-mailing 'I love you' more often), physically (no need to explain this) or through other behaviours (like kindness). I once heard a family expert say, 'A spontaneous kiss while doing household chores can do wonders.'

Second, communicate your admiration and gratitude directly. This is something that most of us don't do often enough. Recall the large German study, which showed that it takes an average of two years to adapt to the wonderfulness of marriage; after that, we start taking each other and the relationship for granted. Giving genuine praise (e.g., 'I'm so proud of what you did') not only makes your significant other happy but inspires her to strive for greater heights. Indeed, in the most flourishing relationships, partners evoke the best in one another, helping each other to come closer to reaching their ideal selves. This has been termed the 'Michelangelo effect'.[30] Just as Michelangelo unearthed an ideal form by sculpting a block of marble, romantic partners can support and facilitate each other to do the same. Because satisfied and stable couples are relatively more likely to idealize one another,[31] they may be more likely to mutually reinforce each other's positively biased perceptions, helping make them come true.

Third, to increase respect, value and admiration for your partner, there are some exercises that can be accomplished on your own on a weekly basis. Here's a sample four-week plan. During week 1, you could write a list of attributes that initially attracted you to your partner or that you appreciate right now and, for each characteristic you generate (be it honesty, sense of humour, intelligence, punctuality or charm), come up with at least one episode that illustrates it well. One couple told me that the secret of their relationship – she's an intelligent, sweet-tempered former model and he's an outgoing, funny, self-described geeky journalist – is that each of them thinks they have the better deal. Contemplate how you might have the better deal.

During week 2, try to remember and write about a good time in your marriage – when you first met or fell in love, when your partner showed support, when you successfully endured a difficult time together. The flip side of this exercise – try this in week 3 – is to consider a recent or memorable thing your partner did that angered or disappointed you. Then (and this is hard) write down two or three charitable explanations for his or her behaviour that attribute the behaviour to forces other than your partner's bad character or motives (e.g., stress, misunderstanding, well-meaning intentions, etc.). A final exercise, for week 4, is to sit down and write about particular goals, values or beliefs that you and your partner share.

Capitalize on good fortune
This strategy involves taking delight in your friends', family members' and partner's windfalls and successes. Social psychologists have shown that what distinguishes good and poor relationships is not how the partners respond to each other's disappointments and reversals but how they respond to *good* news.[32] Recall the last time something really good happened in your life – perhaps you earned a promotion, received a commendation

or award, were invited for a special trip, or won tickets to a sold-out show. How did your partner react when you broke the news to him? Was he thrilled and enthusiastic on your behalf, or did he ignore, criticize or scoff at your good fortune? And how did *you* last respond to your partner's sharing of good news? Personal triumphs and strokes of luck can be threatening or intimidating to close others, evoking envy ('How come he gets to go to Europe when I've wanted to go all my life?'), jealousy ('She cares more about what her boss thinks now than about me') or anxiety ('Does this mean we'll have to move again?'). As a result, the fact that your partner appreciates and validates your good news means not only that he is pleased for you, but that he respects your dreams and values your relationship. Thus, how people respond to things going right for others may be diagnostic of the sense of connection between them. If your close friend or romantic partner shows genuine pleasure, support and understanding, the relationship receives a boost in intimacy and closeness.

Starting today, resolve to respond 'actively and constructively' – that is, with interest and enthusiasm – to your friends' or loved one's good news, however small. One study showed that people who tried to do this three times per day over the course of just a week became happier and less depressed.[33] So, if your partner is excited to tell you something, pay close attention, ask lots of questions and relive the experience with him. If you're happy for him, express it and, if appropriate, insist on celebrating and tell others about it. Researchers find that people who are only 'silently supportive', as well as those who seem disinterested or who point out the down sides of the good news, have relationships that are less close, less intimate and less trusting.

Manage conflict
Observations of hundreds of couples have revealed that unhappy marriages are characterized by a particular style of handling conflict – a harsh start-up in the disagreement (e.g., immediately launching into accusation or sarcasm), criticism (impugning the

partner's entire character, like 'what's wrong with you?'), con-
tempt (expressing disgust with the partner by sneering,
eye-rolling, name-calling or demeaning), defensiveness ('I'm not
the problem, it's *you*') and stonewalling (eventually tuning out,
disengaging or even leaving the room).[34] Happy couples don't
necessarily fight any less or any less loudly, they just fight differently (see below).

If any of these behaviours characterize your relationship, it may
seem daunting to face up to them. But I believe that most people
instinctively know how *not* to do these things. It may take thirty
seconds (and a lot of self-control) to look up (rather than look
down) when your spouse is sending a signal to make up, to voice
a complaint ('Why didn't you call?') instead of a criticism ('You
never remember anything'), or to make a tiny gesture to stay connected while fighting (as simple as eye contact or touch or a 'Got
it'). One of the secrets of the happiest couples has been found to
be something very powerful but actually quite simple. It involves
doing a little thing in the middle of a row that de-escalates tension and negativity – an attempt at patching up. One of the most
common such behaviours is friendly (as opposed to hostile)
humour (e.g., screwing up your face like your two-year-old).
Another is expressing affection or saying something directly (e.g.,
'I see your point'). You've heard it before – the happiest partnerships are also strong friendships.

However, a caveat is in order here. Sometimes, no matter what
you do, your primary relationship will not improve, in which case
it's time to make some hard decisions. If your relationship is damaging to your self-esteem, degrading or abusive, it's imperative to
see a counsellor without delay and/or to consider leaving.

Share an inner life
Even if you and your partner excel at doing all the other things
on this list, it won't necessarily mean that you are happy and fulfilled together. In truth, a deep sense of shared rituals, dreams and
goals underlie thriving relationships. These are all elements that
connect you to each other and create a singular inner life shared

by just the two of you. You grow together, explore new directions and take risks together, challenge your assumptions together and take responsibility together.

Every week, try to do at least one thing that supports your partner's roles (e.g., as parent, skier, manager, chef) and dreams (to travel abroad, to climb the corporate ladder, to go back to school and so on). The goal should be to honour and respect one another and one another's life dreams and interests, even if you don't share all of them.

What if you don't have or don't want a romantic partner?

Scientific research leaves no question that relationships are exceedingly important to well-being. But I don't believe that those relationships have to be romantic ones. Although in almost every study, married people have been found to be happier than their divorced, separated, widowed or single peers, this doesn't mean that happiness is only reserved for them. Deep, long-term friendships are also important for happiness, as are other critical relationships, including those with pets.[35] Indeed, people who are single (and, in particular, women who have always been single) often have close, positive and lasting interpersonal relationships particularly with siblings, friends and nieces and nephews. Studies have found, for example, that, relative to married people, singles are closer to their friends and have more frequent contact with them, and that lifelong single older women tend to have close to a dozen devoted decades-long friends. This evidence for the flourishing of many single people has led some psychologists to challenge the assumption that 'the sexual partnership is the only truly important peer relationship'.[36] Other partnerships matter too. Take note then that a strategy to invest in relationships can bring happiness not only when directed at lovers and spouses, but at almost any significant relationship in your life.

Strategies for making friends

Friendships don't just happen, they are made. One prominent psychologist suggests that the magic number is to have three friends or companions you can really count on. Here are some suggestions for how to get your friendship number up to three and to make them thrive.[37] Select *one* strategy for now and take it upon yourself to implement it as soon as possible.

Make time (again)

Show interest in other people and offer them encouragement. Once a friendship forms, create rituals that allow you to get together and be in touch on a regular basis – a weekly date to go to the gym, a book club, a monthly dinner out, a joint holiday, or a daily e-mail. In this way, friends become as much a priority as all the other areas of your life. However, don't control all your interactions (let your friends decide which movie to see at least half the time) and don't overdo it – give them space when they require it.

Communicate

Self-disclosure – revealing intimate thoughts and feelings – is difficult for some individuals, but it's critical to friendships, especially women's friendships. This is because honest self-disclosure, when it occurs unhurriedly and appropriately, breeds more self-disclosure and cultivates intimacy. The flip side is to listen to your friends' disclosures and problems. Make eye contact, give your full attention and acknowledge his or her statements. Hold off giving unsolicited advice or turning attention back to yourself by recounting your own story ('I know just how you feel'). Sometimes this is appreciated and welcomed and sometimes not. Finally, just like with a romantic partner, convey feelings of affection and admiration from time to time in whatever way feels comfortable to you – 'I've missed you', 'We always have a good time getting together', 'I'm so happy for you that you're expecting', 'Thanks for being there'. It may appear sentimental, but people are amazingly gratified to hear such words. 'A kind word is like a spring day.'[38]

Be supportive and loyal

Be helpful and supportive when your friends need it and affirm their successes. As I mentioned earlier, we often feel threatened by our friends' triumphs. So, instead of feeling envious, try to bask in their reflected glory. Other universal rules of friendship include standing up for your friends when they're not there, keeping secrets, not putting down their *other* friends and reciprocating favours.[39] In the words of William Shakespeare, 'Keep thy friend under thy own life's key.'

Finally, hug

Frequent hugging is enthusiastically endorsed by popular magazines and web sites as a means to increase happiness, health and connectedness to others. If this is your cup of tea, the science is there to prove it. In a one-of-a-kind study, students at Pennsylvania State University were assigned to two groups.[40] The first group was instructed to give or receive a minimum of five hugs per day over the course of four weeks and to record the details. The hugs had to be front-to-front (non-sexual) hugs, using both arms of both participants; however, the length and strength of the hug, as well as the placement of hands, were left to their discretion. Furthermore, these students couldn't simply hug their boyfriend or girlfriend half a dozen times – they had to aim to hug as many different individuals as possible. The second group, the controls, was instructed simply to record the number of hours they read each day over the same four weeks.

The hugging group (who partook in an average of forty-nine hugs over the course of the study) became much happier. And, not surprisingly, the students who merely recorded their reading activity (which averaged a not-too-shabby 1.6 hours per day) showed no changes. So, hugging is an excellent intimacy and friendship booster. The author of the study told me that some of the students – the guys, in particular – were a bit uncomfortable and embarrassed at first, but ended up generating creative ways to hug (such as embracing teammates after successes on the field).[41] So, try it. You may find that a hug can relieve stress, make you feel closer to someone and even diminish pain.[42]

COMPLEMENTARY ACTIVITIES

If you benefit from this activity, you may also want to try:

1) Practising acts of kindness (Happiness Activity No. 4, p. 125)

2) Taking care of your body (Happiness Activity No. 12, p. 250)

Chapter 6

Managing stress, hardship and trauma

~

'But we also boast in our sufferings, knowing that suffering produces endurance, and endurance produces character, and character produces hope, and hope does not disappoint us.'

ROMANS 5:5

~

No life – if we live long enough – is without stress, adversity or crisis. The possibilities are endless – the death of a loved one, a grave illness, an accident, victimization, a natural disaster, a terrorist attack, domestic violence, poverty, stigmatization, divorce and job loss. Close to half of US adults will experience a severe traumatic event during their lifetimes.[1] In the wake of acute challenges like these, many people become depressed, fearful or confused. They may find it difficult to concentrate on the daily tasks of living and they may not be able to sleep or eat well. Some have such intense and long-lasting reactions to a trauma that they are unable to return to their previous ('normal') self for many months or even years.

Some people ask me: 'How can I even *begin* to think about how to become happier before I am able to tackle the many problems in my life?' There isn't a simple answer. Becoming a happier person means rising above your happiness baseline or set point. If a terrible event or chronic problem has undermined that happiness baseline and is absorbing all your resources and attention, then your priority is to cope. Fortunately, most, if not all, of the strategies that help you to be happier – counting your blessings, cultivating optimism, practising religion, nurturing relationships, savouring life's joys and so on – are also strategies that help you to manage life's lowest ebbs. Furthermore, the two strategies described in this chapter, coping and forgiveness, are valuable not only in response to severe traumas but also as a way of dealing with the normal and expected daily challenges of life. For this reason, coping and forgiveness are foundational strategies that embody the potency of the 40 per cent solution – the fact that how you behave and how you think has a great deal to do with how happy you ultimately become, no matter what hurts, stresses and tribulations life doles out to you.

Happiness Activity No. 6: Developing strategies for coping

'We deem those happy who from the experience of life have learned to bear its ills, without being overcome by them.'

JUVENAL

Coping is what people do to alleviate the hurt, stress or suffering caused by a negative event or situation. Psychologists call this 'managing stressful demands' and everyone has done it. When faced with a difficult or painful circumstance, how do you generally contend with it or sort it out?

The varieties of coping

Your beloved pet has died. You're under terrific pressure at work. Your baby has a heart problem and has to have surgery immediately. Your car is totalled and you don't have adequate insurance. A close friend isn't returning your calls. These are all situations that can range from stressful to traumatic. How do you cope? A long-standing convention in psychology has been to divide coping into two types – 'problem-focused' and 'emotion-focused'. Some people tend to be problem-focused copers – they try to take the situation into their own hands, to act on it, resolve it somehow and make a bad thing go away. This isn't always possible, of course. When a loved one has died, you cannot 'fix' the problem. The only coping you can really do is to manage your emotional reactions to the event. If you are overwhelmed by grief, you can take steps to alleviate it or work through it, perhaps with psychotherapy, by spending more time with family, or by absorbing yourself in a meaningful project. It's not surprising then that people are more likely to use problem-focused coping when they feel that something constructive can be done about their situation and to use emotion-focused coping when they feel that the negative event is something that simply must be endured.

Problem-focused coping

So, problem-focused coping, as its name implies, basically involves solving problems. Suppose that you are having great trouble meeting deadlines in your job and are feeling overwhelmed. You need to generate solutions, weigh the costs and benefits of each, then choose one and act on it. Your solutions to your problem might be to confer with your supervisor about a change in duties, to create a new, feasible work schedule for yourself, or even to look for a new line of work. People who use problem-focused coping experience less depression during and after stressful situations.[2]

Below are some examples of how people describe themselves when using problem-focused coping strategies. They come from a popular scale that measures the ways that people cope.[3]

- I concentrate my efforts on doing something about it.
- I do what has to be done, one step at a time.
- I try to come up with a strategy about what to do.
- I make a plan of action.
- I put aside other activities in order to concentrate on this.
- I try to get advice from someone about what to do.
- I talk to someone who could do something concrete about the situation.

That's problem-focused coping, in a nutshell.

Emotion-focused coping

The items on this list all sound very well and good, but if the event or situation that you're facing is uncontrollable, or if you are so overwhelmed by negative emotions that you're unable to begin to take action, then emotion-focused coping is the appropriate and often the only available approach.

There are many emotion-focused strategies, some behavioural and others 'cognitive' (or involving different ways of thinking). Behavioural strategies, for example, might entail distraction or physical exercise (e.g., a walk to lift your spirits) or seeking emotional support from people close to you (e.g., getting sympathy and understanding from a friend). Basically, people who involve themselves in pleasant activities, like going to a movie or a picnic with friends, give themselves a breather from their sadness, anxiety or distress and are thus more ready and better equipped to act on their problems.[4] Cognitive strategies, in contrast, may include positively reinterpreting the situation (e.g., trying to learn from the experience or looking for something good in what is happening), acceptance (e.g., learning to live with it or accepting the reality of what has happened) or turning to religion (e.g., finding solace in beliefs about the afterlife). With the exception of social support, researchers have overwhelmingly focused on studying the effectiveness of – take a breath – cognitive emotion-focused coping strategies. The rest of this chapter reflects that history, but for a good reason – the coping techniques I introduce are the most malleable and learnable. And potent.

Teaching problem-focused and emotion-focused coping

It's clear that both types of coping are valuable, depending on the situation and the person. Some researchers have actually attempted to teach people how to use both strategies. In one study, highly distressed widows and widowers were offered seven sessions of counselling to learn how to cope with their losses. Everyone reported some relief from their distress, but men benefited more from emotion-focused strategies and women from the problem-focused ones.[5] Presumably, these widows and widowers obtained the greatest advantages when they learned something that they didn't already habitually do. This means focusing more on emotions among men and focusing less on emotions (and trying to problem solve) in women.

Other research shows that *both* problem-focused and emotion-focused coping are essential when coping with a chronic problem. For example, women experiencing long-term infertility attended six weeks of training sessions to learn how to use the two kinds of coping.[6] Learning emotion-focused strategies led these women to become less distressed about their situation (e.g., they were relatively less depressed when followed up after the study ended), and learning problem-focused strategies led them to resolve their problems (e.g., the majority who learned such strategies ultimately became mothers).

Construing benefit in trauma

Imagine being the mother of four and watching your husband die of Lou Gehrig's disease, as he slowly and painfully loses his ability to play with his children, dress and feed himself, talk, nod and smile. Lynn was confronted with this heartbreaking situation.[7] As the end was nearing, she told a doctor that she 'felt that there was a freight train coming'. 'There *is* a freight train coming,' he replied.

Lynn's response was to cherish the remaining moments with her husband:

> I don't mean to be a Pollyanna, but I had twenty wonderful years with that man. There are people who don't have one day as happy as I had. It took me six months after Charley died to realize that that feeling will never go away. It's like the Grand Canyon. There's this big hole, and it hurts like hell, but it's beautiful.

A colleague I know lost his dearest friend and closest collaborator, a brilliant scientist, abruptly and cruelly to cancer, cutting short a twenty-seven-year-long magical partnership. 'I am the luckiest man I know,' he said recently at an event honouring his friend, 'I wish on each of you the marvellous collaboration that I had.'

Construing benefit in trauma involves seeing some value or gain (a 'silver lining', if you must) in your loss or negative life event – for example, a change in life perspective, a feeling that one's life has greater value, or a sense of personal growth. Although, at first glance it would seem extremely difficult, if not impossible, to come to believe that your life has improved in many positive ways after a major trauma, psychologists have observed such benefit-finding in numerous studies and populations, in bereaved individuals, cancer patients, stroke victims and HIV-positive men, among others.[8] Indeed, 70 per cent to 80 per cent of people who've lost a loved one report finding some benefit in their experience.[9]

For example, a ground-breaking and now classic study found that female breast cancer survivors reported that their lives had been altered, and often for the better, after developing the disease.[10] Indeed, two-thirds of the women interviewed (many with poor diagnoses) claimed this. What precisely were the supposed 'benefits' of having breast cancer? The women spoke of a wake-up call, prompting them to reorder their priorities and to realize what was truly important in life (a common one was family over work), of deciding to devote more time to their most significant relationships and to spend less time on things like housework and garden chores.

Interestingly, many of these same women seemed to have biased perceptions of themselves and their illness, for example, claiming that they could control the course of their cancer (e.g., by preventing a recurrence through nutrition or exercise) when the medical evidence clearly revealed that they couldn't, or feeling extremely optimistic about their prognosis (e.g., reporting that they had 'beat' the cancer) when the reality was that they were dying. Furthermore, fully seventy out of the seventy-two cancer survivors who were interviewed alleged that they were coping better than the average person in their situation (which, of course, is statistically impossible). Could these views be possibly adaptive? The empirical evidence shows that they were. Women who held such optimistic beliefs were described by their oncologists and expert clinical psychologists, as well as by themselves, as being perfectly mentally healthy and well-adjusted. Furthermore, these women's overly positive views did not seem to hurt them even when their beliefs were flagrantly disconfirmed (e.g., when the cancer returned). Interestingly, these women's remarkable ability to perceive benefits in their ordeal have been observed in individuals who are coping effectively with a variety of illnesses, including HIV, AIDS and heart disease.[11]

In sum, construing benefit in negative life events is a tremendously effective coping strategy, which involves seeing some value in a loss or trauma. Some people claim that their relationships have benefited, that they are more profound, significant and meaningful after the trauma than they were before. For example, in a study of care-givers of hospice patients in the San Francisco Bay area, recently bereaved individuals reported that 'there was a rallying of support, and a camaraderie that I think only shows itself . . . when something like this happens' and 'I have learned and seen a lot of positive things in people – they just glowed.' Other care-givers find guilt-free solace in the ending of the unrelenting care-giving that a death naturally provides.

Still others assert that they have grown enormously as a result of their traumatic experience, discovering a maturity and strength of character that they didn't know they had, for example, reporting having found 'a growth and a freedom to . . . give fuller expression to my feelings or to assert myself'. A new and more positive perspective is a common theme among those enduring traumas or loss – a renewed appreciation of the preciousness of life and a sense that one must live more fully in the present. For example, one bereaved person rediscovered that 'having your health and living life to the fullest is a real blessing. I appreciate my family, friends, nature, life in general. I see a goodness in people'.[12] A woman survivor of a traumatic plane crash described her experience afterwards: 'When I got home, the sky was brighter. I paid attention to the texture of sidewalks. It was like being in a movie.'[13]

Construing benefit in negative events can influence your physical health as well as your happiness, a remarkable demonstration of the power of mind over body. For example, in one study, researchers interviewed men who had had a heart attack between the ages of thirty and sixty.[14] Those who perceived benefits in the event seven weeks after it happened – for example, believing that they had grown and matured as a result, or re-valued home life, or resolved to create a less hectic schedule for themselves – were less likely to have a recurrence and more likely to be healthy eight years later. In contrast, those who blamed the heart attack on other people or on their own emotions (e.g., having been too stressed) were now in poorer health.

Post-traumatic growth

Friedrich Nietzsche's exhortation, 'That which does not kill me makes me stronger', is familiar to many of us. The experience of pain, loss and trauma can indeed make us stronger, or, at least, lead us to *perceive* that we are stronger and more resourceful than we had thought. A woman who cared for her eighty-three-year-old father before he died of cancer described her realization this way:

> I saw myself acting in a role of competence where I had to pull on all my resources just to get through sometimes. I would have to be directing the medical people about what I wanted to do. A person like me who hates showing anger and can't stand conflict. I would have to stand and demand care from the nursing home, and it was necessary and I did it. So I came away with a feeling of competence and strength and gratitude . . . I was forced to grow.[15]

Some psychologists believe that finding benefit in a trauma represents a true personal *transformation*.[16] When you think about it, a major loss can catapult a person into new roles and novel situations. A new widow, who has always thought of herself as a 'wife' and has been greatly dependent on her husband financially, emotionally and socially may be abruptly propelled to learn numerous assorted skills. She may be surprised to find herself rising to the occasion and accomplishing things that she's never judged herself capable of doing – selling a used car, playing catch with her son, calculating her taxes or attending a party solo. This can certainly lead to new self-perceptions, enhanced self-esteem and possibly even growth. But is it a transformation?

The available data say 'yes'. When a challenge or trauma is profound, unsettling a person's foundations and forcing him to confront his personal priorities, sense of meaning and identity, a subset of individuals report personal growth, strengthening and even thriving. Researchers have studied people's responses to a variety of traumas: terminal illness, loss of a home in a natural disaster, divorce, military captivity, sexual assault and having a low-birth-weight child. Some of the common transformative experiences reported by such trauma survivors are as follows:[17]

- Renewed belief in their ability to endure and prevail.
- Improved relationships – in particular, discovering who one's true friends are and whom one can really count on; some relationships pass the test, while others fail.
- Feeling more comfortable with intimacy and a greater sense of compassion for others who suffer.
- Developing a deeper, more sophisticated and more satisfying philosophy of life.

The last item on the list is likely to be triggered by traumas that force people to face mortality – their own or that of others. It's not uncommon to become absorbed in life-and-death existential questions: 'What is the meaning of my life? Why did this trauma happen? What reason is there to go on?' Of course, people rarely find simple and satisfying answers, but the very process of grappling with such philosophical or spiritual questions leads some to report experiencing life at a heightened level of awareness.

The research on post-traumatic growth offers much-needed good news to those of you facing hardships and crises. Not only can you survive, not only can you recover, but you can flourish. I've seen hundreds, if not thousands, of graphs throughout my career, but there was one that has always stayed with me and I was recently thrilled to rediscover it. As reproduced below, it illustrates three potential paths that an individual can take in the face of a major challenge – survival, recovery or thriving.[18] Survival involves a permanent impairment of functioning. This path shows a person who is merely surviving following a trauma, someone who may have lost much happiness and motivation to enjoy love, work or leisure. Recovery describes a person who suffers in the aftermath of a trauma – perhaps unable to work productively or have satisfying relationships for a period of time – but eventually returns to his original state. Finally, thriving involves someone who also suffers in the aftermath, but who ultimately not only returns to her original state but rises above it! This person has experienced a transformation.

How does one pull this off? Psychologists point to real-life examples, like this one of a woman professor diagnosed with

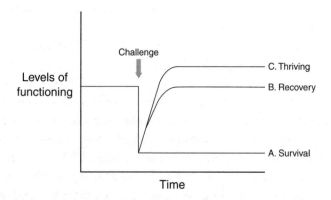

metastatic cancer.[19] Throughout her many treatments – surgeries, radiation, bone marrow transplant, chemotherapy – she continued her life at a brisk pace, teaching, doing research, sitting on committees and travelling for business as well as to ski and scuba dive. When her oncologist expressed puzzlement over the fact that her tumour neither grew nor shrank, noting that 'cancer does not act like that, it never sits still for so long', she replied with a laugh. 'I am living my life so fast that it can't catch up.' Although she seems superhuman, she acknowledges experiencing pain, fear and uncertainty, but reports that her post-cancer life has become more meaningful and that many other women in her cancer support group share a similar view. She reports having more self-confidence and being more easygoing and happier, explaining that her spirituality accounts for some of her post-traumatic growth. She now believes that everything she faces, whether positive or negative, affords an occasion for redemption.

Sometimes, however, the barriers to thriving are massive, calling for demanding and creative strategies. A woman concentration camp survivor was asked how she could possibly carry on and prevail in the aftermath of her calamitous experience. She replied that, in order to function, she makes a 'sort of schizophrenic division ... a compartmentalization between her memories of the camp and what she describes as her so-called normal life'.[20] Compartmentalization is a strategy that people facing a variety of woes, big and small, have found effective, including, most publicly, a recent US president confronting a sordid scandal.

I hope these portraits of flourishing individuals are inspiring and not discouraging. The higher you aim in terms of how you cope with trauma, the more you will achieve. Recovery is good. Indeed, it is excellent. Thriving and flourishing are even better. But remember that post-traumatic growth, and happiness for that matter, is not the same as always being joyful and carefree. Indeed, most survivors experience a great deal of distress *at the same time as* reporting strengthening and progress. So the uphill road that leads to a more fulfilling and more meaningful life may be laid with stones and punctuated by troughs. There's absolutely nothing good about tragedy and loss, but something of value can come from the struggle in their aftermath.

Social support

When twenty-three-year-old Sylvia lost her daughter Sierra to an unexpected, accidental death, she turned to her companions for consolation and support. Bereavement has been found to be associated with an elevation in stress hormones called glutocorticoids, and friendly social contact can lower these hormones.[21] This phenomenon has been observed in both baboons – like Sylvia – and humans.

Turning to social support, the comfort and contact offered by other people (or monkeys) in times of strain, distress and trauma, is one of the most effective coping strategies that exist. Social support not only makes us happier and less anxious and depressed, but it even affects our bodies. In one study, researchers located men and women who'd lost their spouses about a year earlier either to an accidental death (like a motor vehicle crash) or suicide.[22] Perhaps not surprisingly, they found that the sudden death of a spouse was related to an abrupt decline in their physical health. However, those widows and widowers who had confided in others who are close to them had fewer health problems and were less likely to ruminate about their situation.

Another study focused on women facing a very different kind of stressor – life-threatening cancer.[23] Those patients who actively sought social support as a coping strategy immediately after surgery showed greater natural killer cell activity. Remarkably, this finding indicates that using social support may have triggered these women's immune systems to fight their cancer more aggressively. Indeed, women cancer patients who attend weekly support groups have been found to live an average of eighteen months longer.[24]

In sum, social support is pretty incredible – a strategy of almost magical proportions. Except that it's not magic at all. Friends, partners, companions, confidant(e)s – they give you a place to belong, room to share feelings, opportunities to discover that you're not alone in your troubles. Talking to others about a traumatic experience not only helps you cope and see the event with a new perspective, but it ultimately reinforces and strengthens your relationship. How many times have you been plagued by intrusive worries and ruminations about a recent problem and then observed those worries almost palpably lift from your shoulders after talking to an understanding friend? Women especially tend to rely on social relationships as a key to their resilience in the face of stress and trauma. From childhood on, girls are encouraged to value and even define themselves in terms of connections with others.[25] As we grow up, those connections bring us many benefits.

Is all social support beneficial? Of course not. Not every person from whom you seek sympathy or confide in will be responsive in a helpful way and some may do downright damage. If your confidante is hostile, puts you down, makes you even more miserable and anxious, or obsesses right along with you, find a more helpful partner. Studies show that the *quality* of social support is just as important as whether you have it. People who endure problematic, conflictual relationships, or abrasive interactions with others who are close to them, suffer in terms of their emotional and physical well-being.[26]

Finding meaning

A traumatic event, like a serious illness, a death in the family, an unexpected loss of status or employment, or being the victim of a crime, can shake your assumptions to their foundations. 'Why me?' you might ask, or 'How could God let this happen?' Psychologists call this a threat to your 'assumptive world'. It's critical, they say, that in its aftermath you gain an understanding of the trauma and of its implications.[27] In Western cultures, people tend to believe that their world is generally a controllable and predictable place, that bad things don't happen to good people, that people get what they deserve and deserve what they get.[28] This belief in a just world, where things don't happen at random, is implicit but very potent. When a bad thing does happen to a good person, her assumptions about the justice, control and benevolence of the world is exposed as an illusion. What's more, a traumatic event can threaten a person's self-worth (e.g., a victim of random violence might blame herself) and her dreams (e.g., a mother who has lost a child has to envision an entire new childless future).

As a result, coping with a terrible event may require you to rethink your assumptions and beliefs in order to find some meaning in the loss or trauma. This can be a difficult and painful process. How does one make sense of an event that can seem senseless? Studies have found that people make sense of loss in many ways, for example, by acknowledging that life is short and fragile (as one bereaved person said, 'My basic attitude to life was that there's a beginning and an end, and it's going to happen to one or the other of us sooner or later'), by attributing the tragedy to God's will ('I think that my father's illness was meant to be, and that was God's plan') or by explaining a death in terms of the deceased's behaviour ('It always made sense to me. I mean, he smoked for years').[29] Other ways that people have been able to find meaning in a tragedy is to accept the fact that sometimes things happen for no reason or to construe benefits in the negative event, for example, that it put an end to a loved one's suffering, or that they've learned a great deal about life and about themselves, or that the event has spurred them to do good in their community. Finally, some people may interpret a loss or trauma as sending them an important signal (e.g., 'She would have wanted me to turn my life around' or 'The accident was a sign that I should stop drinking').

In sum, it is undoubtedly terrifically hard to find meaning in a traumatic and often seemingly meaningless and arbitrary occurrence. Those who do, however, are better able to cope. One study followed individuals who had lost their loved ones from before the loss to a year after.[30] Those who reported finding some meaning in their loss (it didn't matter how) showed less depression and fewer symptoms of post-traumatic stress disorder twelve months later. The benefit of finding meaning in a loss extends to physical health as well. In another study, HIV-seropositive men who had lost a friend or partner to AIDS and had found some meaning in the death showed healthier immune systems and themselves lived longer over a two- to three-year period.[31] The 'meaning' included gaining a new perspective on themselves and their own lives (e.g., that they should spend more time with friends and family, that they should live life to the fullest, that they should take more risks) as well as growth in their spirituality or faith.

Specific strategies for coping

If coping is a strategy that you wish to develop, then choose one of the following three recommendations.

Finding meaning through 'expressive writing'

About twenty years ago, James Pennebaker embarked on research to explore whether writing about a traumatic or upsetting experience could affect people's health and well-being.[32] The procedure he developed has now been adopted by scores of other researchers, including myself. If you were to participate in one of Pennebaker's typical studies, you would be invited to a laboratory, presented with a sheaf of paper (or, in more recent years, a computer screen) and, with assurances of confidentiality, asked to write about one of your most distressing or painful life experiences. You would be urged to describe the experience in detail and to explore your personal reactions and deepest emotions fully. The writing would go on for fifteen to thirty minutes and you would be asked to come back and continue writing about the experience for a total of three to five consecutive days. Participants in a control condition usually would be asked to do the same amount of writing but on neutral topics, like their daily schedule, their shoes or the layout of their living room.

The growing body of results in this area reveal that such 'expressive writing' about past traumatic events has many beneficial consequences. Compared with control groups, people who spend three days exploring their deepest thoughts and feelings about ordeals or traumas in a journal make fewer visits to a doctor in the months following the writing sessions, show enhanced immune function, report less depression and distress, obtain higher grades and are more likely to find a new job after unemployment.[33] These effects have been found among a wide variety of individuals – healthy and sick, young and old, poor and rich and those residing in Europe, East Asia and North America.

Initially, researchers believed that the benefits of expressive journal writing about trauma were due to 'emotional catharsis' – that is, because the act of writing allows us to overcome our inhibition over the trauma by venting and letting go of our emotions. This hypothesis has now been widely challenged. The critical mechanism appears to be the nature of the writing process itself, which helps us to understand, come to terms with and make sense of our trauma. Finding meaning in the trauma through writing also seems to reduce how often and how intensely we experience intrusive thoughts about it.

I've wondered quite a bit about what makes journal writing so special and effective. What is it about converting our emotions, thoughts and images about a highly distressing event *into words and sentences* that alters the way we think about it? Suppose that you have had your heart broken, or you have experienced a harrowing physical assault, or your healthy and active mother has been diagnosed with Alzheimer's. You might find yourself ruminating about the experience, even when you're supposed to be focused on something else, and you might be troubled with intrusive images and thoughts. Writing about the experience in a journal forces you to organize and integrate those thoughts and images into a coherent narrative. Language by its nature is highly structured. Indeed, the very act of writing sentences may prompt you to think in causal terms (e.g., A may have led to B, which may have led to C), thereby triggering an analysis that could help you find meaning, enhanced

understanding and, ultimately, a sense of control. When an experience has structure and meaning, it seems much more manageable
and controllable than when it's represented by a chaotic and painful jumble of thoughts and images. For example, Pennebaker and his
colleagues found that the more people used causal words (e.g.,
'because', 'infer', 'cause') and insight words ('understand', 'realize',
'see') over the course of their writing sessions about a distressing
topic, the bigger improvements they experienced in t heir health.[34]

It makes sense that if writing helps people find a modicum of
meaning and resolution in their trauma, they might find their
emotional reactions to it more manageable and might be less disturbed by unwanted ruminations. The process of creating a
narrative about your experience – or telling a story – can lead you
to accept it. Furthermore, writing involves recording your
thoughts externally, whether on a page in your diary or a Word
document. This may allow you to unburden yourself by chron-
icling your emotions, thoughts and memories outside of yourself
and thus allowing yourself to move past your troubles.

So, for your first exercise in coping, get out a notebook,
PowerBook, diary or a sheet of paper and follow the directions
of Pennebaker's participants:

> For the next four days, I would like for you to write about
> your very deepest thoughts and feelings about the most trau-
> matic experience of your entire life. In your writing, I'd like
> you to really let go and explore your very deepest emotions
> and thoughts. You might tie your topic to your relationships
> with others, including parents, lovers, friends, or relatives, to
> your past, your present, or your future, or to who you have
> been, who you would like to be, or who you are now. You
> may write about the same general issues or experiences on all
> days of writing or on different traumas each day.[35]

At minimum, you should spend fifteen minutes writing each
day, and you should write for several days in a row, for as long as
needed. Be patient and persistent and watch the benefits unfold.

Construing benefit in trauma through writing or conversing

As you can tell, expressive writing is fairly open ended. You can write whatever you want about your loss or trauma, as long as you strive to express your emotions honestly and fully. The second coping exercise I'd like to introduce also involves journal writing, but in a more guided form. Alternatively, it can be done in conversation with a supportive confidante. A sequence of three general steps is taken, with the ultimate goal of finding benefit in pain.

First, whether through writing or talking, acknowledge that your loss or trauma has caused you a great deal of pain and suffering. Then, consider what you have done during your loss or in response to it that you are proud of. If a family member has died, perhaps you worked extremely hard to make his or her last days comfortable. If your marriage fell apart and you sunk into a depression, perhaps you bravely slogged through your workdays and kept it together, at least in front of people who depended on you.

Next, consider how much you have grown as a result of your loss. Do you feel that you have a new perspective on life (even if it's a negative one)? Do you feel that you are more compassionate now, or more grateful, or sensitive, or patient, or tolerant, or open-minded?

Finally, think about how the trauma has positively affected your relationships. Have any of them been strengthened in any way? Have any of them become closer, more intimate or more supportive?

Coping via thought disputation

This last strategy, derived from cognitive therapy for depression, involves disputing or challenging your own pessimistic thoughts. When bad things happen, we are often overwhelmed with negative emotions and negative beliefs, which exacerbate and feed back into each other – 'I'll never get a boyfriend', 'I'm so unattractive', 'My son doesn't respect me', 'It was my fault that our night out was a disaster', 'My job is going to be eliminated any day now'. These are often automatic thoughts that are overly pessimistic, distorted and negatively biased. A valuable exercise is to follow in writing the five elements of the 'ABCDE disputation' technique – A for adversity, B for belief, C for consequence, D for disputation and E for energize.[36] Here are the steps, in order:

1. Write down the nature of the *adversity*, the bad event or problem you are facing, e.g., 'My best friend hasn't called me in three weeks.'
2. Identify any negative *beliefs* triggered by this problem, e.g., 'She must hate me' or 'I'm terrified that she thinks that I'm too boring.'
3. Record the *consequence* of the problem, how you are feeling and acting as a result, e.g., 'I feel miserable and lonely' or 'I've never been good at keeping friends' or 'I'll skip the dinner party this weekend.'
4. *Dispute* the negative belief, challenging it, thinking of other possible reasons for the problem, e.g., 'Perhaps my friend has been extremely busy (I remember her mentioning a big contract at work).' Or, 'Maybe she's feeling down herself and wants *me* to call.'
5. Considering the more optimistic explanations for your problem can *energize* you and lift your spirits, so that you become less anxious and more hopeful.

So, ABCDE disputation basically involves arguing with your own overly pessimistic thoughts rather than letting those thoughts control you. You may have noticed how the different parts (A to E) are related. Our reactions (the *consequence*) to the bad event (the *adversity*) are in great part determined by our *beliefs* and interpretations about why the bad event has happened and what it means to us. A more optimistic, more encouraging, more charitable interpretation changes our reaction and our outlook (the *consequences*), by *energizing* us.

The hardest part, of course, is the *disputation*. To challenge your automatic negative thoughts, you basically need to take the role of a detective, hunting for evidence that might disconfirm your initial hunches. Say that your bad event is 'My husband has been distant lately' and your belief is 'He's not attracted to me anymore'. Below are questions you should ask yourself and answer, preferably in writing and preferably when you're in a neutral mood.

- What precise evidence do I have for this belief?
- What alternative explanations are there for his recent behaviour?
- Even if my belief is true, what are the implications? Put another way, what is the worst possible thing that could happen? How likely is it?
- What is the best possible thing that could happen and what is the likelihood of that?
- What do I *honestly* think is the most likely outcome?
- Is this belief useful to me? What do I get out of having it?
- And, finally, what do I plan to do to address the problem?

COMPLEMENTARY ACTIVITY

If you benefit from this activity, you may also want to try:

1) Committing to your goals (Happiness Activity No. 10, p. 213)

2) Learning to forgive (Happiness Activity No. 7, see below)

Happiness Activity No. 7: Learning to forgive

When I was a doctoral student at Stanford, a twenty-six-year-old woman, Amy Biehl, who had graduated with a BA in International Relations and had taken a Fulbright Scholarship to research women's rights and fight segregation in South Africa, was pulled from her car and stabbed to death by a mob in Guguletu township, near Cape Town. It happened two days before she was coming home to be reunited with her family and her longtime boyfriend in California. She didn't know that he was planning to ask her to marry him. It was a tragedy – one that unnerved several people close to me, especially parents of children just about her age. They tried to put themselves in the heads of her parents, an effort that was agonizing. Two years later, Amy's parents returned to the township where she was killed and met with some of the killers' families to console them.

To *console* them?

Four young men had been sentenced for eighteen years for Amy's murder. The Biehls came to witness their testimony in front of the Truth and Reconciliation Commission, during which the four men expressed remorse and pleaded for amnesty. The Biehls supported their release. They were able to bury their anger, hurt and hatred.

Amy's father died shortly after that trip, but Amy's mother ended up returning to South Africa yet again, this time to forgive one of the four killers – a man named Ntobeko Peni. He saw himself as a young freedom fighter, growing up poor and segregated in South Africa's townships, taught from childhood that whites were the enemy. But she didn't only forgive him. She gave him a job and, with the job, a future. He works as a guide and peer educator for HIV/AIDS awareness at the Amy Biehl Foundation, which has programmes in townships outside of Cape Town. He also travels the world with Amy's mother to tell their story of forgiveness and reconciliation. Amy's mother says that Ntobeko is part of her family now.

This might appear at first glance as an extreme example and few of us would aspire to hold the reservoir of forgiveness that Amy's mother seems to have. But research suggests that we can learn from her.

What is forgiveness?

I've been describing in this chapter how to respond to a variety of adverse life experiences. One particular kind of painful ordeal comes when you are wronged, hurt or attacked by another person. The injury or abuse could be physical, sexual or emotional. It may involve an insult, an offence, a betrayal or a desertion. It appears that the natural first inclination of human beings to such injuries is to respond negatively, to reciprocate with an equal harm.[37] The two other typical responses are a desire to avoid the person or to seek revenge. It would seem obvious that such responses breed negative consequences. Trying to distance yourself from the transgressor and especially trying to retaliate ultimately makes you unhappy, damages or destroys relationships and may even harm society at large. Throughout history, and continuing to this day, the drive for revenge has motivated numerous ills and horrors of our world, including murder, rape and pillage, but also war, terrorism and genocide.

The focus of this book, however, is on the individual – on you. What does forgiveness mean and is it worthwhile to learn and practise it? Forgiveness may be the one factor that can disrupt the cycle of avoidance and vengeance in which we often find ourselves. Advocated by many if not most of the world's religions (a common notion is that people should be forgiving in their life on earth because they have been forgiven by God), forgiveness involves suppressing or mitigating one's motivations for avoidance and revenge (which often bring with them accompanying emotions of anger, disappointment and hostility) and, ideally, replacing them with more positive or benevolent attitudes, feelings and behaviours.[38] It's worth noting that we forgive another individual; the term 'forgiving ourselves' refers to a separate process of bolstering self-worth, *not* reducing drives for avoidance and revenge.

Psychologists who study forgiveness use a definition that differs a bit from that of the average person on the street. So it's important to understand what they mean by it and what they don't mean by it. Forgiveness is *not* reconciliation, that is, it does not necessarily involve the re-establishment of the relationship with the transgressor. Nor is it equivalent to pardon (which is a legal term, something usually accomplished within the justice system) or condoning (which implies justifying, minimizing or tolerating the victimization or hurt, thus eliminating the need for forgiveness entirely). Forgiveness does not mean excusing (which offers extenuating circumstances or a 'good reason' – 'He did it when he was high on drugs') or denial of harm (which connotes the Freudian concept of 'repression', or an unwillingness to accept what has occurred). Finally, 'forgive and forget' is a misnomer, as forgiving does not involve a decaying of memory for the hurt. Indeed, truly forgiving someone involves contemplating the injury at some length while forgetting the injury would make that process rather difficult.

So, how then do you know if you've forgiven someone? It's when you have experienced a shift in thinking, such that your desire to harm that person has decreased and your desire to do them good (or to benefit your relationship) has increased. Consider how much you agree with the following statements, borrowed from a forgiveness scale:[39]

- I'll make him/her pay.
- I want to see him/her hurt and miserable.
- I live as if he/she doesn't exist, isn't around.
- I keep as much distance between us as possible.

The more you agree with any of these items, the first two tapping revenge and the second two measuring avoidance, the more work you still need to do in order to forgive.

Why forgive?

Both research evidence and anecdotal observations suggest plentiful good reasons why we should forgive those who hurt, offend or victimize us. Before I go on to depict this very powerful evidence, I want to underscore that forgiving is something that you do for *yourself* and not for the person who has wronged you. Wise people surely disagree about when forgiveness is or is not appropriate, about tough questions of justice and morality, and about

which acts are unforgivable. If you have strong reasons not to forgive, those reasons must be respected. However, many of you are
reading this section precisely because you have already ascertained
that forgiveness would be a successful or necessary and fitting
strategy for you. Just remember that forgiving does not mean that
you should necessarily restore the relationship with the transgressor, nor does it mean excusing or condoning. Some acts may
indeed be inexcusable.

There are a number of folk sayings that all carry something like
the following message: Clinging to bitterness or hate harms *you*
more than the object of your hatred. (The Buddha said, 'Holding
on to anger is like grasping a hot coal with the intent of throw-
ing it at someone else; you are the one getting burned.')
Empirical research confirms this insight[40] – forgiving people are
less likely to be hateful, depressed, hostile, anxious, angry and
neurotic. They are more likely to be happier, healthier, more
agreeable and more serene. They are better able to empathize
with others and to be spiritual or religious. People who forgive
hurts in relationships are more capable of re-establishing closeness.
Finally, the inability to forgive is associated with persistent rumination or dwelling on revenge, while forgiving allows a person to
move on.

None of these findings are surprising, but they don't tell us if
forgiveness is the causal agent behind all these good things.
Fortunately, a number of interventions have been done to test
whether training in forgiveness brings about improvements in
well-being and mental health. For example, in one such study,
women over age sixty-five who felt considerably hurt by a particular interpersonal experience were randomly assigned to either
a 'forgiveness' group or to a 'discussion' (or control) group.[41] The
groups met for eight weeks. Women in the forgiveness group
reported learning to forgive more than did the controls, and had
lower anxiety and higher self-esteem. Other such interventions
have been done with individuals experiencing a variety of injuries
and offences, for example, men who were hurt over their partners'
decisions to have abortions, women survivors of incest, people

experiencing romantic infidelity and adolescents who perceived their parents as neglectful. In each of these studies (whether forgiveness was taught as part of group workshops or one-on-one) those in the forgiveness conditions were generally more successful in forgiving and showed diminished negative emotions and higher self-esteem and hope after the interventions, even months later. Not surprisingly, the longer that people are given to think about and learn forgiveness in these studies, the more they benefit. Also, interestingly, women appear to benefit more than men, with men holding on to hurts and grudges longer.[42]

So, the answer to why people bother to forgive is pretty straightforward. In the long run, the preoccupation, hostility and resentment that we harbour only serves to hurt us, both emotionally and physically. Furthermore, forgiveness can be regarded in the larger context of community and society. It can deepen our sense of shared humanity (that we are not alone in experiencing hurts) and strengthen our personal relationships and our wider connections with others. Indeed, studies show that simply remembering someone you forgave compels you into a 'we' frame of mind, to feel closer to others and to desire to help them.[43]

How to practise forgiveness

Of all the happiness-promoting strategies described in this book, I believe that forgiveness is one of the most challenging to carry out. But, as they say, 'no pain, no gain'. What you reap may be enormous. The following techniques can be carried out in a journal, letter, conversation or by using your own imagination. If forgiveness fits your personality, goals or needs, select just one activity from the list below for the time being and give it your best shot.

Appreciate being forgiven
Before you are able to forgive another person, a good first exercise is to appreciate an instance of when you yourself have been

forgiven.[44] Recall a time that you have done harm to another person. Perhaps it was being hateful to your parents, betraying a lover or avoiding a friend. If those individuals forgave you, how did they communicate it to you and what was your response? Why do you believe they did it? Do you think they benefited from forgiving you? Did you and your relationship with the person benefit as well? Did the experience teach you anything or change you in any way? And, finally, what insight do you have about the experience right now? This exercise will help you see the benefits of forgiveness and perhaps provide a model for your own forgiving.

Another way to appreciate being forgiven is to *seek* forgiveness for yourself. Whether it's for a past or present wrong, write a letter of apology. Recognizing and accepting that sometimes *you* are the transgressor may give you empathy and insight into people who are the transgressors in your own life. In this letter, describe what you have done (or *not* done, when action was called for) and acknowledge that it was wrong. Describe the harm it has done to the other person or to your relationship with that person. Apologize for the behaviour, either directly (by saying 'I'm sorry . . .') or by affirming the value of the relationship and your desire to restore it. You may wish to pledge to change your behaviour, to offer some way to 'repay' the person, or to enquire what it would take to re-establish the relationship.

Whether you send the letter of apology is up to you. Sometimes this may not be possible, if you are no longer in contact with the person; sometimes it may be risky or unwise.

Imagine forgiveness
In this exercise, try to imitate the participants from an intriguing study on the role of imagination in forgiveness.[45] First, identify a particular person whom you blame for mistreating or offending you. Second, engage in an imagination exercise, during which you imagine empathizing with the offender and granting him or her forgiveness. Trying to feel empathy involves viewing the situation through the offender's eyes and ears, seeing him as

a whole person rather than defining him solely by the offending behaviour. Granting forgiveness does not necessarily imply excusing or tolerating the offender's behaviour, but it does entail trying to let go of your hurt, anger and hostility and adopting a more charitable and benevolent perspective. While doing the imagining, make an effort to consider your thoughts, feelings and behaviours in detail. For example, when you imagine forgiving your father for abandoning you, what would you say to him? What emotions would you feel and how intensely and in what order? What would your facial expression look like? Which physical sensations would be triggered in your body?

If you do this successfully, you might experience what the participants in this study experienced. The practice of empathic and forgiving thoughts (compared to the practice of nursing grudges and painful memories) led them to feel a greater sense of control over their thoughts, less sadness and anger, and less reactivity in terms of their physiological stress responses (such as lower heart rate, lower blood pressure and less furrowed brows). In other words, the bodies of participants who practised empathy and forgiveness experienced less stress, and yours could too.

Write a letter of forgiveness
This exercise involves letting go of your anger, bitterness and blame by writing, but not sending, a letter of forgiveness to a person who has hurt or wronged you. Sit down and consider the people throughout your life who have injured you or abused you and whom you have never forgiven. (These individuals may or may not still be part of your life; they may even no longer be alive.) Does this experience, and the lack of forgiveness, lead you to persist in dwelling on the person or the circumstances of the hurt or offence? Does it keep you from feeling happy, tranquil and free of intrusive images and thoughts? If the answer is yes, then you would do well to work on forgiving this person.

One of the best strategies is to write a 'forgiveness letter'. In the letter, describe in detail the injury or offence that was done to you. Illustrate how you were affected by it at the time and how you continue to be hurt by it. State what you wish the other person had done instead. End the letter with an explicit statement of forgiveness and understanding (e.g., 'I realize now that what you did was the best you could do at the time and I forgive you'). Below are some real-life examples I have come across from a variety of people who have successfully forgiven:

- I forgive my father for his alcoholism.
- I forgive my undergraduate writing teacher for telling me that I couldn't write.
- I forgive my boyfriend for not being there for me when I got depressed.
- I forgive the guy who crashed into my car.
- I forgive my wife for having an affair.
- I forgive my brother for humiliating me in public.
- I forgive my friend for using me.

The second one is mine.

You may have a hard time writing the forgiveness letter. You may feel that the act is unforgivable or that the person doesn't deserve to be forgiven or that you are too overwhelmed by negative emotions about the event to even begin to think about letting it go. If this is the case, put the letter aside and try again in a few days or weeks. Another approach is to choose another person (or act) to forgive – one that is a bit less painful. Forgiveness is a strategy that takes a great deal of effort, will power and motivation. It must be practised. So, starting with an 'easy' forgiveness exercise might be best for some of you. You can move on to more and more difficult cases with time.

Another strategy to help you overcome a block in writing the forgiveness letter is to learn about other people who have successfully forgiven. Perhaps you know someone in your life for whom forgiveness is a strength. Write or phone them and ask them about their experiences of forgiveness and how they do it. Alternatively, read about public figures who are famous for practising forgiveness, like Mahatma Gandhi, Nelson Mandela, Bishop Desmond Tutu and Martin Luther King, Jr.[46]

Practise empathy

Empathy is the vicarious experience and understanding of another person's emotions and thoughts. It often, but not always, involves feeling sympathy, concern, compassion or even warmth for that individual. The importance of learning and practising empathy for the person who has hurt you is underscored by findings that empathy correlates highly with forgiveness.[47] The more successful you are at achieving understanding, concern and consideration of the other person's perspective, the more likely you are to eventually forgive him or her.

One way to practise empathy in your daily life is to notice every time someone does something that you do not understand. Try to work out such a person's thoughts, feelings and intentions. Why did he behave the way he did? What factors might explain it? If possible, ask him yourself and (assuming that he is self-insightful) you might learn something.

Consider charitable attributions

Besides empathy, one of the key factors that facilitates forgiveness is positive or charitable attributions about the transgressor.[48] An effective way to generate generous attributions is to write the letter that you'd *like* to receive from the transgressor in response to your forgiveness of her – her apology letter, if you will. What explanation (or explanations) might she offer for her conduct? (One technique is to imagine that *you* had been the transgressor in this exact situation and consider what might have driven you to do harm and whether you expect to be forgiven.) Do you buy this explanation? Do you find it reasonable and adequate? Would you believe her? Would you give her the 'benefit of the doubt'? As you write down her response to you, you may sense your perception of her and the situation shifting. The circumstances that caused you so much anguish may be seen from a new perspective.

Why are apologies so helpful in fostering forgiveness? Because they produce empathy.[49] They humanize. When the person who has caused you pain, suffering or harm apologizes, he is showing you a side of him that is vulnerable and imperfect. An apology often includes an explanation of what he was thinking when he hurt you – perhaps he made a huge mistake, perhaps he under-estimated the harm, perhaps he was motivated by good intentions, and so on. No matter what, you end up seeing the situation a little more from his perspective. This makes forgiving easier.

Ruminate less

In Chapter 4, I discussed the pernicious nature of rumination. Dwelling on how badly you're feeling, or on a worry, or on how much better a tennis player your friend is, makes you unhappy, anxious, pessimistic and insecure. It turns out that rumination is also a considerable barrier to forgiveness. People who brood or obsess over a transgression are more likely to hold on to their hurt and anger and less motivated to forgive.[50] Many of you are prob-ably well aware what form these ruminations take. You go over the event (or series of events) in your mind, you feel angrier and angrier, more and more resentful, humiliated, put upon. You imagine what you want to say or do to the person who has hurt you.

Some people believe that this kind of imagination exercise – an exercise in 'vicarious aggression', if you will – will make them feel better, much like hitting a punchbag or knocking around foam bats might defuse anger or blow off steam. A long tradition of research has now shown that this notion, which psychologists call 'catharsis theory' is dead wrong. Fantasizing about how you might physically or verbally cause pain to someone may make you immediately feel better or release some tension, but it actu-ally increases rather than decreases hostility. This is because each time you remember the offence, you are triggering all over again the old feelings of hurt, blame, antagonism or rage.

When thoughts and images of the injury or offence become

intrusive and may even interfere with your daily life, it's time to do something about them. You may borrow the techniques described at the end of Chapter 4 like distraction (immediately diverting your attention to another thought, or absorbing yourself in an engrossing activity) or saying 'Stop!' Although putting a stop to the ruminations will not automatically lead to forgiveness, it is a necessary first step.

Make contact
I mentioned earlier that you shouldn't actually send your forgiveness letter. Here is where I get to change my mind. *Sometimes* it is appropriate and healthy and happiness-promoting to send the letter. The act of forgiveness (writing the letter *and* believing in it) is something you do for yourself. It will make you happier in the long run. *Communicating* that act (if it's even possible) is something that you do to benefit the other person and your relationship with that person. Prepare for it to backfire (maybe even very badly), but also know that communicating forgiveness might end up restoring your relationship and ultimately bringing more joy than you had possibly imagined. Only you will know whether to send the letter or make that call. Finally, remember that there's an alternative, even if you don't send the letter – simply be kind to the person you've privately forgiven.

Remind yourself
An instructive story about forgiveness was told about former US President Bill Clinton. Apparently Clinton once asked Nelson Mandela how he was able to bring himself to forgive his jailers. 'And Mandela said, "When I walked out of the gate I knew that if I continued to hate these people I was still in prison." Clinton believes it, but he has to keep reminding himself. That story [for him] is a little bit of a prayer.'[51] If you have chosen forgiveness as your happiness activity, you have chosen a difficult but ultimately meaningful and rewarding path. When you find yourself slipping into the old furies and bitternesses, remind yourself on a daily basis. Make forgiveness a habit, like you would a prayer.

COMPLEMENTARY ACTIVITIES

If you benefit from this activity, you may also want to try:

1) Developing strategies for coping (Happiness Activity No. 6, p. 154)

2) Cultivating optimism (Happiness Activity No. 2, p. 100)

Chapter 7

Living in the present

There's a clever cartoon from the *New Yorker* that has three panels. In the first, a man is sitting at his desk and daydreaming about playing golf. In the second panel, the same man is playing golf while fantasizing about sex. In the third, he is in bed with a woman while thinking about work.[1] Like the man in the cartoon, we habitually fail to enjoy, savour and live in the present, as our minds are often somewhere else.

However, when you think about it, the present moment is all we are really guaranteed. In this chapter, I describe two strategies that promote living in the present – 'flow' and savouring. Both are states of mind associated with positive emotions and well-being. Putting them into practice is one way that you can overcome your genes and your life circumstances and take a step into transforming yourself into a happier person by making the most of the 40 per cent solution.

Happiness Activity No. 8: Increasing 'flow' experiences

Have you ever been so absorbed in what you're doing – painting, writing, conversing, playing chess, woodworking, fishing, praying, web surfing – that you have completely lost track of time? Perhaps you have even failed to notice that you were very hungry or that your back ached from sitting for so long or that you needed to use the loo? Did nothing else seem to matter? If the answer is yes, then you have experienced a state called 'flow'. Coined by Mihaly Csikszentmihalyi (chick–SENT–me–hi), flow is a state of intense absorption and involvement with the present moment.[2] You're totally immersed in what you're doing, fully

concentrating and unaware of yourself. The activity you're per-
forming is challenging and engrossing, stretching your skills and
expertise. When in flow, people report feeling strong and efficacious – at the peak of their abilities – alert, in control and
completely unselfconscious. They do the activity for the sheer
sake of doing it.

The concept of flow came to Csikszentmihalyi in the 1960s,
when he was researching the creative process. During his interviews and observations of dedicated artists, he was struck by how
they would often ignore hunger, discomfort and fatigue while
working on a painting, yet lose interest in the work as soon as
they were finished. These artists clearly found the process of
painting intrinsically rewarding. In describing their subjective
experience of painting, they used the metaphor of a current
gamely carrying them along. This is flow.

Csikszentmihalyi argues that the good life, a happy life, is one
that is characterized by flow, by 'complete absorption in what one
does'.[3] The key to creating flow is to establish a balance between
skills and challenges. Whether you are rock climbing, perform-
ing surgery, doing your taxes or driving on the motorway, if the
challenges of the situation overwhelm your level of skill or
expertise, you will feel anxious or frustrated. On the other hand,
if the activity is not challenging enough, you will become bored.
Flow is a way of describing an experience that falls in just the
right space between boredom and anxiety. Your happiness
depends on your ability to find that perfect space – to extract flow
from what you are doing.

Indeed, we can experience flow in almost anything we do,
however monotonous or tedious it might appear – waiting for the
bus, changing a nappy, working on an assembly line, listening to
a lecture, even standing at baggage claim. I often experience flow
while analysing data. Sometimes five hours will go by and they
feel like five minutes. On the other hand, some of us fail to experience flow (feeling bored or anxious instead) even during
apparently exciting or captivating events – a sailing adventure, an
action movie or a dance recital. If we train ourselves to obtain

flow in as many circumstances as possible, we will have happier lives.

The benefits of flow

Why is flow good for you? The first reason is obvious – because it is inherently pleasurable and fulfilling, and the enjoyment you obtain is generally of the type that is lasting and reinforcing. Flow provides a natural high which, unlike artificial highs or pure hedonistic pleasures, is a positive, productive and controllable experience, which does not cause guilt, shame or other damage to the self or the society at large.

Second, because flow states are intrinsically rewarding we naturally want to repeat them. However, therein lies a seeming paradox. As we master new skills (e.g., skiing, writing, speech-making, gardening, etc.), our experience of flow diminishes, because the task at hand is no longer as stimulating and demanding. Thus, to maintain flow, we have to continually test ourselves in ever more challenging activities. We have to apply focused mental discipline or strenuous physical exertion. We have to stretch our skills or find novel opportunities to use them. This is wonderful, because it means that we are constantly striving, growing, learning and becoming more competent, expert and complex. One study followed talented teenagers over a four-year time span. Those who, at age thirteen, had identified their talent area (whether music, maths or football) as a source of flow, and who experienced relatively more flow and less anxiety during school activities, were more likely to stay committed to their talent through the teen years (as opposed to disengaging from it).[4] Presumably, these teenagers continued to develop their talents and to expand their abilities and interests.

One of the primary themes running through this book is that we cannot allow our happiness to depend on our external circumstances, for every positive event and accomplishment we experience is accompanied by rapid adaptation and escalating expectations. Even as we attain greater heights, we begin to want even more. Here is Csikszentmihalyi's solution to this dilemma: 'There is no inherent problem in our desire to escalate our goals, as long as we enjoy the struggle along the way.'[5] However, when we are preoccupied with the goal (the graduate degree earned, the children grown up, the kitchen remodelled), we will no longer derive pleasure and contentment from the process of achieving it – that is, from the present moment.

The experience of flow leads us to be involved in life (rather than be alienated from it), to enjoy activities (rather than to find them dreary), to have a sense of control (rather than helplessness) and to feel a strong sense of self (rather than unworthiness). All of these factors imbue life with meaning and lend it a richness and intensity. And happiness.

How to increase flow experiences

I discovered the concept of flow in 1990, in my second year of graduate school. I remember reading Csikszentmihalyi's classic work and my roommate and best friend asked me one day what had possessed me to read a whole book about menstrual flow! Needless to say, Csikszentmihalyi's *Flow* opened up to me a world of a very different kind of flow, a world of a thousand possibilities and opportunities. Finding flow involves the ability to expand your mind and body to its limits, to strive to accomplish something difficult, novel or worthwhile, and to discover rewards in the process of each moment, indeed in life itself. Choose at least one recommendation, below, and adopt it in your day-to-day life.

Control attention

To increase the frequency and length of flow experiences in your daily life, you need to become fully engaged and involved. Whether it's writing a letter, making phone calls on behalf of a client, or playing a round of golf, seek work, home and leisure activities that engage your skills and expertise. How exactly do you accomplish this? The secret is *attention*. William James, the 'father' of psychology (and brother to Henry James), once wrote, 'My experience is what I agree to attend to.' This is a revolutionary thought. What you notice and what you pay attention to *is* your experience – it *is* your life. There's only so much attention that you have to go around, so how and where you choose to invest it is critical. To enter the state of flow, attention needs to be directed fully to the task at hand. When you're intensely concentrating on doing something, you're essentially directing your attention to the task (e.g., drawing) as opposed to other things (i.e., thoughts like 'What time is it?' 'What will I have for dinner?' and 'This is not going as smoothly as last time').

Maintaining the state of flow also involves the control of your attention. If the challenge is too low and you become bored or apathetic, your attention drifts elsewhere. If the challenge is too high and you become tense or stressed, your attention shifts to yourself and your limitations, making you self-conscious. So, your aim is to gain control over what you pay attention to – in a sense, to gain control over the contents of your consciousness moment by moment. Controlling your consciousness means controlling the quality of your experience. Although this may be difficult or even painful, in the long-term it can provide a sense of mastery and participation in life. Like with all the other strategies described in this section, you will need to exert effort and creativity.

Adopt new values

Happy people have the capacity to enjoy their lives even when their material conditions are lacking and even when many of their goals have not been reached. How do they do it? By using the following values as their guide: 1) Be open to new and different experiences (cooking for ten, joining a sports team, hiking to a remote location, learning to play squash); and 2) Learn until the day you die – be it barbecuing, Spanish, knitting, the history of World War II, a more effective way to maintain friendships, a new word game, etc. Try to imitate the rapt concentration on the face of a small child who is learning wonderful new things every day – walking, jumping, doing a jigsaw puzzle, learning the meanings of words, or understanding for the first time how things work (traffic, eyes, school, mail). The state of flow comes naturally to the child, but you may have to work at it.

Learn what flows

In one study, adult workers were given pagers that beeped them at preprogrammed intervals as they went about their days.[6] Each page was a signal to the participants to consider their behaviours at that very moment and to complete several rating scales – that is, how much were they concentrating, did they want to continue what they were doing, and how happy, strong and creative were they feeling. Interestingly, though perhaps not surprisingly, the study found that *while at work* (relative to home/leisure) these individuals spent a great deal more time in high-challenge high-skill situations (that is, those situations that foster flow) and less time in low-skill low-challenge situations. Indeed, they were inclined to experience a sense of efficacy and self-confidence during work hours but to experience apathy at home. However, when probed about what they'd *rather* be doing, these participants uniformly stated that they'd rather be doing something else when working and that they prefer to continue what they're doing when at leisure.

The workers in this study clearly showed a disconnection between their beliefs about work and leisure (e.g., the former as a duty that one is forced to do, the latter as a chosen, and thus valued, activity) and their actual experiences, which were powerfully more positive during work hours. Similarly, many of us may not even recognize when we experience flow. Thus, one of your first steps in applying this strategy is to establish the precise time periods and activities during which you find yourself in flow . . . and then multiplying them.

Transform routine tasks

Even seemingly boring and tedious activities – waiting for the bus, listening to a dull presentation, getting one's teeth cleaned,

or vacuuming – can be transformed into something more meaningful and stimulating. What you need to do is to create
'microflow' activities with specific goals and rules.[7] For example,
you could solve puzzles in your head, draw cartoon characters,
tap melodies to favourite songs, or compose funny limericks. So,
while sitting in a doctor's waiting room, your goal might be to
draw an intricate design and a rule might be that all lines must be
symmetrical. German-born Philipp recounted to me his
microflow strategy while driving in heavy traffic:

> I listen to a lot of music while I am driving . . . trance/techno
> and Japanese video game and anime soundtracks, sometimes
> called Jpop. [Most of these] have very good and methodical
> bass lines, melody lines, and even some drum or bass guitar
> lines . . . I picked a particular beat, whether it was a bass of a
> trance song (it's the 'thump' of a trance song if you have ever
> heard one) or a bass guitar riff of an anime rock song, and did
> my best to tap my finger or foot with the exact rhythm in
> synchrony of the particular riff or beat I was concentrating
> on . . . I was able to alternate songs and then the different
> parts of the same songs to really explore and keep up with . . .
> I did this while driving for long periods of time on the free-
> way . . . When I was running short errands, I found myself
> getting equally frustrated, so I did it every time I was stopped
> at a red light or stop sign or even if the lane was just moving
> a bit too slow for my liking. I was able to take this micro
> activity of keeping in perfect tapping synchronicity of a song
> to wherever I went with my car, whenever I felt like I was
> beginning to feel too many negative emotions . . . I found
> that with this microflow activity I was able to drive perfectly
> but at the same time be able to concentrate on the song and
> my tapping.

Philipp came up with a fairly idiosyncratic and rarefied microflow activity. Whether yours is unique or mundane doesn't
matter, as long as it's somewhat challenging and interesting and

yields a richer, and less boring and stressful, experience of daily life.

Flow in conversation

Depending on your job and lifestyle, a significant percentage of your days may be spent in conversations with others. Do you usually experience flow when you are talking with another person? Are you frequently so interested in the conversation that you almost feel yourself step into a different reality, not noticing time passing or the sights and sounds around you? If the answer is 'no', you may benefit from implementing the following exercise designed to promote flow during conversations.[8] During your next tête-à-tête, whether by phone or face-to-face, focus your attention as intensely as possible on what the other person is saying and your reactions to her words. Don't be too quick to respond, rather, give her the space to expand on her thoughts and prompt her with brief follow-up questions (e.g., 'And then what happened?' or 'Why did you think that?'). One way to smooth this process is to give yourself the goal of learning more about the speaker. What is on her mind? What emotions is she experiencing right now? Have you learned something about her that you didn't know? If you're more of a talker than a listener, then this exercise might be difficult and awkward at first – and might inhibit flow by making you self-conscious – but the strategy should get easier with time.

Smart leisure

Many of us feel that our 'free' or leisure time is precious. There is much too little of it, so we save it for something really special, something that gives us joy. Or do we? Consider the hours of the day during which you are free of obligations and have freedom to choose what to do. Do you watch TV? Read an entertainment magazine? Chat on your phone? Send text messages? During what percentage of your leisure activities are you truly concentrating, using your mind or exercising your skills? If the percentage is low, this means that you're unlikely to be in flow during much of your leisure time.

Of course, after a long and stressful day, vegging out in front of the evening news, *Seinfeld* reruns, or Sky Sports might be your idea of heaven. I agree – that decompression time is sorely needed. But be honest with yourself about how long it truly takes to decompress. I would bet forty-five minutes is enough. After that, you're not vegging, but vegetating, and might end up emerging from the sofa hours later, in time for bed, and wondering where the evening has gone and why you're in such a rut.

Smart work

'We're playing work,' my then-kindergartener announced to me one night right before dinner. She and her three-year-old brother were having a blast. He was sitting at his Barney laptop ('I have to check my e-mails,' he announced) and she was writing and talking earnestly into the phone ('Let me call you right back'). Work can be rewarding, gratifying and enjoyable, if you're lucky and if you make it so.

One fascinating study of workers found that people tend to see their work in one of three ways – as a job, as a career or as a calling.[9] Those who place their work in the 'job' category essentially perceive it as a necessary evil, a means to an end – the job is needed to support themselves and not something positive or rewarding. Accordingly, they labour in order to have the money to enjoy their time away from work. By contrast, the category of 'career' is essentially a job with advancement. People who report having a career may not see their work as a major positive part of their life, but they have opportunities or ambitions for promotion. They invest more time and energy in their work, as the opportunities they create for themselves may bring the rewards of higher social status, power and self-esteem. Finally, those who see their work as a 'calling' report enjoying working and find what they do to be fulfilling and socially useful. They work not for the financial rewards or for advancement, but because they want to; it is inseparable from the rest of their lives.

You might wonder whether certain kinds of occupations are more conducive to 'callings' versus 'careers' or 'jobs'. This is probably true. Artists, teachers, scientists and neurosurgeons might be relatively more likely to enjoy their work and to believe that it makes the world a better place. However, by no means do these occupations have a monopoly on callings. Indeed, researchers have found that people are remarkably adept at crafting their jobs to derive maximum engagement and meaning. For example, interviews with twenty-eight members of a hospital cleaning crew revealed that some of the hospital cleaners disliked cleaning, felt that it entailed low-level skills and did the minimum amount of work required; others, in contrast, transformed the job into something grander and more significant.[10] This second group of hospital cleaners described their work as bettering the daily lives of patients, visitors and nurses. They engaged in a great deal of social interaction (e.g., showing a visitor around, brightening a patient's day), reported liking cleaning and judged the work as highly skilled. It's not surprising that these hospital cleaners found flow in their work. They set forth challenges for themselves, for example, how to get the job accomplished in a maximally efficient way or how to help patients heal faster by making them more comfortable. They added extra tasks outside their formal duties, such as rearranging the paintings on the walls or fetching wildflowers. They saw themselves as part of a larger, integrated whole – not just mopping floors and emptying bins – but serving as part of a system that improves people's lives. People in other occupations – from hairdressers and engineers to computer techs and kitchen workers – have also been observed crafting their jobs in ways to maximize flow and meaning. It's worth considering how your own job can benefit from a new perspective.

Strive for 'superflow'
At times, you may experience flow by fully immersing yourself in music, becoming one with nature, or losing track of time during a phone call. At other times, you may experience some-

thing even more magnificent. Let me propose a related state, which I'll call 'superflow'. This is when you are not only completely absorbed and unselfconscious, but absolutely transcendent. This happened to me one Saturday morning when my son learned how to do a new kind of maths problem and we worked on maths computations – both of us exhilarated, energized, suspended in time – for an hour or maybe two hours; I don't know, because the experience rushed by in an instant. Another time I remember chatting to a colleague at a conference. We were sitting in a busy, crowded, noisy bar area and we talked and talked, oblivious to the presentations and meetings we were missing, not noticing a single passer-by. I was utterly and joyfully unaware of my surroundings or worries or any thoughts other than our conversation during the entire time. Both of these experiences left me feeling happier, more creative, more amiable. They bolstered my sense of belonging, vigour and self-confidence. Strive to achieve the state of 'superflow' whenever you possibly can.

Caveat

If you discover particular activities that reliably deliver for you the experience of flow, you are fortunate. But be aware that such activities, even those viewed as constructive by the wider culture (like volunteering for a charity, playing with one's child, or working on a contract at the office), can become addictive. When you notice yourself consistently ignoring the needs of people close to you, that should be a warning signal. We are all aware that hobbies such as playing video games can prompt people to avoid or disregard their responsibilities, not to mention other sources of satisfaction.[11] But this can happen with socially desirable behaviour as well. I learned this lesson when my husband pointed out to me that I had become so absorbed in my daily reading of the *Harry Potter* books with my daughter, that I was ignoring other pressing responsibilities.

COMPLEMENTARY ACTIVITIES

If you benefit from this activity, you may also want to try:

1) Savouring life's joys (Happiness Activity No. 9, see below)

2) Committing to your goals (Happiness Activity No. 10, p. 213)

Happiness Activity No. 9: Savouring life's joys

~

'My advice to you is not to inquire why or whither, but just enjoy your ice cream while it's on your plate.'

THORNTON WILDER

~

Parents tell their children to be good, so that they can grow up to be moral adults and responsible citizens. Teachers tell their pupils to study hard, so that they can earn high marks, get into a good college and find a decent job. Supervisors tell their employees to work hard and aim high, so that they can win pay increases and promotions. Senior citizen friends tell their still-working chums that the golden years of retirement are near. And, if you're a little like me, even when the present *is* wonderful, you can't take pleasure in it, as you're already imagining being nostalgic for it in the future.[12] We rarely seem to live in and savour the present moment, believing that what counts most will happen in the future. We postpone our happiness, convincing ourselves that tomorrow will be better than today.

Yet the ability to savour the positive experiences in your life is one of the most important ingredients of happiness. Most people truly understand what it means to savour after overcoming uncomfortable or painful symptoms, or following a brush with mortality or a major scare. When you have a toothache and it's gone, you suddenly delight in the absence of the toothache. When you're overwhelmed with terrific allergies, which abruptly dissipate, you truly relish breathing freely. After a near-death experience or an alarming diagnosis, you may also feel able (at least temporarily) to truly appreciate and savour the good things in your life – to live each day as if it were your first day and your last day.

You can think of savouring as having past, present and future components. You savour the past by reminiscing about the good old days – your first love, your wedding, the acceptance letter, the phone call when you learned you got the job, your summer road trip, and so on. You savour the present by truly living in, being mindful of and relishing the present moment – whether it's having lunch with a colleague, listening to grandma's stories, playing football or immersing yourself in a book, song or project at work. This type of savouring overlaps a great deal with flow and with gratitude. Finally, you savour the future by anticipating and fantasizing about future positive events. This is an element of optimistic thinking. Notably, although it may appear that the past and future components of savouring don't belong in a chapter titled 'living in the present', they both involve ways of heightening and preserving pleasure by bringing the pleasure of the past and future into the present moment.

Researchers define savouring as any thoughts or behaviours capable of 'generating, intensifying, and prolonging enjoyment'.[13] So, when you 'stop and smell the roses' instead of walking by obliviously, you are savouring. When you bask and take pride in your own or your friends' accomplishments, you are savouring. When you suddenly emerge out of a frazzled or distracted state (e.g., while talking on the phone or running errands) and become fully aware of how much there is to enjoy of life, you are savouring. This is the slight difference between savouring and flow – savouring requires a stepping outside of experience and reviewing it, whereas flow involves a complete immersion in the experience. Of course, ideally you need not step outside of experience too much or too often in order to savour the moment, for after all frequently asking yourself 'Am I savouring yet?' or 'Am I appreciative enough?' will ultimately detract from your enjoyment.

Whether it involves a focus on the long ago, the present

moment or future times, the habit of savouring has been shown in empirical research to be related to intense and frequent happiness. Moreover, savouring is associated with many other positive characteristics. For example, in several studies, people who are inclined to savour were found to be more self-confident, extroverted and gratified, and less hopeless and neurotic.[14] Interestingly, those adept at savouring the present versus the future versus the past experience different benefits. Those skilled at capturing the joy of the present moment – hanging on to good feelings, appreciating good things – are less likely to experience depression, stress, guilt and shame. People prone to joyful anticipation – skilled at obtaining pleasure from looking forward and imaging future happy events – are especially likely to be optimistic and to experience intense emotions. In contrast, those proficient at reminiscing about the past – looking back on happy times, rekindling joy from happy memories – are best able to buffer stress. Although these studies do not speak to whether savouring causes these good things versus the reverse, the investigator was confident enough to provide the following recommendations to individuals who are sad or unfulfilled:

> Rather than merely reacting to positive events when they happen to occur, [people] can learn to savour proactively – to consciously anticipate positive experiences, to mindfully accentuate and sustain pleasurable moments, and to deliberately remember these experiences in ways that rekindle enjoyment after they end.[15]

Of course, this is easier said than done. First, like all happiness-enhancing strategies, effort and motivation are necessary in order to truly savour. Our attention is often brimming with intrusive and persistent thoughts about the past and present (conversations, tasks undone, problems unsolved) and the future (to-do lists, plans), and committed effort is required to redirect our mind to positive experiences in the here and now. Second, as we already know, the process of hedonic adaptation leads us to obtain less and less pleasure from initially thrilling experiences, be it the view of the snow-capped mountains on the way to work, the song of bagpipes in the town square, or the smell of our new leather jacket. With time, such sights, sounds and aromas simply fade into the background. It takes dedicated will power to re-appreciate those things and stop taking them for granted. The next section describes a number of specific suggestions for accomplishing just that.

Strategies to foster savouring and the research behind them

If savouring life's joys is one of the happiness activities that fits you best, don't be daunted by the many ways to realize it. For now, select just *one* of the options in this section and get started right away.

Relish ordinary experiences

The first challenge in using the strategy of savouring is to learn how to appreciate and take pleasure in mundane, everyday experiences. As a model, consider what participants were asked to do in recent research aimed at exploring the extent to which making savouring a habit can produce tangible benefits. In one set of studies, depressed participants were invited to take a few minutes once a day to truly relish something that they usually hurry through (eating a meal, taking a shower, finishing the workday or walking home). When it was over, they were instructed to write down in what ways they had experienced the event differently as well as how that felt compared to the times when they rushed through it.[16] In another study, healthy students and community members were instructed to savour two pleasurable experiences per day, by reflecting on each for two to three minutes and trying to make the pleasure last as long and as intensely as possible.[17] In all these studies, those participants prompted to regularly practise savouring showed significant increases in happiness and reductions in depression.

Starting tomorrow, consider your daily routine activities and rituals. Do you notice and savour the pleasures of the day or do you dash through them? If the latter, then resolve to seize those pleasures when they happen and take full advantage of them. Linger over your morning pastry or your afternoon snack, absorbing the aroma, the sweetness or the crunchiness (rather than mindlessly consuming). Strive to bask in the feeling of accomplishment when you've finished a task at home or work, rather than distractedly moving on to the next item on your to-do list. Luxuriate in a long hot shower after a brisk walk in the cold. That perfect moment can last a few seconds or an entire weekend. 'Enjoy the little things, for one day you may look back and realize they were the big things.'[18]

Savour and reminisce with family and friends
Often it's easier to savour when you share a positive experience with another. Whether you're visiting a Japanese garden together, hiking to the top of a mountain or listening to jazz in front of a fire, the pleasure of the moment can be heightened in the company of others who similarly value the experience. Marvel at the present moment with the other person. Set aside an hour, an afternoon or an entire day for this activity.

Another person can also bolster the power of positive reminiscence. For example, you might reminisce together about a party you both attended or a holiday or job or friend you shared. You might make a pilgrimage together to a meaningful place from your past, or flip through a scrapbook or photo album together. You might listen (or sing along) to a piece of music associated with a particular memory. Researchers suggest that using a specific technique to trigger or intensify one's recall of the past may be successful at producing vivid, engaging reminiscence. For example, you might use guided imagery to vividly recreate the details of a pleasant memory in your mind. This strategy allows you and a close other to revisit pleasant times.

The advantages of savouring and reminiscing with others have empirical support. Researchers have found that mutual reminiscence – sharing memories with other people – is accompanied by abundant positive emotions such as joy, accomplishment, amusement, contentment and pride.[19] Interestingly, this appears to be particularly true for older individuals. Indeed, the more time older adults spend reminiscing, the more positive affect and higher morale they report.[20] These studies suggest that everyone – but especially older people, who have a wealth of life experiences – is able to extract positive feelings from reminiscence.

Transport yourself
The ability to engage in positive reminiscence, to transport yourself at will to a different time or place, can provide both pleasure and solace when you need it most. I know someone who conjures up the mental image of herself on her mountain bike whenever she is under stress or feeling down or bored. It's an imagination skill that can be honed with practice. Consider one study that successfully taught people how to travel to a mental destination through recall of positive images and memories.[21] Participants were first asked to make a list of happy memories and personal mementos (such as photographs, gifts and souvenirs) and then instructed to engage in positive reminiscing twice daily for a week. Specifically, they were told:

> First, turn to your list of positive memories and choose one to reflect upon. Then sit down, take a deep breath, relax, close your eyes, and begin to think about the memory. Allow images related to the memory to come to mind. Try to picture the events associated with this memory in your mind. Use your mind to imagine the memory. Let your mind wander freely through the details of the memory, while you are imagining the memory.

As the researchers predicted, those participants who reminisced on a regular basis showed considerable increases in happiness, and the more vivid the memories conjured, the greater gain in happy feelings.

Positive reminiscence boosts happiness in several ways. Focusing on positive aspects of past experiences may prompt you to feel that you are attaining your ideals or dreams, and help reinforce your sense of identity. For example, as you recall past experiences and life transitions, you may come to recognize continuity with the past, gain insight into yourself and appreciate your uniqueness. Furthermore, retelling experiences in positive ways can boost self-esteem and compel you to present a positive self-image. Positive reminiscence can also produce pleasure and enjoyment for its own sake – by laughing at funny moments, revelling in the memory of the wind in your hair or reliving a beautiful day. Doing this can also provide comfort and respite from stress during difficult or painful times.

Supporting some of these arguments, a recent study found that, after positive reminiscence, 29 per cent of people reported a new perspective and self-insight towards current problems, 19 per cent reported positive affect, 18 per cent reported 'escape from the present', and only 2 per cent claimed that it did nothing for them.[22] Most important, the more time that these respondents reported reminiscing about happy events or images from their past, the more they felt able to enjoy their *present* lives. Here's what a female participant observed about her experience reminiscing:

> Thinking of good times from the past makes me feel better about the present. It helps me appreciate things more. It gives me an idea of where I was then, where I am now, and where I ultimately want to be. It helps me understand the present and deal with it . . . These memories also give me a sense of confidence, kind of a 'you did it before, you can do it again' type of thing. If things are bad, I use my memories to start thinking of ways to make it better rather than thinking about how bad it is.[23]

Best of all, if you master this strategy, you 'will always have Paris', even when you haven't been back for decades.[24]

Replay happy days

In a recent study, my graduate students and I showed that the practice of repetitively replaying your happiest life events serves to prolong and reinforce positive emotions and make you happier.[25] So, think about one of your happiest days – graduation day (yours or your child's), the first time you heard 'I love you', the first day of your holiday, the day you brought home a puppy – and replay it in your mind as though you were rewinding a videotape and playing it back. Think about the events of the day and remember what happened in as much detail as you can. What exactly did you (or other people involved) say or do? What were the thoughts and emotions running through your head at the time? Don't analyse this day – just replay and revel in it. We found that people who performed this exercise for eight minutes per day on three consecutive days felt more intense positive emotions four weeks later.

Celebrate good news

In Chapter 5, I described research on 'capitalizing' or sharing good news with close family and friends. Sharing of successes and accomplishments with others has been shown to be associated with elevated pleasant emotions and well-being.[26] So, when you or your spouse or cousin or best friend wins an honour, congratulate them (and yourself) and celebrate. Try to enjoy the occasion to the fullest. Passing on and rejoicing in good news leads you to relish and soak up the present moment, as well as to foster connections with others. Researchers advise that you shouldn't shy away from pride – pat yourself on the back, tell yourself how hard you've worked for this moment, imagine how impressed people might be.[27] Or do the same for your spouse or cousin or best friend.

Be open to beauty and excellence

This strategy involves allowing yourself to truly admire an object of beauty or a display of talent, genius or virtue. Strive even to feel reverence and awe. Positive psychologists suggest that people who open themselves to the beauty and excellence around them are more likely to find joy, meaning and profound connections in their lives.[28] It may appear immensely challenging to experience awe in response to mundane daily life but it's an ability well worth cultivating. Don't go through life wearing blinkers to everything that is touching, beautiful, virtuous and magnificent. Consider the example of the poet Walt Whitman, whose 'favourite activity was to stroll outdoors by himself, admiring trees, flowers, the sky, and the shifting light of day, and listening to birds, crickets, and other natural sounds'. Here's a description of Whitman by a contemporary:

> It was evident that these things gave him a pleasure far beyond what they give to ordinary people. Until I knew the man, it had not occurred to me that any one could derive so much absolute happiness from these things as he did . . . Perhaps, indeed, no man who ever lived liked so many things and disliked so few as Walt Whitman. All natural objects seemed to have a charm for him. All sights and sounds seemed to please him. He appeared to like (and I believe he did like) all the men, women, and children he saw.[29]

Be mindful

Many philosophical and spiritual traditions stress the cultivation of 'mindfulness' as a critical ingredient of well-being. The practice of Zen Buddhism, for example, emphasizes clearing one's mind and grounding oneself in the present moment. Given the vast anecdotal evidence of the benefits of mindfulness, psychological researchers have begun to study this phenomenon in the laboratory. A series of studies conducted at the University of Rochester focused on people 'high in mindfulness', that is, those who are prone to be mindfully attentive to the here and now and keenly aware of their surroundings.[30] It turns out that such individuals are models of flourishing mental health. Relative to the average person, they are more likely to be happy, optimistic, self-confident and satisfied with their lives, and less likely to be depressed, angry, anxious, hostile, self-conscious, impulsive or neurotic. Furthermore, people who are habitually mindful of their current experiences are more likely to experience frequent and intense positive emotions, to feel self-sufficient, competent and to have positive social relationships, while those who are *not* usually mindful report more illness and physical symptoms.

In the words of William James, 'Compared to what we ought to be, we are only half awake.'[31] So how does one wake up to the present moment? As it happens, researchers have begun to train people to develop the habit of mindfulness, showing, for example, that a standardized eight-week mindfulness-based intervention can boost well-being and reduce psychological distress, pain and physical symptoms in ill persons.[32] The intervention teaches specific techniques, like learning relaxation, paying attention to breathing through stretches and postures, and becoming aware of bodily sensations, thoughts and emotions. Many of these techniques are integrated in the practice of meditation, which is described in greater detail in Chapter 9.

Take pleasure in the senses
'Luxuriating' – or indulging the senses – is one of the key ways to promote savouring.[33] Pay close attention and take delight in momentary pleasures, wonders and magical moments. Focus on the sweetness of a ripe mango, the aroma of a bakery or the warmth of the sun when you step out from the shade. Take in the cool fresh air after a storm, the brush strokes of an impressionist painting or the crescendo of a symphony. One laboratory experiment revealed that people who focused their attention on the sensory experience of consuming chocolate reported more pleasure than those who were distracted while eating.[34] This means making eating (whether chocolate or steak or a banana) into a ceremonial occasion – with an attractive presentation, a quiet and comfortable setting and no distractions (no TV, reading material or intrusive thoughts). To sharpen your perceptions, you may need to focus concentrated attention on certain elements and

completely block out others. For example, close your eyes and keep still when listening to music or enjoying a massage, or wear ear plugs to a museum. Stay absorbed in the present, in a state of flow, and try not to think of anything else. Some people call this 'rolling in' the moment, just sensing.

An extraordinary illustration of this strategy comes from a story of prisoners in a concentration camp who met regularly to share a fancy dinner in their minds, imagining all the details of the lighting of the room, the stiffness of their clothes and the flavours of the food:

> My friend, a French painter and Resistance fighter, was put in a concentration camp by the Nazis. Every evening during his long incarceration, he and two or three of his fellow prisoners ... entirely by means of conversation and gestures ... dressed for dinner in immaculate white shirts that did not exist, and placed, at times with some difficulty because of the starched material that wasn't there, pearl or ruby studs and cuff links in those shirts ... They drank Châteauneuf-du-Pape throughout the meal and Château d'Yquem with the dessert pastry.[35]

Remarkably, these individuals were able to experience 'pleasures of the mind' even under conditions of severe deprivation. With practice, we all can learn how to luxuriate and transport ourselves, using our five senses, no matter how ordinary or unstimulating our current setting.

Create a savouring album

Whenever I travel for business, even for a day, I carry a little photo album that has photos of my kids at different ages (the husband is relegated to the back). I look at it a lot – in planes, hotel rooms and in the audience of conference talks – and it never fails to give me a happiness boost. You can create such a 'savouring/memory' album yourself. It can have photos of your favourite people, places or things – family, friends, pets, famous paintings, etc. (One of my friends has a beautiful panorama of her home town of Barcelona, Spain.) Or it can have other happy-inducing or meaningful items – your acceptance letter to college, a love note, a favourite recipe, a niece's drawing, or an article about your favourite actor. Look at this album on a regular basis – but not too often, so as to stave off adaptation to its pleasure. You don't want the same thing to happen to the items in your savouring album as might happen to a special photo on your night stand or computer screen. When it's up for a long enough period of time, you fail to notice it altogether. This 'savouring album' is essentially a strategy to create and savour the memories (the 'mental photographs') of your positive experiences. It's also valu-able to review the album in less happy times, when you're especially needful of a boost.

Savour with your camera

An innovative idea is to train yourself to use a camera as a savour-ing tool.[36] Many people take numerous photos while travelling or on holiday or during significant life celebrations to preserve the experience for the future, but the role of photographer may actu-ally detract from their delight in the present moment. I know a father who devoted himself earnestly to photographing the birth of his first and only child. The photos were beautiful but, he lamented afterwards, he felt that he missed out on the most impor-tant first moment of his son's life. Looking through the camera lens made him detached from the scene, an observer and not an ex-periencer. Teach yourself to use your camera in a way that enhances your ongoing experiences, by truly looking at things and noticing what is beautiful and meaningful. Don't just create as many pic-tures as possible – try to take, print and frame the best picture you know how. This will make you more mindful and more appre-ciative, and will lead you to enjoy your experiences more.

Seek bittersweet experiences

A bittersweet experience is one that involves mixed emotions, usually happiness and sadness mixed together. Such events are

usually characterized by the fact that they will soon end – a holiday, a friendship, a phase of life, a sojourn in a particular place or
time. When we are fully mindful of the transience of things we
are more likely to appreciate and savour the remaining time that
we do have. So, although bittersweet experiences also make us
sad, it is this sadness that prompts us, instead of taking it for
granted, to come to appreciate the positive aspects of our holiday, colleague or home town – it's 'now or never'.

Researchers have attempted to foster savouring in the laboratory by drawing people's attention to the bittersweet or
transient nature of some positive life experiences by pointing
out that many such experiences will eventually end. To test this
notion, they recruited college seniors nearing the close of their
undergraduate careers to participate in an experiment.[37] These
seniors were instructed to write about aspects of their college
experience (e.g., their friends, the campus, etc.) twice a week
over a two-week period. Furthermore, while writing, some of
the students were asked to focus on the fact that graduation is
imminent (i.e., that they only had '1,200 hours left'; this was
the 'bittersweet' group), whereas others were asked to focus on
the fact that it's still far away (i.e., that they had 'one tenth of
a year left'; a control group). The researchers expected that
pondering the imminence of one's graduation from college
would elicit feelings of appreciation for college life and to
prompt students to savour the present moment as there is so
little time left. By contrast, the 'graduation is far away' group
would not be compelled to savour the present, as they would
be made aware that there's plenty of time left to enjoy college.
The results confirmed these expectations: Compared to the
control group, the bittersweet group was more likely to show
increases in happiness and to engage in savouring-type behaviours (e.g., spending time with friends, taking photos,
participating in college clubs or taking a scenic route to lec-
tures).

So, don't shy away from the bittersweet. In some sense, all of
our life experiences are bittersweet ones. All good things (and bad

things) come to an end, and the acknowledgement of this truth can prompt you to stop and smell the roses.

Wax nostalgic

Although many people associate nostalgia with homesickness, it is actually a positive emotion, albeit a poignant one. Being Russian-born I should know, as Slavic peoples are famous for their nostalgia. When you feel nostalgic about a past time in your life, a person you were close to, a seashore you once haunted, you may feel a wistful pleasure, a yearning that is at once joyful, affectionate and tinged with sadness, as you are fully aware that it is bygone. From time to time, nurture those nostalgic feelings – they will make you feel warm about your past and bring back cherished memories of beauty, pleasure, goodness and love. Don't compare these feelings with the present; focus only on the positives and how they have enriched your life. My students and I have found that, when recalling their most wonderful moments from the past, the happiest people are apt to put them in their 'psychological bank account' or experiential treasure chest – that is they experience them as adding meaning and richness to their lives rather than focusing on how the good old days were so much better than today.[38] 'Nostalgia is memory with the pain removed.'[39] Studies have shown that nostalgic experiences spawn positive feelings, reinforce our sense of being loved and protected, and even boost our self-esteem.[40]

Nostalgia can be triggered spontaneously – a conversation with an old friend, a birthday party, a photograph, an e-mail – or deliberately, through active reflection. It makes us feel good not only because of the positive memories we might recall but because it protects and strengthens our identity (e.g., by putting together pieces of the past into a coherent whole), fosters pride (e.g., through memories of a past triumph), regenerates a sense of meaning (e.g., through an improved understanding of where we fit in our culture and generation) and buttresses social connections (by celebrating past and present relationships).

A note about writing

Some psychologists advise savouring through writing, perhaps by keeping a journal in which you describe a memorable past experience or an exciting time in the present. I recommend against this. The reason is that writing, while an invaluable tool to foster gratitude or come to terms with traumas, stresses or hurt feelings, is counterproductive when savouring or relishing the present. Research from my and other laboratories shows that writing is inherently a structured process, which forces a person to organize and integrate his thoughts, to reflect on what causes what, to create a coherent narrative about himself and to consider systematic, step-by-step solutions. So, as we saw in Chapter 6, writing is an effective strategy when one needs to cope with negative experiences as it helps a person make sense of them and to get past them. But you don't want to 'get past' a positive event! When it comes to the best experiences in life, it's repetitive replaying and savouring of the experiences that maintains the positive emotions surrounding them and enhances your happiness.[41] In contrast, writing about a positive life event may very well prompt you to systematically analyse that event which is likely to reduce the pleasure associated with it and may even evoke negative emotions, such as guilt or worry. So, don't savour through writing but, instead, reflect, relish and share with others.

COMPLEMENTARY ACTIVITIES

If you benefit from this activity, you may also want to try:

1) Increasing 'flow' experiences (Happiness Activity No. 8, p. 185)

2) Committing to your goals (Happiness Activity No. 10, p. 213)

Final words

It's possible to overdo living in the present. A flourishing life involves contemplating and planning for the future and learning

from the errors of the past. One study found that homeless individuals live almost completely in the present,[42] and observations
of Alzheimer's patients suggest that they do as well.[43] People
whose orientation is overwhelmingly present-focused have been
found to be less capable of delaying gratification and more likely
to engage in a host of risky behaviours.[44] So, as with anything,
strive to strike a balance between absorption in the here and now
and, as I discuss in the next chapter, the conscious appraisal of the
progress you're making towards your goals.[45] As a famous states-
man once described how he changed after a brush with his own
mortality, 'I try . . . in a funny way, simultaneously to think more
about the future in constructive ways but to live more in the
moment.'[46]

Chapter 8

Happiness Activity No. 10: Committing to your goals

~

'An aim in life is the only fortune worth finding.'

~

In 1932, weighed down by the sorrows and agonies of his self-absorbed and aimless clients, an Australian psychiatrist named W. Béran Wolfe summed up his philosophy like this: 'If you observe a really happy man you will find him building a boat, writing a symphony, educating his son, growing double dahlias in his garden, or looking for dinosaur eggs in the Gobi Desert.'[1] He was right. People who strive for something personally significant, whether it's learning a new craft, changing careers or raising moral children, are far happier than those who don't have strong dreams or aspirations.[2] Find a happy person and you will find a project.

Some devote themselves to lifelong goals vis-à-vis their work, while others commit themselves to making their family, social or spiritual lives more meaningful. It turns out that the process of working towards a goal – participating in a valued and challenging activity – is as important to well-being than its attainment.[3] Indeed, numerous anecdotes reveal that people often feel an enormous letdown after having attained something that they have been striving towards for years. After spending a decade helping to build the architecturally exquisite Walt Disney Concert Hall, the seat of the Los Angeles Philharmonic, music director Esa-Pekka Salonen recounted feeling joy, but also a 'sadness that he doesn't seem able to shake. Now that the impossible dream has been realized, how to move on to the next thing? And what could possibly top this'.[4] Although most of us don't share the problems of famous composers, we are privy to the general phenomenon – that working towards a meaningful life goal is one of the most important strategies for becoming lastingly happier.

Committed goal pursuit is different from the other eleven happiness activities that I describe in this book. The reason is that, no matter what our level of happiness and fulfilment, *all* of us have some kinds of goals. Furthermore, our goals vary from one person to another and across time. So how do you adapt this happiness strategy for your particular unique situation? Perhaps you have plenty of goals, but you lack motivation and passion for them. Then your priority should be to develop that missing passion and impetus. Perhaps you are following the wrong kinds of goals. The goals that you have set for yourself may be ones sold to you by the larger culture – 'Make money! Own your own home! Look great!' – and, while there may be nothing inherently wrong with striving for those things, they mask the pursuits more likely to deliver true and lasting happiness. In this case, your priority should be to discern which goals will make you happy in the long term and to follow them.

Six benefits of committed goal pursuit

Our first charge is to turn to the question of why the process of pursuing goals in the first place is so critical to our happiness. One way to think about this question is to consider what happens when a person doesn't hold any significant dreams or aims in life. Such a person is lost, with no direction, no incentives to act, no *raison d'être*. So, first and foremost, committed goal pursuit provides us with a sense of purpose and a feeling of control over our life.[5] Whether our valued activity is becoming a musician or having a baby, it gives us something to work for and to look forward to. In author G.K. Chesterton's words, 'There is one thing which gives radiance to everything. It is the idea of something around the corner.'

Second, having meaningful goals bolsters our self-esteem, stimulating us to feel confident and efficacious. Furthermore, the accomplishment of every subgoal (on the way to the big goal) is yet another opportunity for an emotional boost. Such lifts in joy and pride are important not only because they reinforce happiness, but because they motivate us to continue striving. Consider the unhappiest people you know: they are likely to be apathetic, bored, unmotivated and devoid of aspirations, whether it's the idea of changing careers or changing wardrobes. Some elements of goal striving might require tedium or hard work, but the boosts along the way are worth it.

Third, pursuing goals adds structure and meaning to our daily lives. Notwithstanding the myth of the man in the grey flannel suit, structure and meaning is good! It grants responsibilities, deadlines, timetables, opportunities for mastering new skills (e.g., building a wooden deck) and for social interactions with others (e.g., taking a wood turning class). This is valuable for just about everyone, but it's particularly critical if you are older and retired (and thus may lack the structure and sense of purpose supplied by a profession) or if you have disabilities or health problems that prevent you from doing what you used to do. If you find yourself in one of those situations, you would probably benefit emotionally from pursuing goals with a social, cultural or political flavour, for example, strengthening friendships and family relationships, participating in cultural events, fundraising for a political cause, or enrolling in an online class.

A fourth fringe benefit to being committed to our goals is that it helps us learn to master our use of time by identifying higher-order goals (e.g., to visit every continent), subdividing them into smaller steps or subgoals (e.g., to plan the next trip to South America), and developing a schedule to accomplish them (with Palm Pilot or diary in hand). This is a genuine life-simplifying and life-improving skill. Your life can fall apart pretty quickly if you bungle to-do lists and make a mess of well-laid plans.

Some of us might wonder whether it is feasible or even possible to continue striving towards our goals during times of crisis. Research suggests that not only is it possible, but commitment to goals during such times may help us cope better with problems. So, there is the fifth benefit of goal pursuit. Of course, sometimes traumatic or challenging situations may require surrendering no longer tenable goals. A serious injury or grave financial loss will have us rethinking whether we should relinquish our dream of becoming a ski instructor or attending law school. If we can bring ourselves to replace the old goals with new ones, we'll be happier.

Finally, the pursuit of goals often involves engaging with other people – teachers, clients, friends, colleagues and partners – and such social connections can be happiness-inducing in and of themselves. As I discussed in Chapter 5, human beings have a strong 'need to belong' and participating in relationships, social groups and networks not only makes us happy but contributes to our continued thriving and survival.

What kinds of goals should you pursue?

There is persuasive evidence that following your dreams is a critical ingredient of happiness. But does it matter what the dream is and how you follow it? Indeed, it does. It turns out that the type of goal or 'valued life task' (in psychological jargon terms) that you pursue determines whether the pursuit will make you happy. Consider whether your life goals and dreams have the properties depicted in this section.

Intrinsic goals

As self-evident as it may sound, working towards goals that are personally involving and rewarding to you is more likely to bring you happiness than working towards goals that are not freely chosen. Numerous psychological studies have shown that, across a variety of cultures, people whose primary life goals are intrinsically rewarding obtain more satisfaction and pleasure from their pursuits.[6] 'Intrinsic' goals are those that you pursue because they are inherently satisfying and meaningful to you, which allow you to grow as a person, to develop emotional maturity and to contribute to your community. For example, one of the most intrinsic activities has to be the pursuit of goals while on holiday. More and more, people are choosing to engage in worthwhile and effortful tasks while away from work – for example, travelling to Rome for an architecture class, doing voluntary work, training for a triathlon, or doing an internship to learn how to run a winery. After all, no one, besides yourself, is rewarding you or pressuring you into such efforts. You do it because it's diverting, it's pleasurable and it's meaningful.

By contrast, 'extrinsic' goals reflect more what *other* people approve or desire for you – for example, pursuing goals for superficial reasons such as making money, boosting your ego, seeking power or fame or bowing to manipulation or peer pressure. People usually aim for extrinsic goals as a means to an end such as, working hard to obtain a reward (e.g., wealth or social approval) or to avoid a punishment (e.g., shame or loss of income).

Knocking the pursuit of money, beauty and fame may smack of a value judgement, but my argument is based squarely in research. The truth is that following intrinsic goals makes us happier, in part because such goals are relatively more inspiring and enjoyable, hence we are more likely to invest in them, persevere at them and succeed at them. Another reason is that personal goals that we intrinsically value directly satisfy our most basic psychological needs in life. I'm not talking about food and sex here, but, rather, about our need for 'autonomy' (feeling in control of our behaviour), for a sense of 'competence' (feeling efficacious in dealing with the world around us) and for 'relatedness' (feeling satisfied with our interpersonal relationships). Researchers have shown that the pursuit of intrinsic goals is more likely to fulfil *all* of these needs.[7] Let's say that your intrinsic goal is to become more fit and qualify for a marathon. Training for the marathon is hard and even painful at times, but you persist and relish the 'runner's high' (which we'll learn in the next chapter is probably a myth, but you enjoy the feeling anyway). Running brings a sense of independence and mastery, you connect with others training for the same event, and your high spirits spill over to your marriage. You are not just killing two birds with one stone, but three or four. The benefits of intrinsic goal pursuit are indeed great.

So, does this mean that extrinsic goals are always bad? Not necessarily. Sometimes we pursue extrinsic goals (like material wealth) in order to obtain the resources and opportunities that will allow us to pursue our cherished dreams or intrinsic goals. For example, I'm friendly with an entrepreneur who works very hard to earn a high salary and bonus because, he says, it will permit him to take time off from his work (which is not very satisfying) to write short stories (his true love), to garden (a second passion) and to spend more time with his fast-growing kids (whom he adores). At other times, we need extrinsic motivation in the form of awards, money or social recognition to persist at an important but difficult goal (e.g., survive the grinding work required to attain the job we really want) or, simply, to pay the rent.

Authentic goals

Do you value and truly 'own' your goals, or are they really the goals favoured by your parents, spouse or neighbours? I knew a lot of people in college in the latter category who were med students because their parents really, really wanted them to be a doctor. For the better part of a decade, Ken Sheldon and Andrew Elliot have been studying what they call 'self-concordant' or authentic goals, that is, goals that are rooted in a person's lifelong deeply held interests and core values. Not surprisingly, they find that people are happier, healthier and more hard-working when they are following goals that they truly own, and that these people show bigger increases in happiness after attaining their authentic goals.[8] Presumably realizing authentic goals satisfies our true values and innate needs, thus delivering powerful emotional benefits. If you have ever met a happy medical student, she probably genuinely and authentically desires to minister to the sick. She owns that goal.

One way that you can own your goals is to choose ones that fit you well. We are happier and more likely to persist at a goal when our striving towards it consistently makes us feel good. The more a goal 'fits' your personality, the more likely that its pursuit will be rewarding and pleasurable and increase your happiness. So, for example, if you are an extrovert, you may do well pursuing goals that involve interactions with other people. If you have a dominant personality, you might wish to take on a leadership activity. If you are on the nurturing side, choose a goal that allows you to take care of others. If you are competitive and achievement-oriented, strive for something that satisfies that spirited drive in you, like winning an athletics tournament or aiming to be the most productive worker in your division. Knowing which goal will fit you best takes a bit of self-awareness and emotional intelligence. If you understand your guiding values and have a clear sense of your preferences and desires, you will probably instantly recognize when there's a match between you and a particular activity or life task. And if you don't, then contemplate whether you feel 'authentic' when pursuing a particular goal. When you're doing your thing – writing a song, playing with children, telling a joke, learning about global warming – do you feel like you're *more* the person that you want to be . . . or less?

Approach goals

As an exercise, consider the most important and meaningful goal that you are currently pursuing, whether big or small. Does this goal involve *approaching* a desirable outcome (e.g., seeking novel and thrilling experiences, redecorating your bedroom or making three new friends) as opposed to *avoiding* an undesirable outcome (e.g., trying not to feel guilty, avoiding arguing with your girlfriend, or making sure your house doesn't fall apart). Interestingly, the same goal can be conceptualized as an approach goal (to be a fit and healthy eater) and an avoidance goal (not to be fat). A growing number of studies have shown that people who chiefly pursue or construe avoidance goals are less happy and more anxious, distressed and unhealthy than people who generally pursue approach goals.[9] Not surprisingly, people with many avoidance goals perform relatively more poorly on whatever it is that they're pursuing.[10] One of the reasons may be that it's relatively easy to identify a single path for an approach goal (e.g., to eat three healthy meals per day); an avoidance goal, by contrast, usually requires many paths (e.g., to avoid all obstacles to snacking). Focusing on avoidance goals may also lead you to view things with a negatively biased perspective (e.g., 'I'm prone to feeling guilty') and to be ultra-sensitive to threats or failures,[11] which could become self-fulfilling. All that thinking about how you don't want to feel guilty may backfire on you and soon you'll *really* start feeling guilty.[12]

Harmonious goals

It is fairly self-evident that your goals should complement one another. Simultaneously striving for conflicting goals (like 'build my business' and 'spend more time outdoors') will make you so aggravated and discouraged that you'll relinquish both goals and end up feeling stressed out and unhappy.[13] Unless your business is construction or kayaking, the adaptive solution is to change one or both of the goals to make them more harmonious with one another (e.g., resolving to work on your paperwork in the sun or partitioning your day into work and leisure). That's easier said than done. If it's not possible, you may very well have to give up on one of those goals, but that's preferable to sacrificing both.

Flexible and appropriate goals

As we get older, our opportunities for pursuing goals are bound to change, sometimes opening up and other times diminishing.

An empty nest suddenly affords time for travel or new hobbies or changing careers. A chronic illness prompts us to rearrange our entire perspective and face new roles and challenges. Furthermore, our culture (our native country, ethnicity or religion) 'expects' certain life tasks to be accomplished during certain stages of life, for example, establishing our identity and sense of self, finishing school, getting married, buying a home, attaining career success, having children, retiring and so on. It's no surprise that we obtain maximum happiness when we take on flexible and appropriate goals, that is, the 'right tasks at the right time'.[14] Of course, if we don't fulfil the cultural prescriptives, we are not necessarily doomed to failure or misery, but we must adapt our goals to the opportunities that we do have.

As we get older, what is important to us also changes. The goals that we set for ourselves in our twenties are different from the goals we set for ourselves in our forties and our sixties. Studies have shown, for instance, that young people are more likely to have goals that involve seeking new information, acquiring knowledge and experiencing novelty.[15] When faced with a choice between having dinner with their favourite author and their favourite aunt, they choose the former. Older people, by contrast, make the opposite choice.[16] They are more concerned with emotionally meaningful goals – maximizing positive emotions and avoiding unpleasant ones – than with expanding their informational horizons. In sum, the priorities that we place on our goals change with time but, no matter the substance of the goals, one certainty remains across every age – pursuing goals brings greater happiness than abandoning them.

Activity goals

Which goal is more happiness inducing, seeking to better your circumstances or taking up a new activity? Research suggests, and we already know, that when people strive to change their circumstances (e.g., buy a high-definition television, move to Florida, acquire a tidier roommate) by defining and then achieving their goal, they certainly feel happier, but they risk experiencing hedonic adaptation. In other words, you are likely to adapt quickly to your new situation and begin to desire ever-higher levels of pleasure simply in order to recapture your previous level of happiness. However, the process of pursuing 'activity' goals (e.g., joining a rambling club, volunteering as a blood donor, learning about art) allows a person to continually experience new challenges, take on new opportunities and meet a variety of experiences. So, to answer my previous question, sustained pursuit of activities that you value is more happiness inducing, with its ability to deliver a stream of positive events and regular boosts in happy mood.

Ken Sheldon and I demonstrated this phenomenon empirically in a field study.[17] Participants were instructed to describe two goals that they had recently pursued and realized – one goal that involved a positive change in their circumstances (e.g., moved to a nicer apartment or received some unexpected income) and one goal that involved taking on a new activity (e.g., started studying harder or made God a bigger part of life). The participants actually told us that they had 'gotten used to' their positive circumstantial changes much *more* than to their positive activity changes. Accordingly, the results showed that both activity changes and circumstantial changes made our participants happier six weeks later, but that only activity changes continued to make them happier twelve weeks later. The reason, I'm convinced, is that, despite the fact that circumstantial changes are often more momentous than activity changes, the participants adapted to their positive circumstantial changes such that they no longer boosted their happiness, but not to their activity changes. So, pursuing new activities can indeed produce a steady inflow of positive feelings and experiences.

Recommendations for committed goal pursuit

At the heart of this chapter is a happiness-boosting strategy that involves picking one or more significant goals that are meaningful to you and dedicating time, effort and passion to pursuing them. Obviously, there are as many ways to accomplish this as there are different goals. However, research suggests that the most successful 'strivers' share several characteristics. I've designed a set of suggestions, below, to help you begin and maintain a programme of committed goal pursuit.

Choose wisely

To revisit the previous section, the pursuit of goals that are intrinsic, authentic, approach-oriented, harmonious, activity-based and flexible will deliver more happiness than the pursuit of goals that are extrinsic, inauthentic, avoidance-oriented, conflicting, circumstance-based or rigid. This mouthful of words is based on decades of research. As a first step, then, consider your significant goals and strivings.[18]

MY MOST IMPORTANT GOALS

Instructions: Please think about the goals that are currently important to you or have been important in your life recently. 'Goals' include intentions, wishes, desires and motives. List at least one and up to eight of your most significant and meaningful goals below.

_____

_____

_____

_____

_____

_____

Date: _____

Now, for *each* of the goals that you wrote down, check off which attributes listed in the left-hand column characterize it and which attributes on the right.

CHOOSE THESE TYPES OF GOALS:	. . . NOT THESE:
___ intrinsic	___ extrinsic
___ authentic	___ inauthentic
___ approach-oriented	___ avoidance-oriented
___ harmonious	___ conflicting
___ activity-based	___ circumstance-based
___ flexible/appropriate	___ rigid/inappropriate

If any of the descriptors on the right apply to your goals, then you may need to reconsider them – modify them, perhaps, or grant them lower priority. For example, if you discover that your goals at work are generally extrinsically motivated and inauthentic, contemplate how you might change your perspective. Keep a diary of the ways that your work has made the world a better place today. Perhaps you've comforted a troubled co-worker or client, made a room, garden or street more beautiful, clarified something that's inscrutable, increased neighbourhood safety, helped someone solve a problem, improved the environment and so on. A study of 1,018 working women found that they spent almost exactly 50 per cent of their waking hours working.[19] You may do well to either change your perspective about your work or to change the nature of your work. You'll know if you're successful if hearing that statistic fills you with joy (or at least reassurance) rather than regret.

In general, you are more likely to persevere and succeed at goals that have a larger purpose or long-term importance. So, make sure that your goals are meaningful to you. Is your only motivation to become an artist because you consider painting to be fun, or do you additionally find a sense of purpose while engaging in it? Pleasure is not enough to sustain most people's interest and commitment for extended periods of time.[20] Value and meaning are vital.

Choose wisely: Reprise

What if you read the preceding section and realized, with dismay, that you don't have a list of goals to consider, let alone to reconsider? What if you are really unsure about what you want to dedicate yourself to, what worthy purpose to pursue? Don't despair; there are a number of exercises that can help you discover the goals that are most meaningful for you.[21] The first is to contemplate and describe in writing the personal legacy that you would like to leave after you die. For example, you might imagine how you would want to be remembered by your grandchildren or great-grandchildren. Write a summary of your life, your values and your accomplishments as you would like them known to your descendants, either in the format of a first-person letter or even an obituary. 'A man should choose with careful eye the things to be remembered by.'[22]

Another approach is to write down what kind of lives you would want your children (or future children) to lead as adults – what kind of people you wish them to become, which values to hold, which goals to attain. Keep working on your summary, adding and subtracting, until you are satisfied with it. This process will prompt you to re-examine your life and priorities and help you gain clarity on what you consider most important. In this way, your goals will naturally be revealed to you. Re-read the summary on a regular basis and remind yourself what really matters.

Own your goals

How do you come to have authentic goals – namely, to 'own' them? Ken Sheldon once attempted to enhance the authenticity of people's personal goals (such as achieving academic success, improving a romantic relationship or mastering a sport).[23] If you had been a participant in his study, you would have been asked to attend two sessions during which you would have been encouraged to think of ways to make your goals more interesting and challenging and to try to value them more, identify with them more and find them more meaningful. You would have been advised to re-evaluate goals that you are forcing yourself to pursue – that is, goals you hold only because either somebody else is pressuring or coercing you or because you would feel guilty or anxious if you abandoned them. Trying to 'own the goal' and 'make it rewarding' would have been suggested to you as being especially important during those inevitable periods when pursuing the goal is frustrating or burdensome and you are tempted to give up. For example, if you are having great difficulty maintaining commitment to preparing an office presentation, you could try reflecting on the deeper value that the goal expresses (e.g., developing your potential in your career, lifelong learning, etc.). You might also try strategies that make the work more rewarding, such as practising the presentation with a friend, learning an inventive new software program to create your slides, or finding a particular setting or time of day when the work is more enjoyable.

The results of Ken's study showed that those who were able to transform their goals into authentic ones not only were more likely to attain their goals but felt themselves to be happier and more authentic with time. It appears that people who have goals they truly own are continually growing and developing and are particularly prepared to take advantage of new opportunities to grow even more. Those who do not own their goals, by contrast, appear 'stalled' and stagnant in their growth.

Commit, with passion

The pursuit of goals – even intrinsically motivated ones – isn't always that easy. To fulfil your dream of becoming a mathematician or a costume designer or a parent, you must endure a great deal of drudgery and hard work, obstacles and stress, and, at times, personal sacrifice and failure. Indeed, developing skills in almost any activity requires a great deal of practice, patience and work. And sometimes you must take risks. Thus, it may be obvious why it's important to commit to your goals – better yet, to commit to them with passion, ardour and zeal. If you don't commit or if you do but lack enthusiasm, then you may quit on a whim or you may give up when you're feeling particularly tired, bored or fearful of continuing.

Passionate commitment in and of itself carries many benefits. It fulfils people's needs to belong and to connect with others, as it often involves social duties and obligations (helping a neighbour's teenager with his essay, listening to a despondent friend, nursing a sick child, etc.). Committing to important goals also reinforces our sense of autonomy because, while it may appear at first sight as a constraint to our freedom, the choice to commit is and should be made freely. Following through on our decision to strive towards something also helps shield us from social pressures (e.g., 'Don't be such a workhorse – come party with us!') as well as from our own self-doubts (e.g., 'This is so hard; maybe I should just give up'). When we avidly dedicate ourselves to the pursuit of a dream, we are taking charge of our destinies and gaining insight into ourselves.

Not surprisingly, commitment is especially potent when made in front of other people. Teens who tell their friends that they will abstain from sex are more likely to keep their pledge,[24] and citizens who tell a survey researcher that they intend to vote are more likely to actually do so.[25] A University of Scranton study found that people who made public New Year's resolutions were a remarkable ten times more likely to succeed at their goal than those who had not.[26] Making public our commitment to a particular goal raises the likelihood that we will carry through that goal, in part because we want to appear consistent to ourselves and others and avoid embarrassment or awkwardness.

Create self-fulfilling prophecies

If my grandmother, Baba Valya, had lived long enough, she would have undoubtedly admonished me with something like (roughly translated): 'The one who makes no mistake is the one who does nothing.' The converse being, if you don't try, if you don't make an effort, you'll achieve zilch. So, in the words of Nike, 'just do it'. If you believe in yourself and are optimistic – 'I can become a successful doctor', 'I'll be a good parent, despite my traumatic childhood', 'I know I can ask her out' – you will increase the chances that you will persevere and that whatever you're aiming for will ultimately come to pass. For example, a study of people who resolved to carry through an important new goal for their New Year's resolution found that those who were confident that they could change were significantly more likely to maintain their resolution over time.[27] This is called a self-fulfilling prophecy.

Social psychologists have amassed piles of evidence that simply doing something can change how we feel about it.[28] So, for example, helping someone can lead us to feel that the helping was worthwhile, and raising money for a political cause can lead us to believe more firmly in that cause. So, take action towards your goals, even when you have lingering doubts. The actions in and of themselves are likely to diminish those doubts or dispel them altogether.

Furthermore, once you begin to succeed at a goal – making one new friend (if the goal is improving your social life) or having a rudimentary conversation in Italian (if the goal is to learn Italian) – you will feel jubilant and satisfied with your progress, which, in turn, will bring about more and more success.[29] The result is an upward spiral. Consciously rewarding yourself for achieving milestones can also increase your chances of future success and happiness.[30]

Be flexible

The ability to be flexible with regard to your activities and your goals is truly a valuable skill. After all, if a new obstacle or constraint or opportunity suddenly arises, you may need to change or adapt your aspirations.[31] Say that one of the chief goals that you've been working on for the past several years is to spend more time with your daughter's family. However, you learn that she will be moving soon with her children to another city two hours away. Psychology researchers describe two kinds of control that people can exert over a situation – primary control and secondary control.[32] Primary control – which is often unfeasible – refers to trying to change the situation (e.g., convincing your daughter to stay or moving yourself), whereas secondary control refers to changing how you *view* the situation (e.g., shifting your goals). Studies show that if you are able to adapt your goals to the new challenge, you will be happier. For example, although your overall, higher-level goal (to spend more time with the grandchildren) might remain the same, your subgoals might be different – for example, to purchase and learn to use a web cam to stay in touch, to learn to take the train to their new city, etc. As another example, a person who has suffered an injury may be unable to continue his regular exercise routine, but he may substitute it with other goals. So, the jogger could take up yoga or the stationary bike. This way the higher-order goal (exercise) is maintained, but the lower-order subgoals are adjusted.

The same logic applies when new opportunities develop. Being flexible involves keeping your eyes and ears open to new prospects and possibilities. If you do so, you'll be more likely to take advantage of such opportunities and to derive greater happiness from them. So, if you learn about a new programme that allows you to earn a valued degree part-time, consider acting on it. Effective secondary control also entails viewing constraints or threats as challenges or opportunities. Your daughter's moving farther away might inspire you to learn to drive so that you could visit her more often. So, one door may close, but another may open.

Don't undermine intrinsic motivation

When you do find a pursuit that is both enjoyable and mean-ingful, be careful not to do anything to undermine your intrinsic motivation. The reason is that we can lose interest and enthusi-asm even for the most valued and gratifying activities *if* we feel pushed or coerced to engage in them. Social psychologists have persuasively shown that rewarding people for what they already enjoy may undermine their enjoyment – that is, it can turn 'play' into 'work'. A woman I know loved reading great works of literature and decided to read a PhD in English. A couple of years later, she was accepted to a graduate programme with a good reputation and began taking the sequence of required literature courses. Suddenly, she found herself being rewarded for doing something that she already enjoyed (and punished for slacking off). The rewards – 'A' grades, impressing the professors – essentially gave her a second (and extrinsic) reason for working on her PhD. 'I'm finding myself reading novels so that I can get a good grade and not because I love it,' she told me the last time I saw her. 'I don't look forward to reading any more.' This is how extrinsic rewards can undermine intrinsic motivation.

A classic and elegant study demonstrated this phenomenon with kids.[33] Nursery school children (who all liked drawing) were divided into two groups. Children in the first group were told that, if they played with magic markers, they would receive an attractive 'Good Player Award'. The other group was just given the opportunity to play with markers (with no promise of reward). A couple of weeks later, the researchers returned to the nursery school and observed what the children were doing during their classroom 'free play'. Interestingly, the kids who'd previously anticipated the reward now played less with the magic markers than those who had not been offered an award. For the 'Good Player Award' group, what was once play had been transformed into a duty – something they did to receive a reward – and not because they sincerely enjoyed and valued it.

'Baby Steps': Break down your goals

To make progress towards your 'higher-level' goals, you must break them down into lower-level, concrete subgoals. This means creating plans to take specific steps regarding where, when and how to pursue a goal. People who have such 'implementation intentions' are more likely to realize their bigger, more abstract goals.[34] But, always, keep the more abstract goals in the back of your mind.

Researchers in Montreal, Canada, wanted to help young community-living retirees to identify, plan and pursue personal goals.[35] So, they did an intervention. Over the course of about three months, the participants met in small groups with a group leader for two-hour weekly 'workshops' to 'learn how to manage their life goals'. The intervention was extremely successful – relative to a control group, the retirees who participated in the workshops became significantly happier after the intervention and maintained that improvement for a remarkable six months after. Given how well the intervention worked to teach people to follow and realize their goals, let's consider what it encompassed. Bear in mind the steps taken by the individuals enrolled in this study, as you might want to draw on them yourself.

During the first few sessions, participants generated a list of their personal aspirations, intentions and projects (e.g., to social-ize more, to become more spiritual, to raise a pet, etc.), and brought up any irrational beliefs about these goals (e.g., 'My friends don't like me around any more' or 'I could never afford a pet').

Second, they identified their highest priority goals and con-templated them at some length. Suppose that your highest priority goal is to move to the city. How much effort will this require? What kind of resources do you need? How much would you enjoy the move? And so on.

Third, they selected a single goal (e.g., learning Spanish), described it in concrete terms (e.g., gaining fluency in speaking and some facility in writing and reading) and personally committed to it. You may consider writing your goal down in a journal, posting it in a visible place or announcing it to your family or circle of friends.

The fourth step involved developing implementation intentions – where, when and how would actions be taken (e.g., complete a Spanish language workbook, take a Berlitz language course on Monday nights, etc.). A critical element here was to anticipate obstacles (e.g., boredom, lack of time, frustration, family disapproval) and to think of strategies to manage them (i.e., switch gears, prepare your family, set aside time to study when energy levels are high, etc.). For example, you might try to watch out for thoughts of quitting or feelings of low motivation and make a conscious effort to divert your attention to the task at hand.

Fifth, participants carried out their plans, persisting through challenges and difficulties, with the group's emotional support. Indeed, at times, it's necessary to revise or change your chosen goal and even to question its priority ('Is moving really the right thing for me right now?').

So, for example, one of the participants, a 'Mrs M', began the intervention with a lot of challenges (her husband had passed away five months earlier, leaving her feeling helpless and astray, and she had recently retired) but, according to the researchers, ended up successfully involving herself in goal pursuit and becoming considerably happier as a result.[36] Her original inventory of priorities comprised four different goals – 'Put my talent to good use', 'Recover my self-confidence and autonomy' 'Re-establish myself either through work or a charitable cause' and 'Join a new circle of friends' – and she selected the last one to focus on. During the planning phase, Mrs M broke up her goal into concrete terms, specifically, 'to attend breakfasts for retirees, to find new activities to participate in . . . with others' and 'to take the initiative to call people instead of waiting for them to call'.

The obstacles that Mrs M faced included moments of feeling like giving up and persistent grief over the two major losses in her life – her husband and her work. In the process, she was encouraged by hopeful thinking, supported tangibly and emotionally by the workshop group, and additionally decided to undertake psychotherapy to work out her grief.

The leaders of the workshops noted that Mrs M demonstrated 'exemplary courage' in pursuing her goal of making new friends (as well as her broader goal of rediscovering the high-energy, decisive woman that she once was). By the end of the intervention, she reported having achieved 75 per cent of her objective and felt strongly that she was progressing towards 'finding the woman from before' and became happier in the process.

So, you see that committed, passionate goal pursuit consists of many elements. Although the process may be difficult it's not really very complicated. All the required steps are logical – you begin with a dream or vision of what you want to do, you break it up into smaller, concrete subgoals, you identify in advance (and prepare for) the doubts or challenges that might compel you to quit, and you go and do it. Whether your goal is to get married, to read every great work of literature, to be an expert skateboarder or scrap booker, or simply to become a happier person, it's within your power to make it happen. Just remember that happiness will come from pursuing goals and not necessarily from achieving them.

Mr Schwengel

Before I end this chapter, I want to tell you a story about a guy I interviewed who happens to be a teacher. His name is Kurt Schwengel and he is well known as one of the most innovative and talented teachers in his school district. I had heard from a variety of sources that he is a fantastic reception teacher, winner of a Crystal Apple ('Best Educator') Award, who has developed his own curriculum, which he constantly updates and reworks on his web site. 'Mr Schwengel doesn't follow the rules,' a little girl from his school had warned me, so I should have guessed that he'd be a genuinely happy person. And he is. He is pure energy, enthusiasm, ingenuity, hard work. 'I love my job. I'd do it for free,' he told me, and it shows. His job is a calling.

The happiness-enhancing strategy of 'Committing to goals' may sound boring, but it is anything but. To say that Mr Schwengel has committed to goals is an understatement. He is fairly bursting with goals. He makes digital movies of his pupils and creates new games that make them 'explode with happiness'. Every three weeks, he changes the curriculum to a new theme, with accompanying costumes, music, thematic school work and field trips ('Star Wars' is the kids' favourite, but so is 'baseball', 'Japan' and 'The mystery of the missing swordfish'.) He takes the reception children to college basketball games, the beach, the dinosaur museum and introduces them to bowling and sushi. Every morning, when the classroom door is opened promptly at 8:30 am, the kids rush in like he's a rock star. He plans and designs and writes and imagines and talks all day long. He is a phenomenal disciplinarian. ('You never *ever* hear a kid say, "So-and-so was mean to me today" in his class,' a former Schwengel mum informed me.) He's teaching five-year-olds how to read, how to use scissors, how to play Uno, and how to putt. And when he's not working hard, he's playing hard.

Let me make something clear. Mr Schwengel is not manic or off his rocker. He doesn't even necessarily *look* happier than you or me. He is just engaged, in flow, in constant interaction with children and adults, making his work and life as enjoyable and meaningful as anyone could imagine. I'm sure excellent reception teachers are underpaid. And, unlike Mr Schwengel, I'm sure some of them bemoan the drudgery, the bratty kids and the anxious, pushy parents. Elsewhere in this book, I've raised the notion that there are multiple perspectives of the world – of yourself, your family, your job, your living situation. Deciding to become happier entails making a choice about which perspective you take and acknowledging that the choice is *in your hands*. Mr

Schwengel has made the choice to commit to being the best teacher he can be. You make your own choice.

COMPLEMENTARY ACTIVITIES

If you benefit from this activity, you may also want to try:

1) Savouring life's joys (Happiness Activity No. 9, p. 196)

2) Developing strategies for coping (Happiness Activity No. 6, p. 154)

Chapter 9

Taking care of your body and your soul

This last chapter on happiness-increasing activities covers a set of strategies that appear, at first glance, qualitatively different from the rest. After all, most people don't commit to a religious faith, join a gym, or smile at strangers *in order* to become happier. Happiness, however, happens to be a significant byproduct of all of these behaviours, which is true regardless of how fortunate (or unfortunate) you have been with regard to your 'happiness genes' or your position in life. This very fact makes the strategies described in this chapter a vital part of a programme to maximize the amount of happiness in our day-to-day lives. If any of them happen to fit your traits and lifestyle, choose one today and begin implementing it without delay.

Happiness Activity No. 11: Practising religion and spirituality

Psychological researchers have often been hesitant to study spirituality and religion. On the face of it, science and religion cannot mix – God cannot be investigated in the laboratory and the sacred cannot be quantified. Just because religious beliefs can't be empirically tested or falsified, however, doesn't mean that the *consequences* of having religious beliefs, participating in religious life, or searching for the sacred cannot be studied. Indeed, a growing body of psychological science is suggesting that religious people are happier, healthier and recover better after traumas than non-religious people.[1] In one study, parents who had lost a baby to sudden infant death syndrome were interviewed three weeks after their loss and then again after eighteen months.[2] Those who attended religious services frequently and who reported religion as being important to them were better able to cope eighteen months after the loss, showing relatively less depression at this time and greater well-being than non-religious parents. Two reasons were found to underlie the benefit of religion on adjustment – those active in their churches reported greater social support (perhaps through the church itself) and were able to find some meaning, however elusive, in their children's deaths.

Religion's returns for health and well-being

Other studies have shown that, relative to non-religious folks, those who are active in their religion live longer with a variety of diseases and are healthier in general.[3] For example, if you are having serious cardiac surgery and receive strength and comfort from your religious faith, you'll be almost three times more likely to be alive six months later.[4] The trouble is that we don't really know why. One seemingly obvious reason could be that religious people are more likely to practise healthy behaviours. Indeed, many religions prohibit such unhealthy practices as excessive drinking, drug use, promiscuous sex and smoking. Religious people smoke and drink less than their less religious peers.[5] Certain religious groups (like Mormons and Seventh Day Adventists), which encourage healthy diets and prohibit premarital sex, alcohol, tobacco and drug use, are healthier than other groups.[6] Religious groups also encourage positive, low-stress lifestyles – for example, by advocating moderation (versus extreme, illegal or risk-taking behaviour) and by fostering a harmonious family life. Indeed, some studies show that religious involvement is related to reduced risk of crime, delinquency and marital conflict.

This potentially explains the finding that religious people are physically healthier, but what about the fact that they're happier, more satisfied with their lives and cope better with crises? For instance, 47 per cent of people who report attending religious services several times a week describe themselves as 'very happy', versus 28 per cent of those who attend less than once a month.[7] The social support and sense of identity provided by belonging to a close-knit religious organization (church, temple or mosque) could be the operative mechanisms. After all, religion is usually not practised in isolation but within a 'fellowship of kindred spirits', who share one another's burdens, reach out to those in need, and offer friendship and companionship. To be sure, people who attend religious services on a regular basis have larger social networks – that is, more friends and acquaintances on whom they can rely – and actually do receive tangible help from members of their religious group.[8] This isn't surprising, as religious services and the many activities associated with them (such as charities, volunteer programmes and outreach initiatives) bring people together who have a lot in common. Members share not only the basic assumptions and beliefs inherent in their religion, but important political and social values. This fact not only enables one-to-one social, emotional and material support, but it also creates a sense of community among the members of the church, synagogue or mosque, leading people to feel appreciated, respected and provided for. This sense reinforces your identity and affirms your lifestyle. After all, it feels good when people whom you respect and admire share similar roles and values and your approach to daily life.

So, it's possible that the fact that religious people are happier than the non-religious has nothing to do with the substance of their religious and spiritual beliefs (with God, with living life in accordance to their holy texts, with the sanctity of life, or with the sense of meaning that religious faith gives their lives) and everything to do with the simple fact that their religion brings them into contact with other similarly minded and caring people. It could be true, but I don't believe it.

First, we shouldn't ignore the one 'ultimate' supportive relationship for many religious individuals – one that doesn't require any formal participation in religious services or programmes – and that is their relationship with God. This relationship is not only a source of comfort in troubled times but a source of self-esteem, the feeling of being unconditionally valued, loved and cared for. Those of you who feel this way have a sense of security that others only wish for. Your belief that God will intervene when needed gives you a sense of peace and calm. Your identification with God or particular biblical figures can help you interpret and guide your own life ('What would the divine other do in this situation?') and even fuel a sense of vicarious control ('With an omniscient and omnipotent deity, all things are possible').[9]

Second, your sense that God has a purpose in everything helps you find meaning in ordinary life events, as well as in traumatic ones. This is critical. Regardless of whether you are involved with a formal religious organization, your health and happiness may benefit simply (or perhaps not so simply) from having religious faith. This becomes particularly important during challenging times. A health crisis or a death in the family – especially one that is unexpected or premature – may lack a clear secular explanation and can severely challenge your basic assumptions about the fairness and justice of the world. 'Religious coping', which includes praying, re-examining one's sense of meaning and collaborating with a divine other, can help you understand that the event is part of a broader divine plan or that it offers an opportunity for spiritual growth or that you have the ability to handle things. For example, the sense of meaning that you derive from your religion can provide hope (e.g., 'God will ensure that things will get better'), a satisfying explanation via a broader, benign purpose (e.g., 'God brings hardship to make you strong' or 'The will of a loving God cannot be fully understood') and solace (e.g., 'We are more than just a momentary blip in the universe'). Indeed, such religious coping is so powerful that, during hard times, it is the single most frequently used form of coping by older people.[10]

A mother who lost her firstborn son and later gave birth to a healthy second child was able to find meaning in the death in the following way: 'They say there's a reason for God to do everything, you know. I think that's very true because I think I love [my second child] a lot more than I would [have] had our first son been here.'[11] Similarly, studies show that 'God had a reason' is one of the most common responses by victims of a range of traumas, such as paralysis, to the question, 'Why me?' Furthermore, those of us who are able to apply a benevolent religious framework generally adjust better to our ordeal. For example, in a study of patients undergoing chemotherapy, those who believed that God had a measurable control over their cancer had higher self-esteem and were rated as better adjusted by their nurses (e.g., more happy, serene and active, and relating better to others).[12] Interestingly, the belief in God as a controlling force helped these cancer patients cope better than belief in their own personal control. But the control they were talking about wasn't a passive submission to an external force; rather, the patients spoke of using prayer and faith – as well as their own efforts at managing the disease – as a means of obtaining control from God. So, it was an active and interactive give-and-take process between the individual and a higher power.

Even beyond negative or traumatic life events, when our days are merely ordinary, religion and spirituality undoubtedly help us find meaning in life. Why do we need a sense of meaning? Because we need to feel that we matter, that our suffering and our hard work isn't futile, and that our life has a purpose. Because we need to feel a sense of control over our fates. Because we need to be able to justify our actions – why should we forgive, what do we have to be grateful for, why should we turn the other cheek, and so on. Because we need a reason to focus beyond just ourselves. And, finally, because a sense of meaning fuels our sense of self-worth. It makes us feel good about our belief systems, our identity and the community of like-minded individuals to which we belong.[13]

It's also worth noting that religious faith gives rise to a number of positive emotions and experiences that are associated with happiness and this in itself can partly explain why religious and pious people are happier than non-religious ones. One such attribute is the disposition to forgive. A slew of studies has shown that highly religious and spiritual individuals see themselves as more forgiving and value forgiveness more than do their peers.[14] Finally, the practice of religion – private prayer, spiritual pursuit and collective worship – can engender hope, gratitude, love, awe, compassion, joy and even ecstasy, all being happiness-increasing feelings.[15]

Benefits of spirituality

So far, I have been muddling a bit the words 'spiritual' and 'religious'. What's the difference? There is certainly a lot of overlap, but the overlap isn't complete.[16] Spirituality is defined as a 'search for the sacred'[17] – that is, a search for meaning in life through something that is larger than the individual self ('self-transcendence' is a good label). Spiritual individuals refer to God, or to related concepts like divine power or Ultimate Truth. Religion also involves a spiritual search, but this search usually takes place in a formal, institutional context. However, because the majority of spiritual people define themselves as also religious, the benefits of spirituality are essentially identical to the benefits of religion. Spiritual people are relatively happier than non-spiritual people, have superior mental health, cope better with stressors, have more satisfying marriages, use drugs and alcohol less often, are physically healthier and live longer lives.[18] People who perceive the divine being as loving and responsive are happier than those who don't.[19]

However, those of you who do not believe in God may still be able to sanctify ordinary things on earth. If you think of your work as a calling (divine or not), if you perceive your children as blessings, if you understand love as eternal, or if you believe that the body is holy, you are imbuing aspects of life with sacred or divine qualities. Sanctification, it turns out, can provide motivation, meaning and satisfaction. Couples who sanctify their marriage are more satisfied and invested, parents who sanctify parenting are more effective disciplinarians, and college students who pursue goals concerned with transcending the self and committing to a higher power (e.g., 'Be aware of the spiritual meaningfulness of my life' or 'Learn to tune into higher power throughout the day') are relatively happier.[20]

So, spirituality offers something for those of us who are not or do not want to be affiliated with any formal religious institution. Instead of attending church or temple, we can work at searching for the sacred in many different ways – through meditation, prayer or by instilling a spiritual dimension into our daily lives. First, as I'll describe in the next section, meditation is a powerful technique that can boost both physical and psychological well-being, and many people who practise it do so by using a spiritual mantra. The ability to transcend your ordinary life through meditation appears to be one of the reasons for its many benefits.

Although undoubtedly there are different ways to pray, the type of prayer most closely linked with spiritual practice – and the most beneficial – is meditative prayer. This is a type of prayer through which you try to maintain a divine relationship. For example, you might spend time just being 'in the presence' of God. People who practise meditative prayer are happier overall and feel closer to God than those who practise other kinds of prayer (such as petitioning for relief or beseeching for forgiveness).[21]

Finally, people for whom spirituality is important try to experience a sense of the divine in their day-to-day existence – for example, by cultivating feelings of awe, inspiration and wholeness by fostering a sense of the vastness of God's love, by nurturing belief in a power greater than oneself and by developing a connection with the transcendent. This sense of spirituality may come more easily with practice, and during extraordinary circumstances, such as childbirth.

For whom are religion and spirituality most beneficial?

The first answer to this question is consistent with a key theme of this book, which is that particular happiness-enhancing activities will be most effective for people who are open to them and are motivated to practise them with effort and commitment. In other words, if it feels natural to you to practise religion and spirituality, then by all means do it.

In addition, researchers have made several interesting discoveries, including the fact that religiosity is more strongly tied to happiness among women (relative to men), among African-Americans (relative to whites), among older people (relative to younger ones) and among North Americans (relative to Europeans), possibly because their religious faith is relatively stronger. Furthermore, people who actively and publicly participate in religious activity (e.g., attending church or praying) are happier than those who simply espouse religious beliefs. (This finding underscores the key role that a support community may play in the happiness-boosting effects of religion.) Finally, and not surprisingly, those who pursue religion for intrinsic reasons (i.e., as a way of life) are happier than those who pursue it as a means to an end (i.e., for instrumental, extrinsic reasons, such as career or status,[22] or to get their children into a church school!).

Are there downsides to religion?

Freud argued that religion can create an 'obsessional neurosis' whose symptoms include suppressed emotions, repressed sexuality and guilt.[23] The popular media sometimes suggests that religious people are more prejudiced and closed-minded than their less religious peers, or are rather passive about their lives and health (relinquishing all control to God), or are incapable of rational scientific thought, or have maladaptive beliefs in divine vengeance, 'righteous anger' and original sin. Furthermore, just like intimate relationships, which can deliver a person's highest highs and lowest lows, religious congregations can similarly be a source of stress and conflict. They may demand a great deal of time, energy, money, sacrifice and conformity to strict expectations for moral conduct and family life.

Do these represent genuine drawbacks and harms of a religion, or are they myths perpetuated by a secular public? Yes and no. Studies support some, but not all, of these observations. For example, people who strongly believe that prayer can cure their ills are less likely to exercise and are less involved in their own health care; and those who passively defer their problems to God show lower levels of mental health.[24] People who perceive God as distant and punitive are more likely to be distressed and ill, and individuals angry at God backslide in their health. Guilt, shame and fear may be experienced when people believe that negative events represent God's punishment for their sins (or, worse, the work of demonic forces), and such beliefs are associated with greater depression and worse health and quality of life.[25] Finally, beliefs in original sin are associated with low self-esteem, perhaps because it's hard to feel good about yourself if you feel incompetent and shameful due to the conviction that you are inherently a wicked person.

Regarding the question of whether religious beliefs can foster prejudice, this has been found in some studies of religious fundamentalists, who sometimes agree with statements like, 'The reason the Jews have so much trouble is because God is punishing them for rejecting Jesus'[26] and 'The AIDS disease currently killing homosexuals is just what they deserve'.[27] However, these findings are fairly weak and the results not very generalizable to today's diversity of views, indicating that the vast majority of religious and spiritual individuals are more likely to be inclusive, compassionate and open-minded than the reverse.

Finally, the search for the sacred can be unsuccessful, triggering anxiety and distress or, in rare cases, can lead to absolute submission to a cult or hostility towards non-believers. To be sure, these are extreme examples. If you choose religion and spirituality as one of the activities to increase and sustain your happiness, you're unlikely to confront such problems. As with all the happiness-boosting strategies I have discussed, moderation and common sense are wisest.

Practising religion and spirituality

I had considered leaving this section blank, as most people who are religious or spiritual have a pretty good idea of how to observe their faith. But perhaps a few suggestions can galvanize someone who is uncertain, at a loss, or feeling despondent and inert. I'll start with a brief list and expand on a couple of strategies in detail. For now, today, you need only choose *one* activity to try. Join (or recommit to) a temple, church or mosque, a spiritual programme or a bible study group. Set as your goal to attend a religious service once a week, or even daily. Spend fifteen minutes every day reading a spiritually themed or religious book, flipping through a volume of affirmations, listening to a spiritual radio programme or watching a religious show. Volunteer for a faith-based charity. And, finally, learn about other religions by doing research at the library or on the web or by talking to friends and acquaintances about their faiths. Not only will you be enlightened, and perhaps stirred to try something new, but you may end up building or strengthening friendships.

Seek meaning and purpose

Researchers believe that a genuine sense of meaning in life must be rooted in a person's own thoughts, feelings and experiences. Blindly embracing someone else's sense of meaning won't bring about happiness and growth. Creating meaning is one of the most difficult things that you can do, and the meaning that you do create is likely to change over the course of your life. Here are six suggestions from researchers on how to strive to find it.[28]

First, life is more meaningful when you are pursuing goals that are harmonious and within reach – for example, when you have the time, the ability and the energy to devote to your most important goals, whether those goals involve rearing children or developing as a writer. If you're not sure what your goals are or how to follow them, read Chapter 8.

Second, greater meaning comes from having a coherent 'life scheme'. Sit back and write down, or share with someone, your own life story. Who are you now and who were you before? What future do you imagine for yourself? What are the obstacles in your path? What assumptions do you hold about the world and why things are the way they are?

Third, creativity – in the arts, humanities, sciences and even in self-discovery – can impart a sense of meaning to many people's lives. Here again, self-transcendence may be critical. What you create may be not only a joyful process for you personally, which lends your life significance, but something, if you're lucky, you may pass on to others for today and for future generations.

Fourth, for many there is sometimes powerful meaning in anguish and trauma (see Chapter 6). Suffering may bring about post-traumatic growth, including spiritual growth, a timeless perspective on possible life paths and a sense that life has renewed meaning.

Fifth, at the heart of religion and spirituality are strong emotional experiences, like the comfort you feel at a religious service or the awe and wonder you feel when in the presence of the mystery and majesty of the divine, or when confronted with the intensity of love, the immensity of the universe or scenes of exquisite natural beauty. Such religious experiences – including conversion and near-death experiences, which may include profound feelings of spiritual awakening, ecstasy or being 'bathed in light' – all serve to deepen your faith and endow your life with greater meaning.

And, finally, an essential path to finding meaning in your life is, almost by definition, to work on developing your faith. In a sense, faith provides the answer to the 'big' questions: Who am I? What is my life for? Where do I fit in? Who is the creator? How do I live a virtuous life and improve the world around me?

Pray

A universal way to practise religion and spirituality is through prayer. Indeed, almost seven out of ten Americans report praying every single day and only 6 per cent report never praying (in England and Wales, 80 per cent of people reported having an affiliation with organized religion [74 per cent being Christian] but only 7 per cent of Christians attend church).[29] Every religion has its own form and tradition of prayer, its own ways of communicating with God or the divine. The following ideas are for how to make prayer a bigger part of life.

- Dedicate a period of time each day – from five minutes to an hour – to prayer. You may use the time to petition God for something for yourself or others, or simply to be 'in his presence', or to read a prayer book.
- Alternatively, you may choose to pray spontaneously throughout the day and in specific situations, for example, when you feel depressed or tense or judgemental or when you witness a beautiful object or a kind act, or when something particularly good (or bad) has happened.
- Say a prayer upon waking or before bedtime or prior to each meal. A prayer of gratitude, if you are so inclined, may be particularly comforting and happiness-inducing (see Chapter 4).

Rosa, a young woman I met at my university, decided to change her life by actively practising prayer. Although she was raised to believe in God and to attend church on Sundays, she told me that she only did it because she was dragged there. When Rosa became an adult, she had stopped doing something that she used to do a lot, and that was praying. This is how she describes her experience of trying to accomplish her new goal and the multiple benefits she incurs:

> The past week I have been praying when I go to bed and when I wake up. I pray for my day and I give thanks for everything that has happened. I tell God of all the things that have bothered me during the day, finding myself wiser and happier when I finish praying, as if I had just told a friend everything that has bothered me for a while. Before I started praying, I felt awkward, as I had to do it in front of my roommate and I did

not know how she would take it, yet when I engaged in praying to God, and closed my eyes, I stopped being aware of my
surroundings. I completely let myself free of all opinions and
biases and thanked him for my day, thanked him for all he had
done for me, and prayed for strength to continue in his path
in the following days. As I finished praying I felt relieved, as if
a huge weight had left me and I felt satisfied.

The activity itself was not hard, *per se*, but doing something I
have not done in many years was hard to pick up, especially since
I started doing it every morning and every night. However, I
enjoyed doing it . . . I did not feel alone any more . . . I have and
will make a habit of repeating my prayers every day, as I know
that every time I do, I engage in better conversations with people,
act more thankful, forgive easier, and make the ones around me
feel like they are in good company. I believe that God is capable
of many great things and he will watch over me wherever I am.
He is my father, my friend, and my brother, and the feeling that
I receive from talking to him is joyous as I get to share with him
all my secrets, and he rids me of all my doubts and anxieties. I am
definitely going to continue doing this every day as it gives me
strength when I wake up and I rest easier as I go to sleep.

Find the sacred in ordinary life
Develop an ability to see holiness in everyday things, both beautiful and plain. A meal can be holy and so can a child's laugh or
a new snowfall. The Big Sky above Montana looks to many
people like it has God's fingerprints on it, but so can ordinary
scenes and situations. Sanctifying day-to-day objects, experiences
and struggles takes a great deal of practice, but it's at the heart of
spirituality and its rewards.

Closing

Scientists can no longer ignore the powerful influences of spirituality and religion on health and well-being. If nothing else, the
statistics should compel them. In the US alone, the vast majority

of individuals – about 95 per cent – believe in God.[30] If you so choose, and in your own way, you can harness the benefits of faith to improve your happiness and your life.

COMPLEMENTARY ACTIVITIES

If you benefit from this activity, you may also want to try:

1) Taking care of your body (Happiness Activity No. 12, see below)

2) Developing strategies for coping (Happiness Activity No. 6, p. 154)

Happiness Activity No. 12: Taking care of your body (Meditation)

‿

'Half an hour's meditation each day is essential, except when you are busy. Then a full hour is needed.'

ST FRANCIS DE SALES, 1567–1622

‿

One of the limitations of the existing research on religion is that almost all of it has focused on Judeo-Christian faiths. Eastern religions – Hinduism, Buddhism, Taoism – offer a distinct perspective At the core of these religions is an explicit contemplative spirituality. In Buddhism, this discipline is achieved through meditation, which helps a person accept life's 'irrefutable truths' – that our lives are constantly changing and that our grasping to control our lives is futile. The regular practice of meditation is said to produce true happiness by realizing a state of awareness and detachment.

Meditation actually comprises a family of techniques that go by different names (Zen meditation, transcendental meditation, Vipassana meditation) and different categories (concentrative, mindfulness, contemplative). The core ingredient that underlies them all is the cultivation of attention.[31] Of course, you can focus attention in many different ways, for example, non-analytically and non-emotionally on a single object (on a flame, your breath, a sound, or a single word – such as is done in concentrative meditation) or nonjudgementally on all thoughts, sights and sounds without ruminating on them (such as is done in mindfulness meditation), or more broadly by opening yourself up to God to contemplate the big questions of life (such as is done in contemplative meditation). Meditation is a very personal experience and may be performed in many different ways, but experts have put together several crucial elements to aim for during its practice:[32]

- Be nonjudgemental – observe the present moment impartially, with detachment, without evaluation.
- Be nonstriving – although, at first glance, this instruction may appear inconsistent with what I advised in the chapter on committed goal pursuit, it's not, as it encourages you not to be too focused on achieving (as opposed to *progressing towards*) your goals.
- Be patient – don't rush or force things, but allow them to unfold in their own good time.
- Be trusting – trust yourself and trust that things will work out in life.
- Be open – pay attention to every little thing, as though you're seeing it for the very first time.
- Let go – set yourself free of ruminations. This is what's called non-attachment.

Why meditate?

I honestly was surprised to learn how many controlled laboratory and field investigations have been conducted to explore the consequences of the practice of meditation.[33] An avalanche of studies have shown that meditation has multiple positive effects on a person's happiness and positive emotions, on physiology, stress, cognitive abilities and physical health, as well as on other harder-to-assess attributes, like 'self-actualization' and moral maturity.

For example, researchers who study the bodies of people during the practice of meditation have confirmed that meditators are able to attain both a profound state of physiological rest (indicated by a reduced respiration rate, for instance) and a heightened state of awareness and alertness (indicated by such things as increased blood flow and other relevant markers in the brain). In my favourite meditation study, healthy workers underwent an eight-week training programme in mindfulness meditation.[34] At the end of the eight-week period, those who had practised meditation (compared to a control group) showed increases in activity in their left prefrontal cortex, relative to the right. If you recall from Chapter 2, this particular pattern of greater brain activation in the left versus right part of the brain is observed in happy and approach-oriented individuals; thus, this finding nicely corroborates other research revealing that a series of regular meditation sessions produces greater happiness and less anxiety and depression.[35] Furthermore, in the same eight-week meditation study, meditators showed a stronger immune response to the influenza vaccine (with which they had been injected) and, the greater the increases in their left-right brain asymmetry, the stronger the immune response. So, amazingly, even a short-term practice of meditation can affect your brain activity and your immune system.[36]

Not surprisingly, such physiological effects may translate into and influence a person's health. Meditation interventions have been shown to be effective in patients with heart disease, chronic pain, skin disorders and a variety of mental health conditions such as depression, anxiety, panic and substance abuse. Besides its direct physiological effects, meditating can help people who are ill (and everyone else, for that matter) because it reduces their reactivity to stress and boosts positive mood, self-esteem and feelings of control. For instance, one study showed that a six-week meditation workshop made working adults happier by augmenting their daily positive emotions which, in turn, produced such benefits as more savouring of the present moment, enhanced quality of their relationships, more social support and a reduction in their illness symptoms.[37]

A number of intriguing studies have even revealed benefits of meditation for such seemingly intractable characteristics as intelligence, creativity and cognitive flexibility in the elderly. For example, in two different studies, college students who undertook a programme to learn about and practise meditation showed bigger improvements on an intelligence test as well as in their course test grades, relative to control groups. And another study with premedical and medical students found that those who were instructed to practise mindfulness meditation reported greater spiritual experiences and empathy for others, and lower anxiety and depression, even during the stressful exam period, than the control group.

These studies make meditation look like a panacea. If the evidence were only anecdotal I'd be sceptical, but it's based on years of empirical work. The data are persuasive that there's something powerful about this technique, *if* you learn to apply it with sedulous effort and commitment. Successful practitioners of meditation cultivate it like physical exercise, as a daily way of being. A woman friend who swears by meditation as the secret to her happiness described it to me this way:

I meditate every morning for twenty minutes. It is a sacred time that I protect from all intrusions or commitments, and, for the rest of the day, I am more centred and open-minded, not as sensitive or irritable or tense. I feel a sense of well-being that lasts all day. A day that I miss doing it is not the same, somehow wrecked.

People meditate for a variety of reasons – to gain inner peace, to explore a higher reality, to heal themselves of disease, to release their creativity or intuition or to attain insight. Or to achieve happiness.

How to meditate in fewer than 300 words

Teachers of meditation advise that meditating involves sitting alone in a comfortable place, back straight. Close your eyes and focus on breathing in and out. As you breathe out, silently repeat a short word (like 'one', 'aum', or 'be'). Or, if you prefer, focus on a specific object, sound or task, like a candle, a tone or your breathing. If your mind wanders (e.g., 'I have to start dinner in twenty minutes', 'Jack looked so handsome yesterday', 'I feel a sore throat coming on'), let your thoughts pass and then restart by bringing your attention back to your breathing. The key is to notice your mind wandering and then to turn inward and 'detach' from your thoughts. Don't let your ruminations and fantasies and plans and memories control you – take charge of them. This will take practice and repetition, as beginners usually can only 'quiet' or 'still' the mind for no more than a few seconds at a time. A common experience is the moment you think you've emptied your mind, it starts to fill up again.

Build the length of time you are able to meditate from five minutes to twenty minutes and try to do it every day. And, ideally, arrange for a meditation space. It can be modest or large, decorated with photos, art works or inspirational quotes, or completely bare. It should be comfortable and, if possible, free of distractions.

Meditation has many rewards, but it doesn't come effortlessly for everyone. Pascal wouldn't have contended that 'All of humanity's problems stem from man's inability to sit quietly in a room alone' if sitting quietly alone was easy. For a boost or encouragement, consider taking a class on meditation, visiting a meditation web site, or buying a how-to CD or book.

Happiness Activity No. 12: Taking care of your body (Physical Activity)

An impressive study of physical activity was published in the *Archives of Internal Medicine* in 1999.[38] The researchers recruited men and women fifty years old and over, and all suffering from clinical depression. They were randomly divided into three groups. The first group was assigned to four months of aerobic exercise, the second group to four months of antidepressant medication (Zoloft) and the third group to both. The assigned exercise involved three supervised forty-five-minute sessions per week of cycling or walking/jogging at moderate to high intensity. Remarkably, by the end of the four-month intervention period, all three groups experienced their depression lift, and reported fewer dysfunctional attitudes and increased happiness and self-esteem. So, aerobic exercise was just as effective at treating depression as was Zoloft (Sertraline or Lustral in the UK), or as a combination of exercise *and* Zoloft. Yet exercise is a lot less expensive, usually with no side effects apart from soreness. Perhaps even more remarkably, six months later, participants who had 'remitted' (recovered) from their depression were less likely to relapse if they had been in the exercise group (six months ago!) than if they had been in the medication group.[39] The researchers named the study the Standard Medical Intervention and Long-term Exercise study. SMILE.

The proverbial 'feel-good factor' in exercise is well known. But the fact that the psychological benefits of physical activity trumped those of antidepressant drugs surprised even me. Could the exercise programme in this study have boosted participants' self-esteem and sense of mastery over their training? Could the antidepressant medication, by contrast, have given participants a less self-affirming explanation for their personal improvement (i.e., 'The drugs lifted my depression' versus 'It was my own effort and commitment to the exercise programme that helped me beat this thing')? In any case, the SMILE study epitomizes a flood of research corroborating the multiple benefits of physical activity for health and well-being. Physical activity reduces anxiety and stress, protects us from dying in general (and from dying of heart disease or cancer, in particular), reduces the risk of numerous diseases (diabetes, colon cancer, hypertension), builds bones, muscles and joints, increases quality of life, improves sleep, protects against cognitive impairments as we age, and helps control weight.[40] In sedentary older adults, a very low-intensity exercise programme (walking or resistance/flexibility training) reduces depression and increases confidence, and maintains the improvement for an astonishing five years.[41] Finally, surveys show – and large-scale randomized interventions confirm – that exercise may very well be the most effective instant happiness booster of all activities.[42] Is that enough?

Why does physical activity make people happier?

Psychologists believe that several explanations underlie the well-being rewards of exercise. First is the self-esteem/mastery explanation I just mentioned. Taking up a sport or fitness regimen makes you feel in control of your body and your health. Seeing yourself get better at something – faster, further, stronger – provides a terrific sense of agency and self-worth. Second is the possibility that physical activity offers potential for 'flow', as well as a positive distraction that turns away worries and rumination. It essentially serves as a 'time-out' from your stressful day, with positive spill-over effects for hours afterwards. Interestingly, this view of exercise makes it sound a lot like meditation and, indeed, the few studies that have directly compared meditation to exercise show that the two activities often show identical effects, including reduced anxiety and increased mood-lifting hormones.[43] Of course, the *experience* of exercise and meditation is very different, most notably, one generally producing so-called 'high-arousal emotions' (energy, enthusiasm and vigour), the other producing low-arousal emotions (serenity, peace and calm). But they are all positive emotions that not only make you feel good but also distract you from hassles and anxieties.

Third, physical activity when performed along with others can provide opportunities for social contact, thus potentially bolstering social support and reinforcing friendships. It can even lift the burden of loneliness or isolation. A former avid footballer in Birmingham, UK, described how taking up football allowed him to take on a new social identity separate from his current one – namely, a person with a mental illness:

> When you have had a bad day . . . then you can go out for football for an hour and a half with complete strangers and

they don't know what I do, they just know me to play football with and that's how I like it. I've got friends who know
about my illness but these people don't know nothing about
me, they just respect that I am a good footballer and they like
me because of that. It's kind of a therapy for myself because
I don't have to justify who I am and what I have done in the
past in terms of illness and they just respect me for being a
damn good football player because I am the captain of the
team.[44]

Of course, the 'feel-good' consequences of exercise could be
physiological in origin. When you exercise, you not only feel
good that you're accomplishing something, but you experience
the fringe benefits of improved physical fitness, including greater
cardiovascular endurance, flexibility and strength. You may be
able to lift heavier objects, walk farther and avoid health problems
into old age. This in itself can bring about greater happiness.
Indeed, exercise has been shown to elevate serotonin levels similar to the effects of Prozac.[45]

But what about the 'endorphin hypothesis'? Doesn't vigorous
physical activity elevate endorphins – the brain's natural pain-
killing and euphoria-inducing opioids – leading to the familiar
'runner's high'? Unfortunately, there is not a great deal of support
for this theory, although central opioids *have* been found to
suppress the unpleasant symptoms of physical exertion, thus
presumably reducing discomfort (though probably not producing an actual 'high').[46]

Finally, I should mention that physical activity really has two
kinds of benefits: the first is the 'acute' immediate boost you gain
from a single bout of exercise and the second involves the
'chronic' improvements from an ongoing exercise programme.
These benefits are not one and the same. For example, you may
feel wretched *during* exercise, but experience feelings of motivation, exhilaration, lifting of anxiety or general well-being
immediately afterwards. Alternatively, you may not encounter *any*
enduring effects (such as the sense of mastery from sustaining

your training or bolstered body image from dropping a trouser size) until much later. The first time I resolved to become fit, back in school, I read in a running manual that it takes eleven weeks for a running programme to 'stick' and to obtain benefit. Eleven weeks is a long time to wait – and endure – and, unfortunately, many people give up before they reach that mark. But when you reach it, physical activity becomes a natural extension of your life, a habitual act that requires no decision making to initiate. When the alarm goes off, you don't contemplate whether you should drift back to sleep or get up and start moving – you just do it. It sure is worth it.

What if exercise makes you feel bad?

Rigorous physical activity, no matter what it is, may cause you to feel terrible. Does this make you a bad person? No, but it probably means that you should change your exercise routine. First, consider finding an exercise that – magic word – *fits* your lifestyle, resources and personality. Don't jog if you live in a rainy climate and hate being wet. Don't join a gym if you can't afford it. Don't participate on a team if you're allergic to competition. Don't do aerobic exercise (e.g., elliptical machine) if you prefer anaerobic (e.g., stretching and toning). Do something that affirms some part of you – if you're a social person, acquire a running partner or join a golf club. If you need more time with your children, buy a jogging stroller or join a baby yoga class. If you like nature, take up hiking or skiing. If you love the water, do a water-based sport. If you have only slices of time during the day, exercise in ten-minute chunks or take the stairs everywhere you go or do callisthenics in your office.

Second – and this is a crucial one – if exercise makes you feel bad, you are very likely overdoing it. Learn to measure your maximum heart rate (see below) and, when you set out for your first session, do *not* exceed 60 per cent of that limit. For some people, this may be walking briskly (running will come later) or simply walking. Too many start out an exercise routine working out too hard, which leaves them feeling discouraged, frustrated and generally unwell, and so they quit.

In one study, participants were asked to cycle at 60 per cent of their maximum heart rate. Over the course of thirty minutes, half of the participants reported feeling progressively better and half claimed feeling progressively worse. Researchers, who tend to study the average person, don't yet know why some people experience pleasure while exercising and others displeasure, but you can take steps to figure out why you in particular feel good or bad.

How to do it

Physical activity is defined as 'energy expenditure above that of resting level',[47] so the field is really wide open, the options limitless. Researchers chide people who use the terms 'physical activity' and 'exercise' interchangeably (as the latter is really only a subset of the former, exercise being a specific kind of planned and structured physical activity, usually with the goal of improving physical fitness or health), but I choose to confound them anyway. If you resolve to undertake a programme of physical activity after reading this chapter, you'll essentially be *moving* more. It's that simple. The moving can be done as part of a formal, organized and refereed sport, or at home alone on a yoga mat.

Exercise professionals traditionally advise that you calculate your maximum heart rate (most simply defined as 220 minus your age) and strive to work out at a level between 65 per cent and 80 per cent of that figure. So, if you are thirty-two, your maximum heart rate is 188 and the range to aim for is between 122 and 150.[48] Don't be a slave to this range, however – it's quite approximate, as the formula is designed for an average person of your precise age.[49]

Few of us don't already have a pretty good idea how to start and implement a physical activity routine. But it doesn't hurt to add these several recommendations:

- Start slow in the 60 per cent to 65 per cent range of your maximum heart rate.

- Decide ahead of time on specific dates, starting times and durations of your exercise, and pencil or stylus them in, treating them like fixed appointments. Would you ever miss a meeting with your boss or fail to pick up your kid from school? Yes, but rarely, and only in exceptional situations.

- If possible, choose a time to exercise during a time of day when you feel most energetic.

- Current guidelines recommend thirty minutes of moderate physical activity on most days of the week. But better to exercise for ten minutes than not at all. The most important thing is to stick with your plan.

- If you already engage in regular physical activity, up the ante. Run faster and longer, lift heavier weights, join a more advanced swimming or dance class.

- An exercise routine is like a diet. It's okay to break it, but don't let guilt and shame so overwhelm you that you give the whole thing up. Get back up on the horse (literally or figuratively) the following day.

Activity and rest

I don't know if it was ironic, coincidental or completely pre-dictable if you knew me, but I found myself reading scientific papers on the benefits of physical activity while exercising on a stationary bike. Admittedly, I'm a bit addicted to exercise and my commitment (if not always my performance) is very high. But one thing that I *don't* get enough of is sleep. 'The world belongs to the energetic,' according to Ralph Waldo Emerson, but the energetic also need to reserve time for rest. No matter how active and vigorous and successful we are during wakeful hours, if we don't obtain an adequate amount of sleep, we'll suffer in terms of our moods, energy, alertness, longevity and health. One prominent sleep researcher argues that if people got just one more hour of sleep each night, our Western 'sleep-sick' society would be much happier and healthier.[50] It's like those ads professing that you can 'Lose weight while you sleep!' You can say you've read it here that you can become happier while you sleep.

Last word

No one in our society needs to be told that exercise is good for you. Whether you are overweight or have a chronic illness or are a slim couch potato, you've probably heard or read this dictum countless times throughout your life. But has anyone told you, indeed, *guaranteed* you, that regular physical activity will make you happier? I swear by it.

Happiness Activity No. 12: Taking care of your body (Acting like a happy person)

It is somehow fitting to complete our discussion of specific strategies for how to become happier with the prescription to simply *act* like a happy person. Remarkably, pretending that you're happy − smiling, engaged, mimicking energy and enthusiasm − can not only earn you some of the benefits of happiness (returned smiles, strengthened friendships, successes at work and school)[51] but can actually *make* you happier. In poet Marge Piercy's words, 'Live as if you liked yourself, and it may happen.'

Facial feedback

This wisdom has been supported by decades of research and by the 'facial feedback hypothesis' in particular − an idea foreshadowed by Darwin's view that 'the free expression by outward signs of an emotion intensifies it.'[52] In other words, show the physical manifestations of happiness (or fear or disgust) and you will come to feel it, at least in mild form. Smooth (or furrow) your brow, fashion smile (or frown) lines, open your hands (or clench them) and you might just experience more joy or more irritation. According to this notion, your face (and body and voice) sends signals ('feedback') to your brain, informing it that you are experiencing a particular emotion and leading you – surprise! – to feel it.

If you ever took a course in Introductory Psychology, you probably learned about a study in which participants were asked to hold a felt-tip marker in their mouths, either gripped directly between their teeth (simulating a smile) or between their puckered lips (simulating a frown).[53] The participants were not aware that the marker-holding would have any particular impact on them, nor were they truthfully told why exactly they had to do this. Instead, they were instructed to examine a set of *Far Side* cartoons and to judge how funny they found them. Those whose facial muscles were (unknowingly to them) manipulated to resemble a smile found the cartoons more humorous than those whose facial expressions mimicked a frown.

This study, and many others like it, suggests that simply taking on the facial expressions and postures of happiness can go a long way to make you experience joy. Admittedly, the effects are modest. When trained actors were obliged to manipulate their facial muscles (most of us average folk aren't able to do this) into the configuration required for a genuine smile – to be exact, this involves the contraction of the 'orbicularis oculi', the muscle that encircles the eye, and contraction of the 'zygomaticus major' muscles, pulling the corners of the lips upwards – the actors reported feeling positive and happy, though their feelings were closer to '*as if* I were happy' than the real thing.[54] In spite of this, some people swear by a strategy of regular smiling. Recently, a reader named Marsh wrote to me that he makes use of a special wristwatch designed to vibrate several times a day to prompt people to take their medication. He has it set to 10 am, 12 noon, 2 pm, 4 pm, and 6 pm to remind himself to smile. 'Am I happier?' he wrote. 'I think so.'

Permanent smiles or frowns

Another intriguing sort of evidence for 'facial feedback' comes from research seeking to understand the effects of permanent facial expressions on emotion. Mobius syndrome is a birth defect that causes those afflicted with it to lack the ability to move their facial muscles – in a real sense, they have a frozen neutral expression on their faces. Such patients claim that they cannot *experience* emotions, only think them. 'I . . . think happy or I think sad, not . . . actually feeling happy or feeling sad,' reported one man with the condition.[55] So, the inability to physically express emotions powerfully influences the ability to feel them.

Have you noticed that, as people age, they tend to develop facial lines that match their personality? A very old and very happy person appears to have a happy expression fixed on her face, and a person who has been sad (or angry) all his life is trapped with a sad (or angry) look. This is actually a scientifically supported fact. For example, repeated contractions of the orbicularis oculi muscle, which constricts both sides of the eyes, raising the cheeks and gathering the skin inwards towards the bridge of the nose, causes eye wrinkles – the familiar crinkly eye lines that characterize a smile. So, what if you take away the 'sad' or 'angry' wrinkles, would you actually become happier? If the facial feedback hypothesis is right, then yes. A study to test this directly was done not long ago.[56] The participants were ten clinically depressed patients whose depression had not responded to treatment by either drugs or psychotherapy. In other words, nothing had worked. They were all women, thirty-six to sixty-three years of age and they had been depressed for periods ranging from two to seventeen years. All the patients were administered muscle-paralyzing botulinum toxin A – aka Botox – to their frown lines (on the bridge of the nose, between the eyebrows, and slightly above them). Two months later, nine out of the ten participants were no longer depressed and the tenth had much improved. Although it comes from an admittedly preliminary study, this is a stunning finding. Undoubtedly, removal of the frown lines makes other people perceive you as happier (and more attractive) and, as this investigation shows, people actually do *feel* happier.

Social interactions and coping

Of course, in the real world, outside of the laboratory, if you smile the world smiles with you. People respond to you more positively, they may initiate a conversation, engage with you, help you out or comfort you, become your new best friend or the future parent of your child. The smiles of infants have been shown to procure love and attachment, ensuring that the caregiver will continue to care for the child and secure his well-being. Mothers who express positive emotions have infants who begin to express positive emotions as well, an observation that led Eric Fromm to go so far as to contend that 'A mother must not only be a "good mother", but also a happy person'.[57]

Even, or perhaps especially, in the face of stressful events, smiling and laughter can help 'undo' negative emotions, distract and bring about feelings of peace, amusement or even joy. In one study, people who had lost their spouses six months earlier were interviewed and asked to reminisce about their marriage.[58] Those who laughed spontaneously during the interviews reported coping much better with their bereavement and experiencing more enjoyment in their lives, less anger and more positive relationships with others. It was as though the laughter helped them 'dissociate' from their distress. Other work has shown that laughter can lower stress hormones and even the *expectation* of laughter can elevate beneficial hormones. Men who anticipated watching one of their favourite humorous videos had 27 per cent more beta-endorphins in their blood and 87 per cent more human growth hormone than a control group.[59] And these physiological changes happened before the videos had even rolled.

In sum, smiling and laughter – even the insincere 'I don't want to pose for this photo' smile or 'This joke's not that funny' chuckle – gives rise to a mild feeling of positive well-being. But, even more, that little boost jumpstarts a powerful upward spiral of consequences for coping and social relationships, thereby reducing anxiety and distress and bringing you ever greater happiness and joy.

So, go for it – smile, laugh, stand tall, act lively and give hugs. Act *as if* you were confident, optimistic and outgoing. You'll manage adversity, rise to the occasion, create instant connections, make friends and influence people, and become a happier person.

COMPLEMENTARY ACTIVITIES

If you benefit from these activities, you may also want to try:

1) Committing to your goals (Happiness Activity No. 10, p. 213)

2) Savouring life's joys (Happiness Activity No. 9, p. 196)

PART III

Chapter 10

The five 'hows' behind sustainable happiness

It's relatively easy to become happier for the short duration, just as it's a piece of cake to quit smoking for a day or to temporarily keep a tidy desk. The challenge lies in *sustaining* the new level of happiness. You know this intimately if you've tried to turn your life around before (perhaps numerous times) but have found that 'nothing works'. I would wager that your previous attempts *have* worked, just not for long. Why not? This chapter explains that long-term increases in your level of happiness can be attained, but only if you abide by the five 'hows' (or keys) behind sustainable well-being. The six chapters of Part II described in detail a set of twelve activities from which you can adopt one – or two or four – to launch the process of making yourself a happier person. On the other hand, some of you may choose to read about all twelve activities and benefit from each and every one.

With the intentional activities, you have the power to harness the promise of the 40 per cent of our feelings of well-being that are within our control – to improve that large part of your happiness that *can* be improved. You may have begun carrying out these happiness activities already or you may have not. In either case, you may be wondering about the essential secrets of their success. If you understood better *how* and *why* the happiness strategies worked would you be more effective in practising them? Would you be more likely to persist in engaging in them? Absolutely. In this chapter, I describe the critical 'mechanisms of action' (or reasons) for the success of the book's core programme. The five 'hows', grounded in the scientific literature, are assembled and interpreted together here for the first time.

The First How: Positive emotion

~

'Happiness consists more in small conveniences or pleasures
that occur every day, than in great pieces of good fortune
that happen but seldom.'

BENJAMIN FRANKLIN

~

Say that you are reasonably comfortable materially. You may not
have everything you desire, but you have a roof over your head,
plenty of food to eat, clothes that fit and keep you warm and
some security in your income. What if 75,000 dollars suddenly
fell out of the sky and onto your fortunate head? How should
you spend the money to maximize the happiness that you will
obtain from it?

This is by no means a frivolous question, as the answer gets to
the heart of one of the primary ways that particular happiness
activities, or behaviours, make people happier – and that is by
creating many happy moments. Indeed, frequent positive emotions – feelings of joy, delight, contentment, serenity, curiosity,
interest, vitality, enthusiasm, vigour, thrill and pride – are the very
hallmark of happiness.[1] Although all human beings endure negative emotions, happy people experience positive states more
frequently than do their less happy peers. It can even be said that
positive emotions make happy people who they are.

Fortunately, each of the twelve intentional happiness activities
described in Chapters 4 to 9 has the ability to generate a cascade
of positive experiences. To be sure, one of the desirable features
of such activities is that they can be frequently initiated, re-
initiated and adjusted to yield a continual flow of positive
experiences and positive feelings. For example, a person who has
resolved to undertake the twin strategies of committing to
goals and increasing flow may decide to return to school in
middle age. Accordingly, he may vary his reading choices and
course selections in order to develop expertise in multiple areas.
In the process, he will feel strong intrinsic motivation and flow,

and experience the joy of discovering fascinating new areas of knowledge, the pride of mastering new skills and the enjoyment of meeting new people. These ongoing positive experiences, brought about by conscious effort on the person's part, may help him to remain particularly happy over a long period of time.

Consider another individual who embarks on practising the three strategies of gratitude, kindness and religion. If she places sincere effort into these activities, she will feel the gratification and peace that comes from appreciating life's blessings, the satisfaction that comes from helping others and from forging new relationships, and the serenity and awe that comes from being in the presence of God. Notably, however, these surges of positive feeling won't be singular, but recurrent. No happiness-enhancing strategy would be capable of successfully sustaining happiness if it made a person feel happy only once and only briefly.

If you contemplate each of the twelve happiness-boosting activities, you will observe that every one of them has the potential to produce a stream of positive experiences, to increase the number of transient bursts of happiness in your life. Because positive emotions are typically short-lived, many people believe they are trivial. This is a mistake. As Barbara Fredrickson has eloquently argued, moments of pleasure don't just make you *feel* good. They broaden your horizons and build your social, physical and intellectual skills.[2] In this way, positive emotions beget upward spirals – for example, you feel invigorated after aerobic exercise, which boosts your creativity, which gives you a new idea about how to enchant your partner, which strengthens your marriage, which shores up your satisfaction and commitment, which leads you to be more grateful and forgiving, which fuels optimism, which creates a self-fulfilling prophecy, which buffers the sting of a setback at work, and so on. Some of the changes produced by small boosts of positive emotion are small and some are big. But they add up. Positive emotions truly *make* you into a happier person. 'We live in an ascending scale when we live happily,' said author of *Treasure Island* Robert Louis Stevenson, 'one thing leading to another in an endless series.'

So, if you suddenly experienced a financial windfall, you would ultimately be much happier if you spent the money on numerous pleasant, mood-boosting things occurring on a day-to-day or weekly basis – a daily lunch of expensive sushi, a weekly massage, a regular delivery of fresh flowers or Sunday morning calls to your best friend abroad – rather than spending it all on a single big-ticket item that you believe you would really love, like a new top-of-the-line Jaguar or the remodelling of a bathroom with hand-painted tiles. By now you should appreciate the fact, as Ben Franklin did, that you would swiftly adapt to the new car or bathroom, but not to the bursts of intermittent happiness.

But why do we continue to *believe* so strongly that it's the large and dramatic events of our lives – the earthquake, the overseas adventure, the wedding, and the divorce – that are the ones that matter? Because those are the events we anticipate, remember, chew over and discuss with others. We tend to notice and recall only special and important episodes from our lives, the one day that something went very wrong (or extremely right) instead of the remaining 364 ordinary days. However, don't underestimate the positive emotions experienced during those ordinary days, because if properly understood they can change your entire perspective and open up your mind to new possibilities that you didn't know were there just moments before. Consider the now-famous Madeleine cake consumption experience of French novelist Marcel Proust:

I raised to my lips a spoonful of the tea in which I had soaked a morsel of the cake. No sooner had the warm liquid mixed with the crumbs touched my palate than a shudder ran through me and I stopped, intent upon the extraordinary thing that was happening to me. An exquisite pleasure had invaded my senses, something isolated, detached, with no suggestion of its origin. And at once the vicissitudes of life had become indifferent to me, its disasters innocuous, its brevity illusory – this new sensation having had on me the effect which love has of filling me with a precious essence; or rather this essence was not in me it was me. I had ceased now to feel mediocre, contingent, mortal.[3]

Yes, Proust definitely feels a positive emotion upon eating the Madeleine – perhaps more intense and transcendent than that experienced by most of us ordinary folk, but we have all had our share of positive emotions. The fact that the experience feels *good*, however, doesn't end there. It changes him, providing new insight and new understanding. It prompts him to look at the world in an entirely different way. This is an elegant analogy for what happens when you resolve to craft daily kindnesses or smile more or consider the brightest possible future for yourself. By enacting these strategies, you will create happy moments in your life that not only will make you feel happier, but alter your whole way of thinking and being. They will create a sense of possibility and promise, and who knows where that will take you.

Positive emotions and depression

If you've ever had long-lasting or intense periods of feeling down or blue, you may be surprised at the role that positive emotions can play in depression. To be sure, depression has been described as a syndrome distinguished by a *deficit* of positive emotions – a lack of joy, curiosity, contentment, enthusiasm – that is, an empty cup.[4] Indeed, inability to take pleasure in joyful events is a hallmark of depression. This positivity deficit is also evident in how depressed people think about the future and the past. Their problem, it turns out, is not so much that they anticipate bad things will come to pass, it's that they cannot believe that good things will.[5] They also have great difficulty recalling anything pleasant that ever happened to them.[6] The experience of positive events is also important: surprisingly, recovery from depression appears to be jumpstarted by positive events even more than it's thwarted by negative events. For example, researchers in the UK carefully analysed forty-nine instances when women improved or recovered from a depressive episode.[7] These changes of fortune were found to be galvanized by a positive experience, especially something that gave these women the feeling of a 'fresh start'.

All these observations and findings point to multiple ways that happiness-enhancing activities can alleviate the symptoms of depression. The activities that will be most effective in lifting depressive symptoms should be those that increase 1) positive emotions (e.g., joy and relief at overcoming an obstacle) and the positive experiences that will stem from those feelings, 2) positive thoughts (e.g., 'I'm tougher than I thought') and 3) positive experiences or events (making an important deadline at work). It's worth noting that, in our day-to-day lives, emotions, thoughts and experiences are interconnected and typically occur together. Researchers, however, usually disaggregate them, so that they can show the value of each separately. In any case, it's no coincidence that the twelve happiness strategies described in Part II of the book are all designed to accomplish exactly what is needed to ward off depression: increase positive emotions, foster positive thoughts and fuel positive experiences.

First, we have already seen that happiness activities boost positive emotions, but researchers have also shown that positive feelings can foil the effects of negative feelings.[8] For example, in one study, participants were given only one minute to prepare a speech on the topic 'Why you are a good friend'. (Unbeknownst to them, the speech never actually took place.) Immediately, these participants reported being extremely anxious, felt their hearts racing and their blood pressure rise. Then, they were divided into four groups and each group was simply shown a movie that made them feel either joyful, content, neutral or sad. After the films, eventually all the groups returned to their original emotional and physiological state (i.e., no anxiety, normal heart rate, etc.), but the two groups who experienced positive emotions (namely, joy and contentment) showed the fastest recovery in their cardiovascular symptoms.[9] Recent data from my lab extended this finding to depression.[10] People who were instructed to practise various happiness activities reported experiencing more frequent positive emotions (such as contentment and pleasure) for as long as three months after our study had ended. Critically, our analyses revealed that those very positive emotions, in turn, led the same individuals to show reduced depressive symptoms as long as six months after the study.

Researchers argue that positive emotions possess the ability to 'undo' the lingering cardiovascular effects of negative emotions. Indeed, feelings of joy, satisfaction or pride can help people see the 'big picture' of their lives and provide a sort of 'psychological time-out' in the midst of stress or trauma, thus lessening the sting of any particular unpleasant event. In these ways, positive feelings marshalled in the face of adversity can build resilience, by helping people bounce back from stressful experiences.[11]

A second benefit of happiness activities is that they boost positive thinking. As I will discuss in the Postscript, the most widely held theories of depression posit that negative, dysfunctional thoughts are at the root of this disorder.[12] This is because pessimistic, downbeat attitudes and memories fuel negative emotions – sadness, anger, jealousy, fear – which spawn more negative thoughts and so on, in a vicious downward spiral. In contrast, happiness activities can counteract the negative bias by helping us unlearn our patterns of negative thinking. For example, hopeful predictions that result from the optimism strategy replace thoughts of hopelessness and powerlessness. Joyful memories brought to mind by the savouring strategy replace bitter and angry recollections about old hurts. Pleasant, distracting thoughts prompted by the avoiding overthinking strategy replace fretful ruminations about current troubles. Indeed, a study from my laboratory confirmed this reasoning. People who actively and regularly practised either gratitude or optimism over an eight-week period came to regard their routine experiences in more positive ways and to find everyday events (meeting a friend, commuting to work, cooking dinner) more satisfying.[13] These more positive thoughts and interpretations, in turn, triggered improvements in well-being.

Third, happiness activities encourage positive experiences. Practising the nurturing relationships activity yields periods of relaxation and contentment in the company of family and friends. Practising acts of kindness produces moments in which we suddenly feel efficacious and appreciated. Having more flow at home, school and work can lead us to be more successful and productive, producing greater engagement and enjoyment of our daily life.

The majority of conventional depression therapies aim for 'remission', or the virtual absence of depressive symptoms, as their endpoint.[14] Most people recognize, however, that relief of symptoms is not the depressed person's ultimate objective. If you are depressed, your goal is not just to *not* be depressed – your goal is to be happy. However, even after therapy has successfully assuaged sadness, guilt, fatigue and apathy, you still may not be happy and you almost certainly wouldn't be flourishing or thriving. The latest estimate is that 11 per cent of us are 'languishing', that is, not clinically depressed, yet living stagnant, empty lives or, to quote Thoreau, leading 'lives of quiet desperation'.[15] Thus, recovery from depression will probably return you to a hedonic 'neutral' point, to 'languishing' at best. The goal of practising happiness activities is to bolster positive emotions, thoughts and experiences, such that they eventually lift you and sustain you above that neutral point.

If you are currently receiving treatment for depression, the combination of the treatment *and* the use of happiness-increasing strategies will hopefully have the double-whammy effect of relieving depressed mood and elevating happiness. The reasons should be plain by now. The happiness strategies are expected to trigger pleasant emotions and uplifting thoughts, which serve as an antidote to depressive symptoms. And the happiness strategies are expected to bring about a stream of positive experiences, which are also inconsistent with depression.

Positive emotions versus life meaning

Are transient positive emotions really as important to strive for as honour, integrity or meaning in life? The answer is that the very question is misleading. It sets up a false dichotomy between so-called hedonistic pleasures versus the well-deserved gratifications of the mind, heart and soul. In truth, positive emotion is positive emotion, joy is joy, contentment is contentment. Who is to compare the thrill of a helicopter ride to the ecstasy of spiritual awakening, the joy of a lemonade in the high desert to the delight of hearing your baby's first laugh? Experiences that forge a sense of life meaning – whether they involve helping a friend in need, worshipping a higher power, or developing a superior expertise – are *happy* moments, even if the positive emotions surrounding such experiences may not always be evident immediately, or if they differ (which they undoubtedly do) from the positive emotions induced by a sugar high.

So, don't pooh-pooh pleasure. You can find pleasure in a silly TV show or in being wholly absorbed in a lecture on astrophysics. Both types of pleasures contribute to a happy life and both types of pleasures can give rise to the multiple benefits of positive emotions, like feeling more sociable, more energetic and more resourceful. An avalanche of studies has shown that happy moods, no matter the source, lead people to be more productive, more likeable, more active, more healthy, more friendly, more helpful, more resilient and more creative.[16] This means that positive emotions actually help us achieve our goals (reinforcing the feeling that we are working towards something important), as well as helping us strive for meaning and purpose in life. Indeed, a series of intriguing studies at the University of Missouri found that happy moods actually lead people to perceive their lives as more meaningful; for example, the more positive emotion people experience during a particular day, the more meaningful they judge that day.[17] That seriousness and greatness must be accompanied by grumpiness is a myth.

Whence the source

I confess now that I did gloss over something. The *source* of the happy moments does in fact matter, for it influences the ability of the experience to be self-sustaining. Although the bliss of a sinful pleasure can trigger the same kinds of intellectual, social and physical benefits as the bliss of hard-earned effort, the sinful pleasure is over quickly and, what's more, can leave guilt or other negative feelings in its wake. But the pleasure borne of any of the dozen happiness-inducing strategies described here – whether they involve practising optimism, nurturing relationships, developing coping strategies, or living in the present – is lasting, recurring or self-reinforcing. One of the chief reasons for the durability of happiness activities is that, unlike the guilty pleasures, they are hard won. *You* have devoted time and effort to meditating or avoiding overthinking or committing acts of kindness. *You* have made these practices happen and you have the ability to make them happen again. This sense of capability and responsibility is a powerful boost in and of itself. When the source of positive emotion is yourself (as opposed to a televised World Cup game or chocolate or a glass of wine), it can continue to yield pleasure and make you happy. When the source of positive emotion is yourself, it is *renewable*.

The Second How: Optimal timing and variety

~

'To be interested in the changing seasons is a happier state of mind than to be hopelessly in love with spring.'

GEORGE SANTAYANA

~

Discovering which exact strategies you can undertake to become happier won't necessarily blow your mind. Many people intuitively grasp that being grateful for what they have, savouring the moment, strengthening relationships and coping well with hardship are all activities that ultimately bolster happiness. Knowing what to do is an important step, but you also need to know precisely *how* to do it. Fortunately, research has something to say about specifically how a happiness-increasing programme must be carried out to achieve maximum success. In this section, I describe two elements that are critical – timing and variety.

Timing is important

~

'Love is brief, but frequently recurring.'

FRANÇOIS DE LA ROCHEFOUCAULD

~

The pie-chart theory of happiness predicts that no attempt at making yourself happier can work if you eventually adapt to the happiness-boosting effects of your effort. This is why, as we saw in Chapter 2, the strategy of changing one's circumstances – earning more money or switching jobs – is ultimately fruitless. But can't you also adapt to the *activities* you do in order to be happy like counting blessings, dispensing kindnesses or pursuing life goals? Yes, you can, unless you respect the second how of sustainable well-being. As French author La Rochefoucauld intuited, activities, by definition, are episodic – they happen at irregular intervals. Intentionally cultivating optimism, for example, might be something that you do on mornings that you wake up gloomy, or on your way to social get-togethers, or each time you receive an e-mail from your boss. Alternatively, you might choose to practise optimism every Sunday night by writing in a journal about your best possible future self. The bottom line is that for happiness activities, as for humour, timing is important. Accordingly, it's essential to consider your strategies' frequency and duration and to strive to time them in ways that deliver you greatest satisfaction, serenity or joy so that you thwart adaptation. For example, you might choose to 'count your blessings' only after braving a difficult period, or only when you're especially needful of a boost, or only at the week's end. Indeed, a friend of mine actually keeps a handwritten list of the strategies that work especially well for her during particular times (e.g., meditate and practise gratitude before in-laws visit, focus on goal pursuit and avoid overthinking when dealing with supervisor, etc.) and she consults that list during those times. This way, you strive to discover the optimal timing for each activity by establishing the frequency of engagement that allows each activity to remain fresh, meaningful and positive.

How do you accomplish this? Through self-experimentation. Earlier, I described a couple of experiments from my laboratory in which we induced people to practise different happiness-boosting strategies.[18] These experiments offer some ideas for how one might achieve optimal timing. One study showed that people were more successful at increasing their happiness when they counted their blessings every Sunday night than when they did it three times a week. A second study showed that people were more successful at increasing their happiness when they committed five acts of kindness on a Monday than when they spread their kind acts throughout the week. Both of these observations may be true for you as well. However, these findings represent averages – that is, *on average*, people who count their blessings on Sundays only and those who do five acts of kindness in one single day are happiest – and they may not apply to every reader of this book. Furthermore, these general rules may not apply to other ways of expressing gratitude or kindness (such as writing gratitude letters or volunteering weekly for a charitable organization) or to other happiness activities (such as learning coping strategies or practising optimism, forgiveness or flow). So, you need to try different ways of timing your happiness activity, manipulating when and how often you perform it, until something clicks and it begins to work for you.

Interestingly, religious practices and prohibitions make clever use of optimal timing. Jewish Orthodox married couples, for example, are forbidden to touch each other, let alone be intimate, during the seven days surrounding the woman's menstrual period. To ensure that inadvertent physical contact doesn't occur, even such mundane acts as passing the salt must be conducted with forethought and care – the wife must place the salt shaker on the table in front of her husband, leaving just enough time to pull back her hand before his comes close to hers. This might seem absurd to some of us, but the unintended (or perchance intended?) fringe benefit is the maintenance of the flames of love and passion. How wonderful it must be to be able to resume physical contact after the period of prohibition each month! Notwithstanding the origins for such practices, we can borrow their spirit if not their substance to enhance the love and happiness in our own lives.

Variety, the spice of life

Activities, by definition, are also dynamic, that is, they don't tend to stay the same.[19] Being generous and charitable to others on a regular basis requires a multitude of diverse behaviours every week. One day you might leave an extra large tip for a weary waiter, another day you might visit a grieving friend, the following week you might do the dishes even when it's not your turn. The same applies to expressing gratitude or striving for goals or any other strategy you might undertake. This is why we don't adapt very quickly or easily to an activity (and its shifting nature) and this is why another important way that you can bolster the effectiveness of a happiness activity is to *vary* it. By varying it, we ensure that we don't adapt to it. For example, by alternating attention among several projects at work, by varying the route, time of day and speed of your running regimen, or by exploring a variety of software programs and web sites, your activities could remain intrinsically enjoyable and conducive to many rewarding 'flow' experiences. Or if, in expressing gratitude, you choose to vary the domains of life in which you count your blessings (i.e., in relationships, in your profession, in your health or in whatever area of life you've recently been fortunate), then the strategy may remain fresh and meaningful and work indefinitely. Conversely, if you count the very same blessings every day, in a non-varying routine, you may become bored with the routine and cease to extract any meaning from it. Supporting this notion, psychological research suggests that people tend to seek variety in their behaviour, perhaps because change in both thoughts and actions is innately pleasurable and stimulating.[20] No doubt aware of this, the German philosopher Immanuel Kant was said to shift his routine on his daily walks, in order to forestall boredom.

The importance of variety is demonstrated by both empirical and anecdotal evidence. In a 'kindness intervention' from my laboratory, participants given the opportunity to vary their acts of kindness over a ten-week period (do an extra household chore, then help a stranger change a tyre, then help a niece with homework, etc.) became happier and stayed happier. For the participants who performed similar acts each week, however, the kindness strategy completely backfired.[21] An analogous observation was made by US 'obesity czar' Robert Jeffery.[22] Having developed an obesity intervention that is incredibly effective, he soon learned that it works great for about six months, at which point his clients get burnt out or bored with the regime and can't stick to it. So, he has begun to retool the intervention every six months or so in order to give a booster shot for its effectiveness, encouraging his clients to try new and different weight loss routines.

These observations underscore the notion that a crucial method of maximizing the impact of an activity is to attend to its variety. So, sprinkle a little of this and a little of that, revivify your happiness strategies on a regular basis, surprise yourself sometimes. Regard finding happiness as an adventure, full of enterprise, developments and detours. Work on several happiness activities at once, so if one is not going so well, you can relish another.

I was reading a novel not long ago and came upon the assertion that 'to be happy you have to find variety in repetition'.[23] It may seem like puzzling phrasing, even an oxymoron, but it actually comes close to what I mean here by the suggestion to vary the way you implement your happiness activities. On the one hand, there's routine and habit – the habit of initiating the behaviour in the first place – and, on the other hand, there's *how* you do it, which cannot always be the same or you'll adapt to it and end up feeling the same as when you started.

My friend Stephanie told me of a guy in her acting class who had 'tried everything' in his attempts to become a happier person. Every day, he listened to motivational tapes, he prayed, he wrote in a journal and he went on a bike ride to the beach. He was incredibly assiduous about this routine and never wavered from it. But it wasn't working. The classmate was sinking lower and lower, and my friend was just bewildered. Then a light bulb went on. The guy had created such a rigid routine that he was going through the motions in exactly the same way every day. He listened to the same tapes every morning and he prayed for the same individuals using identical words. His route to the beach never strayed. When you take up a happiness activity, be sure to jazz up your routes to the beach, both literally and figuratively. Effort matters, without question, but so does *how* you put it into practice.

The Third How: Social support

Most of us are involved in a wide web of relationships and social connections. We are dependent on other people and we could not accomplish many of our goals if we didn't receive help and cooperation from others. It's not surprising, perhaps, that the third critical factor underlying the success of a happiness activity is 'social support'. This jargon term is used by psychologists to represent all kinds of help and comfort provided by others, especially those with whom we have strong, meaningful relationships. Say you are embarking on a happiness-enhancing programme, which involves the three strategies of regularly expressing gratitude, avoiding overthinking and engaging in regular aerobic exercise. Having a 'buddy' with whom to carry out the programme, or simply the validation of people close to you, is an enormous benefit. Social support partners can offer 'informational' support (e.g., suggesting a new way to show gratitude or cautioning that your current approach might lead you to get stuck), 'tangible' support (e.g., giving you rides to the gym) and 'emotional' support (e.g., providing reassurance, solace and inspiration).

We learned in Chapter 6 that social support is invaluable in helping people cope with life's challenges and misfortunes. For example, women who have at least one friend are better able to cope with problems than those without friends.[24] Whether you're suffering a break-up, a chronic illness or the threat of lay-offs, talking to a caring friend or family member can significantly ease the pain and provide a push to address problems. Confiding your worries and troubles to others can reduce stress if you learn that they have endured similar experiences and have survived or thrived. It can reduce anxiety when other people comfort and reassure.

Emotional or tangible support – whether this involves a sole confidante, a circle of friends, your family or a psychotherapeutic group – may also be crucial in helping people persist at and realize their goals in general.[25] Social support helps motivate and guide you along your path, thus ultimately promoting the realization of a wide variety of goals, including those concerning work, relationships and personal growth. Indeed, many organizations, such as Alcoholics Anonymous (AA) and some large religious congregations, emphasize the importance of having 'teammates' or 'small group members' who work together towards goals, be they abstaining from alcohol or worshipping. Whether they are teammates, buddies, mentors or big sibs, supporting and validating others can make the difference between short-term success and long-term success in your goal of becoming happier. Indeed, group support, such as the kind found in AA, can be extraordinarily powerful in galvanizing conviction, commitment and perseverance:

> An alcoholic could lose his job and his family, he could be hospitalized, he could be warned by half a dozen doctors – and go on drinking. But put him in a room of his peers once a week – make him share the burdens of others and have his burdens

shared by others – and he could do something that once seemed impossible.[26]

What does this have to do with trying to become happier? Any change in behaviour that requires effort and dedication will be made easier if your spouse, children, friends, parents, siblings and co-workers are supportive. They can motivate you and remind you to continue to practise your happiness activities – an indispensable boost when you start to lose momentum or simply forget. They can offer positive feedback, encouragement and warmth – 'Hey, you seem so much happier lately', 'You look great' or 'I know what it's like to feel like quitting.' Sometimes, it's necessary to establish ties with a new group of people – perhaps from happiness-relevant chat groups or web sites – who might share similar goals and concerns as you. Or, you might want to seek out new friends in your own work, school and neighbourhood communities as a way to find partners who support each other's efforts. And remember that you don't need a posse: often, just one caring friend will do.

The research evidence

The importance of social support is demonstrated in copious empirical investigations. In the domain of health, for example, sick patients who have strong social support are relatively more likely to cooperate with their medical treatment.[27] Studies have found that patients with hypertension (who must take medication every day and eat low-salt diets) are much more likely to adhere to their strict regimens if they have family support, especially from spouses.[28] Those with social support are more motivated to cooperate with their doctors' orders, more knowledgeable about their treatments and more likely to maintain their blood pressures.

Moving on to the self-help domain, people who make New Year's resolutions are much more likely to persevere for two years, and even for six years, if they have social support.[29] And one of my favourite studies investigated the extent to which social support can help people with the goal of losing weight.[30] Participants undertook a four-month-long weight-loss programme (involving diet, exercise and behavioural changes) either alone or with three acquaintances, friends or family members. Of those who embarked on the programme alone, 76 per cent completed it and 24 per cent maintained their weight loss in full for an entire six months. In contrast, of those who engaged in the weight-loss programme with social support, 95 per cent completed it and 66 per cent maintained their weight loss in full. Furthermore, those with social support lost more weight and kept more of it off. These numbers are compelling to say the least.

Like these participants, I would expect that those of us who attempt a happiness-enhancing programme without much social support are unlikely to commit for very long to carry it through. Think of social support as essentially a force that works with the behavioural change. Your spouse, friend, life coach or other 'buddy' can encourage you to work hard towards your goals and serve as a sounding board when you lose motivation or get stuck in a rut.

The Fourth How: Motivation, effort and commitment

~

'You have to participate relentlessly in the manifestations of your own blessings. And once you have achieved a state of happiness, you must never become lax about maintaining it, you must make a mighty effort to keep swimming upward into that happiness forever, to stay afloat on top of it.'

ELIZABETH GILBERT

~

Another vital key to a successful happiness-increasing programme, as you already well know, is committed and dedicated effort. When it comes to achieving greater happiness, the steps you need to take are not altogether different from those required for learning French or changing careers or any other goal you might pursue.

1. You must *resolve* to undertake a programme to become happier.
2. You must *learn* what you need to do.
3. You must put weekly or even daily *effort* into it.
4. You must *commit* to the goal for a long period of time – possibly for the rest of your life.

The first and second steps you have already initiated by picking up this book or others like it. They are critical steps, as the sense of mastery and possibility that accompanies the launch of a new chapter for yourself is immensely powerful and transporting. Just think of it, you are on the threshold of altering your life! 'Every time you make a choice,' wrote C.S. Lewis, 'you are turning the central part of you, the part of you that chooses, into something a little different from what it was before.'

The third and fourth essential steps in this process – concerted effort and commitment – may be the hardest. Without them, your journey will be altogether brief. You may become happier for a day, a week, perhaps a month, but it won't last. Most people have had such experiences with New Year's resolutions – come 1 January they know exactly what they need to do, they're determined and motivated to do it, they try for a time, and then they give it up. Following through on new intentions isn't easy, but neither is the work required for all the best and most meaningful things in life.

The wonders of motivated and committed effort

Motivation plays an indispensable role in all four steps of resolving, learning, effort-making and committing. You know that you have high motivation for a new endeavour when you find yourself brimming with enthusiasm and ideas about it. You know that you have high motivation when you do something because you

truly believe that the experience (or its consequences) will ultimately be interesting and challenging and enjoyable. The desire
comes from deep within you. My collaborators and I have tested
directly the question of whether the more motivated a person is
to become happier the more successful he or she will be. For
example, in one study, we directly recruited participants who
wanted to improve their happiness levels (e.g., 'Do you want to
be happy? This is the study for you!') and compared them to participants who signed up for a generic psychology experiment.[31]
The effects were striking. Regardless of whether they were asked
to 'write gratitude letters' on a regular basis or to 'journal about
their best possible futures', the motivated participants became a
great deal happier, whereas the non-motivated participants
improved only slightly or stayed the same. Another happiness
intervention that we did, in which we also induced people either
to practise gratitude or optimism, corroborated this result.[32]
Those participants who found the happiness-enhancing activity
most motivating and rewarding were the ones most likely to practise it and, therefore, the ones most likely to benefit from it.

So, there you have it, the secret ingredient of motivation. The
more motivated you are to do something, the more likely you'll
invest effort in it! And it doesn't take a rocket scientist (or a social
psychologist) to persuade you that, without effort, there is no
result. Plenty of studies confirm this intuitively obvious observation. Even *after* the experimenter has hung up her coat and
packed up the lab, those participants who continue to perform
the happiness-enhancing activity and integrate it into their lives
are more likely to show long-term benefits than those who
quit.[33] Without effort, without trying, without striving, without
tenacity, without constancy of purpose there is only failure, hesi-
tation, 'a faint heart, and . . . a lame endeavor'.[34]

When my students and I first started conducting happiness
interventions, it didn't take long for us to notice that the benefits lasted only as long as the participants practised their assigned
strategies. We initially received stinging criticism for this: 'Your
interventions must not be very strong.' But my colleague down

the hall (an acclaimed methodologist) Robert Rosenthal came to our rescue. He pointed out that the pattern of our results characterizes *every single* kind of pharmaceutical, including life-saving medications and therapeutic drugs taken by millions. The drug may be life-saving while you take it but, interestingly, the moment you stop, it 'fails' to work. Yet, I've never heard someone argue that insulin, aspirin, Lipitor, Claritin (Clarityn), Vicodin (dihydrocodeinone) and Viagra must be weak because they don't have long-term benefits. Again, the lesson here is the importance of practising the life-changing programme you have undertaken, whether that programme involves becoming a happier person, quitting smoking or treating an illness. Effort and commitment are king.

What if you're too busy?

'I'm too stressed out to think about anything else but how to get through the day,' a not-so-happy acquaintance told me when I suggested that she try some happiness activities. She was indeed busy, with two teenagers in the house, volunteering work and her real-estate practice taking off. So, I empathized. But, when it comes to the important things in life, are we ever really too busy? When you decided to have a baby, did you reserve just one hour a month to contemplate it? When you fell in love, did you set your relationship aside to make more time for your job? When you obtained an incredible career opportunity, did you say no because it would spoil your schedule? Hopefully not. Besides, many of the happiness activities do not actually require you to make time. They are simply ways of living your life – observing your job, partner and children with a new, more charitable and optimistic perspective, saying a kind word to your spouse, distracting yourself when you find yourself dwelling, uttering a short prayer before a meal, smiling at strangers during your commute, empathizing with someone who has hurt you, and so on. Most of these strategies aren't a time drain but, by deliberate choice and with some effort, can be woven seamlessly right into your day.

What if you backslide?

There surely will be times when your commitment wavers, when you forget and when you fail to practise the happiness-enhancing strategy you have determined to undertake. This is normal and inevitable and human; none of us is perfect. Furthermore, know that circumstances will arise when being ungrateful, unforgiving, self-focused, pessimistic, traumatized, lethargic or indecisive is completely understandable and acceptable. A continual and perfect state of bliss is not only impossible to achieve but also maladaptive.[35] Plenty of situations (deaths, failures, abuses of power) call for negative emotions, which have the valuable function of promptly triggering action and reaction, whether it's grieving, persistence or work towards reform.[36] In any case, the point for you to remember is that when you lose motivation to continue engaging in your happiness activity, and when you stop engaging in it, you need not feel that all is lost and that your individual situation must be hopeless. There is no crisis here. Your complicated life probably interfered, or maybe the strategy you were using lacked variety, or maybe you needed more encouragement from friends. Simply renew your motivation – reconsider the reasons why you want to become happier – and get back on track. Sometimes, at this point, substituting a new happiness-enhancing strategy might be of value and sometimes it's altering how you practise the strategy you originally chose. Research suggests that the right combination of optimal timing and optimal variety, strong social support and determined effort can be effective for the vast majority of people.

Recommit today . . . and tomorrow

I'm not usually in the habit of quoting Oprah Winfrey, but here I go. When she was reportedly once asked how she is able to run five miles per day, even when travelling, she replied that she has to recommit to the goal every day of her life. The same applies to strategies to make yourself a happier person. Renew your commitment every day. Not only the strategy but also the very act of recommitment will become easier and more automatic with time.

The Fifth How: Habit

I hope you are now convinced that it takes a great deal of effort and determination to become happier. This may be disappointing news for some, especially if lately you've been feeling disheartened, insecure or overwrought and simply aren't sure if you have the energy that this effort calls for. So, here I get to deliver the good news, which is that the effort is greatest at the beginning, but it diminishes with time, as your new behaviours and practices become habitual through repetition.

How do habits form?

We all have habits – some good, some bad. Most people associate the word 'habit' with annoying behaviours like chewing fingernails, sucking thumbs, twisting hair or interrupting conversations. Smoking is a familiar habit and so is changing lanes without using indicators or buying a latte every morning on the way to work. Healthy or 'good' habits are behaviours like always cutting the fat off a piece of chicken, flossing after every meal, carrying a water bottle wherever you go or recycling.

What do these behaviours have in common? They are labelled 'habitual' because you don't have to make the decision to do them. They are not intentional acts. When I wake up in the morning, I immediately get out of bed and put my running clothes on. I don't usually – well, not often – ever think, 'Should I get up and go running or should I stay here under the bed sheets?' So, there's really no decision to make. Similarly, if you have the habit of singing show tunes in the car or getting a takeaway every Friday night, you don't debate the act, you just do it.

Habits form with repetition and practice. Researchers theorize that every time you repeat a behaviour (such as going jogging in the morning), associations develop in your memory between the behaviour and the *context* in which it occurs.[37] For my morning jogging, that context would be the alarm clock going off, my bedroom, my running gear by the door, etc. So, with repetition, the contextual cues (the alarm clock ringing) will automatically trigger the habitual behaviour (donning running shoes), such that the behaviour eventually switches from the direction of 'controlled processing' to 'automatic processing'.[38] To apply this to happiness strategies, the more often you initiate a positive activity the stronger the connection becomes between that activity (savouring or appreciating) and the cues around you (family dinner or daily hassles). So, the next time (or more likely the tenth time) you get together with your family, you might be prompted into savouring simply by the situation of being around your loved ones, and the next time you get stuck in traffic, you might be prompted into an appreciative mode by the surrounding cues. Of course, such connections take time and a great deal of practice to build. As you might expect, habits take time to form and endure.

But aren't habits hard to establish?

When it comes to losing weight or quitting smoking, media reports and research articles are full of failure stories. Indeed, well-controlled treatment studies show incredibly high recidivism rates for people who try to change their behaviour. For example, we're told that 86 per cent of those who try to quit smoking eventually take it up again, and 80 per cent to 98 per cent of those who try to lose weight gain it back (and often gain more than they lost).[39] However, don't we all know people who've successfully turned their lives around, people who have successfully lost weight, quit drinking, given up drugs, renounced lives of crime, gone back to school or become less grouchy? How can we reconcile these two facts – the high recidivism rates from studies of weight control and smoking cessation programmes and the relatively high success rates among our acquaintances and friends?

In a now-classic study, social psychologist Stanley Schachter tried to resolve this paradox.[40] When talking to staff at his Columbia University office and acquaintances and strangers at Amagansett beach, where he spent his summers, he observed that a large percentage of them used to be overweight or smokers. So, the anecdotal evidence – the 'real-world' evidence – suggests that lots of people successfully kick bad habits and form new ones. Indeed, this is what Schachter found in his wide-ranging beach and office interviews – namely, a 63 per cent success rate for self-cure of smoking and obesity. He concluded that the published recidivism data are biased by the fact that they represent the outcomes of the 'hard-core cases' – that is, people who come in for treatment. The rest, who are able to cure themselves, don't seek treatment. In addition, and this is a seemingly obvious but very important observation, in trying to accomplish something (like quitting smoking), people may try (and fail) many times before they ultimately succeed. The 63 per cent of success stories that Schachter found had tried several times before finally accomplishing their goal.

Schachter's fairly informal investigation was replicated in a more recent, much larger and more representative study of 784 individuals with extensive histories of being overweight.[41] These individuals were able to keep off a minimum of thirty pounds (fourteen kilograms) for at least five years. Most tried many weight-loss methods and yo-yoed in their weights until they were finally successful. It took most of these people until their forties to lose the weight and to maintain it; however, once they found what worked for them, the task became much easier. Indeed, the researchers were surprised to learn that 42 per cent of the sample reported that maintaining the weight was much easier than losing it. By the time they reached their weight goal, their weight-loss strategies had probably already turned into true habits.

Two kinds of habits

So, clearly, everyone's goal should be to turn positive thinking and behaviour strategies into habits. But be wary of the wrong kind of habit! Your aim should be to create the habit of *instigating* a happiness activity – go ahead and forgive, savour, thrive, look on the bright side and count your blessings. Aim to do it unconsciously and automatically. This kind of habit helps you get 'over the hump' of implementing a happiness activity on a regular basis. Conversely, the other kind of habit, the habit of doing the activity the same way each time, would eventually become monotonous, prone to adaptation, and deficient in any happiness-boosting potential.

Conclusion

This book's message can be understood as the exhortation to establish new, healthy habits. Because activities such as looking on the bright side, savouring the moment, practising forgiveness and striving for important life goals make a difference in your happiness, it is certainly a good idea to make a habit of doing them. It may be exasperating to know that naturally very happy people, those fortunate to have high set points, seem to have inherited such habits. They don't need to *try* to be optimistic or grateful or forgiving, it's second nature to them. However, if your set point for happiness is not as high and you were blessed with fewer of those good habits, know that with some time and determination, you can develop the same exact habits for yourself.

In the past, you may have felt trapped in the tunnel of your unhappy inheritance, your pessimistic thoughts or your maladaptive habits. I hope the journey that this book has introduced you to will liberate you from the heavy weight of those negative perceptions. You'll find that there's a tremendous freedom in understanding the unifying theory of happiness put forth here – not only in knowing what are the most powerful determinants of happiness but in recognizing how to access that portion of happiness that's in your power to achieve a real and lasting change.

Afterword: The promise of abiding happiness

'It is never too late to be what you might have been.'

GEORGE ELIOT

Writing this book knocked me for six. I'd been investigating happiness for eighteen years. I'd been engrossed in the broader subject of psychology for longer. Much of the research I have described in these pages I know like the back of my hand, and I am fairly well familiar with the rest. And yet, immersing myself in the data about the various activities that people can use to become happier had an unexpected impact on me – an impact that quickly became almost laughingly predictable. When I was working on the gratitude section, I wound up penning a gratitude letter to a colleague (not something that comes naturally to me), and when I was working on the kindness section I was unusually considerate and thoughtful towards my acquaintances and friends. My husband was pleasantly surprised when he found me practising on him the techniques I wrote about in the section on nurturing relationships and, during the writing of the spirituality section, I (the least spiritual person I know) started thinking about the larger questions about meaning and purpose and reading messages into some of the major events of my life. These experiences genuinely surprised me not only because of my intimate familiarity with all these recommendations to boost happiness, such that they were really nothing new, but that I honestly had never been the best subject for receiving these recommendations. I am not the type of person to pick up a self-help book or to try to 'count her blessings'. Yet this is precisely what working on this book made me want to do. And if I, the ultimate reluctant subject, can be transformed in her recognition of the power and efficacy of this book's suggestions, then some of you reluctant readers can be transformed too.

In hindsight, I can now understand why certain chapters affected me more than others. Writing about the strategies that I was already good at – optimism, goal pursuit, coping, physical activity and flow – didn't influence me as much as those for which I needed improvement. For example, the section on living in the present was especially compelling and valuable in teaching me to focus on what really matters in the moment as opposed to fretting about daily irritations. But why would it have such an impact, given that I am *already* well aware (as you might also be) of the copious anecdotal evidence that living in the present makes people happy, not to mention the empirical work supporting it? In some seemingly magic way, seeing all the evidence converge together in one chapter, in one place, magnified its impact. Today, a frustrating, disappointing or painful moment does not go by when I don't ask myself: 'Will this matter in a year?' And it passes.

I hope that you will have a similar experience. You may already be vaguely aware (or even certain) that such activities as meditating, expressing gratitude, pursuing significant life goals and doing random acts of kindness would make you a happier person. But how can you be sure that these strategies would work for you and how precisely should you carry them out? Furthermore, why haven't you committed to practising such activities, or practising them effectively, up until now? Perhaps *The How of Happiness* will be the catalyst that you've been wait- ing for to remake your life. The foundation of science should bolster your confidence that you can be happier *if* you practise happiness activities in an optimal way and with dedicated effort. You may not have known how to do that before and I hope you have a better idea now. You may not have been as fulfilled and happy as you wanted to be for your entire life and now are assured, from the potential of the 40 per cent of our happiness that we can control, that changing your happiness level is entirely in your hands. That your 'unhappy genes' do not doom you to unhappiness or, worse, to depression.

The recommendations in this book for how to become a happier person turned out to possess a surprising power, even for a seasoned happiness researcher like myself. Without a doubt, writing the book has changed my life in some anticipated and many unanticipated ways. I hope that reading it will change yours and help you get the life you want.

Postscript: If you are depressed

If you scored in the 'depressed range' – that is, 16 or above on the depression scale (the CES-D) on pp. 36–37 – you may be wondering what you need to know immediately and what special steps you can take in addition to those described here. I should stress, however, that although a programme to become happier can positively be attempted by those who are depressed, relief from depression is not what this book promises. We'll now take a closer look at depression, what causes it, and what can be done about it.

What is depression?

Depression is an illness, not a failing. It's what psychologists call a 'syndrome', that is, a group of signs and symptoms that form a pattern. Many of you are undoubtedly already familiar with these symptoms. Some of you may only have a few of them, while others may have many. There are nine classic symptoms, with the first two being most diagnostic of depression:[1]

1) Sad mood for most of the day – feeling down, anxious or 'empty', though some of you may feel tense or irritable instead.
2) Being less interested and finding less pleasure in almost all hobbies or activities that you used to enjoy (including sex).
3) Feeling excessively guilty, worthless or helpless.
4) Having little energy and feeling fatigued much of the time.
5) Having a hard time concentrating, remembering or making decisions.

6) Having trouble sleeping – experiencing insomnia, early-morning awakening, or oversleeping.
7) Having trouble eating – overeating and gaining weight *or* losing your appetite and losing weight.
8) Feeling either agitated or 'slowed down'.
9) Having thoughts of death or suicide, making suicide attempts.

It's important to distinguish clinical, diagnosable depression from a passing sad mood. Full-fledged depression involves your whole body and person – your feelings (e.g., 'I feel wretched'), your thoughts (e.g., 'I'm ugly') and your physical state (e.g., 'I can't sleep'). To make things more complicated, there are also different *types* of depression. The most common are the following:

• Major depression, which involves one or more episodes (or periods of time) during which the depression is intense and you suffer a large number of symptoms. These symptoms interfere with your work and your relationships, in addition to disturbing your sleeping, eating and enjoyment of once pleasurable activities.
• Dysthymia, which is a less severe but more chronic (longer-lasting) type of depression. Your symptoms aren't as numerous or as disabling as in major depression, but they keep you from feeling good or functioning very well. And, if you're particularly unlucky, you may have both major depression and dysthymia, a condition researchers call double depression.
• Subsyndromal depression, in which you have some symptoms of depression, but they are not so intense or so long-lasting to earn you a formal diagnosis of either major depression or dysthymia. However, this type of depression deserves attention too, as you may still feel miserable and impaired in your daily life.

And, even within these classes of diagnoses, you may suffer from particular types of symptoms. For example, when women are depressed, they are more likely to experience weight gain, a boost in appetite and increased need for sleep, called 'reverse vegetative symptoms'. Men are more likely to experience the opposite and to feel angry and discouraged instead of hopeless and helpless. Furthermore, approximately one in ten adults (men and women) have depressed moods that cycle with the seasons, inflaming during the winter months. About one in twenty women have depressive symptoms that tend to appear during the week before their menstrual periods. Depression in women is also common after giving birth. Depression in older people is often triggered by a taxing illness or the loss of a loved one.

But, no matter what kind of depression, or what unique constellation of symptoms you have in particular, you must know that you *can* get better. Amazingly, the typical depressed person doesn't seek treatment for an average of *nine years* after experiencing her first symptoms.[2] So, even if you're pretty sure you are depressed, or have been in the past, you may have never received help from a mental health professional. I urge you to do so without delay, for several reasons.

First is a problem called 'co-morbidity'. This means that, if you are depressed, you are very likely to be experiencing one or two or even more other physical or emotional problems. Do you have persistent worries and tension, or irrational fears that you just can't shake? Have you ever had a panic attack, when you've felt that you might die? Do you have frightening nightmares or memories of a terrifying event? Do you have an eating disorder or a problem with smoking, drinking or drugs? These are just some of the conditions that tend to accompany depression and must be managed and treated as soon as possible. Fortunately, several kinds of antidepressant medications have proved to be helpful not only in effectively relieving depressive symptoms, but also in treating these accompanying conditions.[3]

The second reason to seek help for your depression is that it can wreak lasting damage on your life. Indeed, research shows that the toll depression takes is as great as that of a chronic physical disorder, like diabetes, arthritis or high blood pressure.[4] Because the average age at which people develop depression is in their mid-twenties, the illness can have a profound effect on important life transitions, like finishing education, starting out in a career, becoming a parent, and getting and staying married. Furthermore, in the United States alone, the loss of productivity engendered by depression costs $33 billion per year in salary (in England alone, the cost of treatment and loss of productivity is estimated at £9 billion per year).[5]

Some people argue that depression is 'normal', that feeling sad or inadequate or hopeless about everything is not a sign of irrationality or illness. Some even argue that good things can come out of it. There is a kernel of truth in this. Some of the low moods we feel may be what Freud termed 'ordinary human unhappiness', and sometimes pessimism has value. That is, people with negative outlooks may be more vigilant about threats and dangers (indeed overly so), and thus heed warnings that optimists will not. But if you are depressed, you know all too well that what you are experiencing is not just a pessimistic view of yourself and the world – what you are experiencing is utter suffering and pain. Much of this suffering is unrelenting and awful and undeserved, and this is the biggest reason why depression needs to be resolved and relieved.

The causes of depression

Susceptibility and stress (or nature and environment)

Many physical diseases develop when two things are present at the same time. First, we have an inborn susceptibility or predisposition towards the disease and, second, we experience some kind of event or stress in our lives that triggers it.[6] Likewise, depression appears to be a result of both 'nature' and 'environment'. Like heart disease or diabetes or arthritis, depression is rooted in our biology. This is the nature part, involving our genes and brain function. The heritability of depression – that is, the extent to which it is genetically determined – ranges from 20 to 45 per cent[7] for milder forms and is likely to be much higher for severe forms. Indeed, a parent, child or sibling of someone with depression has a two to four times higher probability of becoming depressed than the average person.[8] So, it's clear that some of us are born with a susceptibility to depression. This susceptibility, which could be inherited or simply ill-fated, is likely to be expressed in what happens in our brains. Many studies have found that people suffering from depression show unique symptoms in their bodies.[9] These symptoms include too-low amounts of various brain chemicals (noradrenaline, serotonin and dopamine), a too-high amount of a stress hormone (cortisol), and disturbance of deep dream-related (REM) sleep. Furthermore, new technologies allowing researchers to image the brain have revealed that severely depressed patients have abnormalities in the prefrontal cortex (the region of the brain responsible for thinking and managing emotions), as well as in the limbic regions (i.e., areas involved in sleep, eating, sex, motivation, memory and responses to stress), including the mysterious sounding Area 25.[10] So, in sum, there is now a great deal of evidence that depression is partly rooted in those parts of our physical bodies over which we have minimal control.

However, a genetic or biological predisposition is generally not enough to precipitate depression. It's not the whole story. A stress or some kind of trigger is necessary as well. If your predisposition is very strong, then a relatively minor stress could lead you to fall into a full-fledged depression. If your predisposition is small, then only a major stress or trauma will bring about depression.

So, what do I mean by 'stress'? The trigger that makes you depressed could literally be stress in your life, although it's likely to be severe stress – for example, the stress of poverty or a traumatic life event (like experiencing violence, a natural disaster, or the loss of one's home), separation or divorce, serious or chronic illness, caring for a sick child or ageing parent, and many others.[11] Alternatively, some researchers focus on bad experiences in childhood as the 'stressors' that trigger depression in adulthood.

Indeed, many different kinds of poor parenting have been blamed for later depression, including whether your mother was depressed or anxious while pregnant, as well as whether your parents were neglectful, intrusive, harsh, inconsistent or abusive. Unfortunately, researchers don't know whether it's the inadequate parenting that leads to later depression in their kids, or something else entirely, like depression-prone genes shared by the whole family.

Psychological vulnerability

What else can cause or activate a depression? Many tomes have been written on this subject, and I will only mention the two theories backed, in my judgement, by the most scientific evidence. The first is Aaron Beck's cognitive theory of depression, which forms the basis for the most commonly used psychotherapy for this illness – cognitive behavioural therapy. Beck is a psychiatrist who argues that some people have dysfunctional attitudes that make them vulnerable to becoming depressed in the face of a negative event. These maladaptive attitudes often involve the notion that our happiness and self-worth depend on being perfect or hinge on other people's approval. For example, we might think, 'My teacher's critical comment means that I'm a total failure' or 'If my girlfriend doesn't love me, then I am nothing.' If we share these beliefs, then when something truly bad happens, we tend to have automatic negative thoughts about 1) ourselves (e.g., 'I'm not lovable'), 2) our present experiences (e.g., 'My boss always prefers my co-workers'), and 3) our futures (e.g., 'I'll never outgrow my shyness'). Beck calls these types of thoughts a 'negative cognitive triad'.

A related explanation for depression, called hopelessness theory, came out of the work of Martin Seligman and his students. According to this theory, having expectations that bad things will happen to us and that really good things will *not* happen, and that we cannot do anything to improve the situation, can cause depression. Thus, hopelessness is thought to lie at the root of a depression. How does a person become hopeless? When confronted with a stressful or otherwise negative experience, some people draw harmful inferences or conclusions. For example, when a man fails to get an expected promotion, he may conclude that being passed over 1) 'means I don't have talent', 2) 'will prevent me from ever advancing in my career', and 3) 'proves that I'm unworthy'. These are symptoms of hopelessness and they are likely to trigger depression in such a person. In contrast, another person in the exact same situation may be protected from hopelessness, and thereby from depression, if she alternatively concludes that 1) 'I haven't been putting much effort into my job lately', 2) 'I should work harder, so I could get the promotion next year', and 3) 'this has no bearing on my self-worth'.

Both hopelessness theory and Beck's cognitive theory assume that people who become depressed have a 'cognitive vulnerability', that is, a dysfunctional way of thinking about negative life events that makes it more likely that they'll become depressed. Simply put, how we interpret our life experiences (e.g., current problems in a relationship) influences our feelings about those experiences (e.g., feeling hopeless and inadequate versus confident and optimistic), which ultimately lead to distress and even full-fledged depression.

An exciting recent project, The Cognitive Vulnerability to Depression Project, has followed participants over time, measuring both their maladaptive thoughts and their life stresses. This project has found that, indeed, those participants with hopeless and dysfunctional attitudes at one point in time are more likely to suffer a major depressive episode at a subsequent point in time.[12] Fortunately, cognitive therapy, as you will shortly learn, has been very effective at attenuating these maladaptive attitudes.

Risk factors for depression

A risk factor is something that makes depression more likely, without necessarily causing it. There is now a great deal of scientific support for three risk factors for depression:

1) Poor social skills.
2) Shyness or withdrawal.
3) Excessive dependency on others.

If you recognize any of these qualities in yourself (and it's possible to possess more than one), then obtaining professional help may be extremely valuable. First, if your social skills need improvement, you can learn how to express yourself and communicate better, to control your emotions and be sensitive to others' feelings, and to initiate and hold your own during conversations. Researchers have also found that people who have poor social skills have a tendency to seek criticism from friends and family, indeed, they gravitate towards people who reject them. This is also something that a psychotherapist can help you resolve.

Second, if you are the type of person who avoids social situations or is excessively shy, you may be predisposed to experience depression. This is probably because, in the face of stress or negative events, shy or inhibited people avoid the very thing that can protect them from falling into a negative spiral, namely, companionship and social support.

Finally, if you constantly seek reassurance from other people about your worth and lovability or if you are extremely needy of others' acceptance and support, then you may be characterized by so-called 'excessive interpersonal dependency'. Like with the other risk factors, having this characteristic makes you vulnerable to becoming depressed. So, again, excessive dependency should be worked out in a therapeutic context.

The most effective treatments for depression

This section could take up the space of an entire book because there are many, many treatments for depression. Hence, I will only discuss the four most effective therapies that, in my opinion, have the strongest empirical support. One is pharmacological therapy, otherwise known as antidepressants. The other three are types of psychotherapy (or 'talk' therapy) – cognitive-behavioural therapy, interpersonal therapy, and marriage-and-family therapy. The current wisdom is that people with mild depression do very well with psychotherapy, but those with moderate or severe depression may significantly benefit from antidepressants.[13] Most, however, do best with a combination of medication and psychotherapy – the medication to provide swift relief from symptoms and the psychotherapy to teach skills so that the depressed person can independently solve her problems and manage her depressed feelings and thoughts. We'll begin with the best psychotherapies.

Cognitive-behavioural therapy

As mentioned earlier, Beck's cognitive theory of depression gave rise to this, the most widely used depression therapy. The focus here is on your *thoughts*. Cognitive-behavioural therapists assume that those who are prone to depression are overly negative in their perceptions of themselves, their worlds and their futures (that negative cognitive triad again) and that such people show distorted thinking. For example, a depressed person might come to the therapist's office and declare that she's a failure because it had rained at her son's swimming party the day before. The job of the therapist is to teach the depressed patient to recognize and dispute her negative beliefs and to replace them with more adaptive thoughts. So, the therapist might engage in a dialogue with the patient about the circumstances of the child's party until the patient realizes that her thinking has been irrational and unduly pessimistic. 'Homework' may be assigned between sessions to reinforce the therapist's instruction and guidance.

So that's the *cognitive* part. The *behavioural* part consists of teaching depressed patients skills that they might lack such as problem solving (i.e., teaching you how to define life problems and helping you to generate possible solutions to those problems and choose among them), self-control (i.e., teaching you to set weekly goals and then to monitor your behaviour and reward

yourself for meeting those goals), and so-called 'behavioural activation' (i.e., encouraging you to take action rather than avoiding
difficult situations). The main goal of behavioural therapy, however, is to engage depressed individuals in activities that they
enjoy and that afford them a sense of mastery. Not only will this
strategy increase positive emotions, but it will also distract the
depressed person from overthinking – or 'ruminating' about her
feelings and problems, which makes the depression even worse.[14]

Cognitive-behavioural therapy is relatively short-term, usually
lasting from four to fourteen sessions. However, treatment is
likely to be longer for those with an extensive history of rigid
dysfunctional thinking. Patients with long-standing and
entrenched maladaptive beliefs are taught to recognize that much
of their distress stems from these beliefs and not just from the negative life events that they've experienced. In other words, it may
not be the break-up six months ago that's making you depressed,
but your continued maladaptive ruminations about that break-up.

Is cognitive-behavioural therapy effective? The short answer is
yes. Indeed, this type of therapy has been one of the most exten-
sively tested of all depression treatments and has been shown to
be equally or more effective than other psychotherapies and
roughly comparable to medication.[15] Furthermore, those who
are treated with cognitive-behavioural therapy until the depression has lifted (i.e., until 'remission') are less likely to relapse or
to suffer from a future depressive episode.

Interpersonal therapy

If you're depressed, you are likely to have at least one interpersonal problem. For example, you may be grieving the loss of
someone close to you, dealing with a failing marriage or a stressful life transition, or suffering from a lack of assertiveness.
Although it's loosely based on Freudian psychoanalysis, interpersonal therapy uses an eclectic approach, borrowing the best
techniques from a handful of other therapies. For example, applying the assumptions of medical doctors, the depressed person is

defined in this therapy as having a medical illness, which is treatable and not the result of a personal defect or weakness. Furthermore, like marital therapists, interpersonal therapists help you work on and solve your relationship problems, instilling optimism in you that doing so will both improve your personal situation and relieve your depressive symptoms. Finally, like cognitive therapy, interpersonal therapy is focused on the 'here and now', and not on excavating the unconscious basis of depression in childhood.

This therapy takes three to four months. During the sessions, the focus is on addressing your recent and ongoing interpersonal events, whether those involve marital strife, a child's disability, or the loss of friendship, and the therapist's strategy depends somewhat on the type of event that's problematic. For example, if your greatest concern is conflict with your mother-in-law, the interpersonal therapist will talk with you about the disturbed relationship, the exact nature of the conflict, and what you want to do about it. The therapist will help you re-create your situation so that he or she can fully understand it. The therapist will then go over with you all the options that you have at your disposal to resolve the problem – options that the depression may have kept you from seeing or exploring fully. Together, you may engage in role playing at this point to rehearse possible strategies, such as what you would say when confronting your mother-in-law about a grievance.

Studies have shown that interpersonal therapy is very effective at alleviating depression. Its efficacy is close or equal to that of antidepressant medication and even superior to medication at improving social functioning.[16] If you feel this type of psychotherapy is a good fit for you, then it could be a vital treatment.

Marriage and family therapy

Like interpersonal therapists, marital and family therapists recognize that depressed individuals often have problems with family relationships. Indeed, if you are married and depressed, you are very likely to be experiencing distress in your marriage.[17] If you are depressed and have children in the home, you are probably experiencing difficulty in the area of parenting.[18] So, serious depression can cause pain and suffering not only in the ill person, but in his or her family. But is it the family problems that cause depression or vice versa? According to 'stress–generation theory',[19] whose logic guides most marital and family therapists, the causal arrow runs both ways. There are many ways that depressed individuals can create stress in their interpersonal relationships, and this interpersonal stress can make them even more depressed. For example, depressed women are more negative and pessimistic towards their partners, are more lax and inconsistent mothers, have more strained relationships with their teenage children and are more likely to withdraw during conflicts. All of these factors make it more likely that the depression exacerbates these women's family troubles. On the other hand, marital problems (such as an infidelity or the threat of divorce) and parenting problems (such as constant strife with kids) increase the risk of depression or aggravate the depression that's already present.[20] This vicious cycle – in which depression leads to problems, which lead to more depression and more problems – is where the marital and family therapist can intercede.

I will mention the two most common and successful interventions for the kinds of family troubles commonly experienced by depressed individuals. These are behavioural marital therapy for marital discord[21] and parent training for child management problems.[22]

Behavioural marital therapy is a relatively brief treatment in which the therapist meets regularly with the depressed person and his or her partner. In the first phase of treatment, the therapist tackles the biggest strains on the relationship and helps the couple have more positive interactions. For example, the couple may be given a homework assignment to figure out what activity they have enjoyed doing together in the past and then going ahead and doing it. When this phase is successful, the depressed person is already feeling brighter and both partners are expressing positive feelings towards each other. This boost serves as the foundation for the second phase, whose aim it is to restructure the relationship, for example, to improve the way that the couple communicates, handles problems, and interacts on a daily basis. Sometimes this is done by having the couple literally write a behavioural 'contract', agreeing to change aspects of their behaviour. When successful, this phase will leave the couple feeling more supportive and sensitive to one another's needs, more intimate, and better able to cope with future difficulties. Finally, in the third phase, the therapist helps the two partners prepare for stressful situations that might come to pass and encourages them to attribute their improvement in therapy to their love and caring for one another. Interestingly, behavioural marital therapy has been found to be at least as effective as individual therapy at lifting depression. However, it has the additional benefit of bolstering marital satisfaction. Indeed, a number of studies have shown that the boost in marital happiness (or favourable changes in the marriage related to that boost) is in fact the *reason* why the marital therapy works.[23]

Unfortunately, marital therapy suffers from a considerable obstacle – its success hinges on the depressed person's partner not undermining the whole process or refusing to participate altogether. This does happen occasionally (though less often than it did twenty-five years ago) because some people consider such therapy a stigma. An alternative is to consider parent training as a first step, as depressed individuals are likely to have difficulties in both the arenas of parenting and marriage. Relative to marital therapy, parent training is much more widely accepted, considered less embarrassing and doesn't require the participation of both parents. Different types of parent management training exist, but most teach parenting skills (e.g., the use of reinforcement and time-out with children), provide insight into how parents may be inadvertently reinforcing their children's problem behaviour (e.g., by giving attention to negative behaviour), model warmth and effective communication, and instil confidence in new and not-so-new parents alike. This type of intervention has been shown to alleviate child management problems *and* relieve depressive symptoms.[24]

Antidepressant medication

It would be difficult to find a person who's never heard of antidepressant medications. These drugs have been available to depressed individuals for almost fifty years. Prozac is undoubtedly the most well-known, but there are many other drugs, and they can be divided into several categories. The first category includes the most commonly used antidepressants, called SSRIs. These are the 'superstars' you've heard of, like Prozac, Zoloft (Sertraline), and Paxil (Seroxat). The second category are newer drugs that include Wellbutrin (bupropion) and Effexor (Efexor) The third and fourth categories are older antidepressants, which are still considered effective, but have more side effects. These comprise the 'tricyclics' (like Anafranil and Tofranil) and the 'MAO inhibitors' (like Nardil).

Our society has witnessed a massive growth in antidepressant prescriptions. In 2005, antidepressants were the third most commonly prescribed medications of any kind in the US.[25] Needless to say, the widespread use of these drugs has provoked many strong and polarized opinions. Some argue that everyone, even relatively happy people, should be taking Prozac, while others prophesy that its widespread use will deliver terrible ills. As always, however, there is a middle ground. The fact is that 60 to 70 per cent of depressed patients improve after using a single antidepressant,[26] although it usually takes three to six weeks for a full response.[27] If one drug doesn't appear to work, many depressed individuals ultimately find another one that does. On the other hand, a sizeable percentage of patients do not respond well to such medications or can't tolerate the side effects. It's important to find the treatment that's right for you. Someday, with the help of a new field called psycho-pharmacogenetics, we may be able to do this by matching the best-fitting drug to our unique genetic make-up.[28]

The choices of antidepressants are indeed overwhelming, but your GP or a psychiatrist can help navigate the boundless information and select the type and dosage of drug that is appropriate for each individual case.[29] Indeed, each class of antidepressants is unique, for example, particular drugs attack different brain chemicals (serotonin or noradrenaline or both), differ in their side effects, show different interactions with other medications that the patient might be taking and require different doses and schedules. For example, Prozac is taken once daily and the dosage needs to be adjusted only slightly during the course of treatment. This pill is believed to work by increasing the amount of serotonin in the patient's brain. Its side effects are minor, but include nausea, insomnia and nervousness at the beginning of treatment; sexual side effects may be problematic throughout treatment. Another downside is that Prozac can block the effectiveness or reduce the safety of other medications (e.g., drugs taken for heart disease, migraines or epilepsy) more so than do other antidepressants in its class (such as Zoloft [Sertraline]).

By contrast, the antidepressant Wellbutrin (buproprion) affects the depressed patient's levels of noradrenaline and dopamine (and *not* serotonin), so it's likely to be effective for a different sort of patient than is Prozac. Wellbutrin's most common side effects – insomnia, anxiety, tremor and headache – are also different from that of Prozac and, on the positive side, it has few sexual side effects. However, its drawbacks are that it needs to be taken up to three times daily, and it has a higher chance than other antidepressants of causing seizures. Fortunately, a newer cousin of Wellbutrin, called Zyban, has addressed some of these potential problems – Zyban doesn't carry an elevated risk for seizures and needs be taken only twice a day.

Effexor XR is yet another antidepressant which works biologically in a different way from all the other drugs in its class. Interestingly, it raises the patient's levels of serotonin when taken at low-to-moderate doses, and elevates noradrenaline at higher doses. Some studies show that, when it comes to more severely depressed patients, Effexor XR is more effective than any other drug of its kind.

The older classes of antidepressants are usually not used as first-line agents due to their higher rates of side effects and other complications. However, they may be tremendously valuable for certain types of depressed persons, especially when other drugs don't initially succeed at lifting their depression. So, in sum, there are many choices for pharmacological treatment of depression and the selection process is complex, especially for the roughly one-third of depressed people for whom the first drug tried (the 'first-line agent') is unsuccessful. The fact that many options exist, however, is good news, as doctors can try various approaches. The most obvious one is to switch to another antidepressant, but other options include increasing the dosage or the length of treatment, adding a second non-antidepressant drug and giving two antidepressants simultaneously.[30]

Patients are often curious about how long they need to stay on the medication and whether the depression will return once they stop. The usual recommendation is that antidepressants be taken from four to nine months (fortunately, they are not habit forming), at which point the medication will be tapered over a period of one to two months. If one's depression is severe and recurrent, runs in the family, and started before age twenty, many doctors recommend 'maintenance treatment', that is, to continue taking the medication even after the depression has fully lifted in order to prevent recurrence. Research confirms that this is indeed good advice. For example, in two studies, the vast majority of patients who continued taking the tricyclic Tofranil for five years after experiencing depression did not have a recurrence.[31] Even better news comes from studies showing that antidepressants lower the risk of future depressions even *after* they're discontinued.[32]

Despite the fact that antidepressants now help millions of people, misconceptions about such drugs are still widespread. Some claim, for example, that these drugs provide only 'artificial' relief. This is the notion that depressed people need to work out their problems and deal with their depression by themselves, without help from synthetic agents. A related assumption is that antidepressants prevent people from facing the true sources of their suffering and troubles. In response, I'd like to underscore that depression is an illness that needs treatment. Without treatment, the symptoms of depression can last for weeks, months or even years. People with depression cannot just 'snap out of it' or 'pull themselves together'. Hardly anyone would ever argue that people shouldn't take 'artificial drugs' for cardiovascular disease or cancer or rheumatoid arthritis. It's true that depression is different – it seems to be a disorder of emotion rather than an organ of the body, like the heart or kidney. But, in truth, depression is a disorder of the brain. When a drug begins to relieve the suffering of the depressed individual, only then can she begin to confront her pain.

Which treatments are debatable?

I want to mention two well-known treatments for depression that have been found to be much less effective that the ones I've already described. One is herbal therapy, the most common of which involves taking St John's wort, a fragrant plant draped in yellow flowers in summer. In Germany, this plant is used more for depression than conventional antidepressants and most of the research testing its effectiveness has been done there. This work shows that it can be effective, especially for short-term periods for mild depression.[33] However, flaws in the studies that have been done so far have prompted the US National Institutes of Health to conduct a much larger and well-controlled three-year study, and this study found that St John's wort was no more effective than a placebo at alleviating depression or at boosting overall functioning.[34] Because this herbal medicine can have dangerous interactions with other medications, and because its potency and preparation are not tightly regulated in the US, depressed people should be vigilant when using it as a treatment.

The other treatment that has had mixed results for depression is psychodynamic therapy, which includes traditional Freudian psychoanalysis. Psychodynamic therapists believe that a depressed person's current problems can be resolved successfully only with an intense self-exploration, the goal of which is to give the person a complete understanding of her conflicted feelings and the unconscious basis of her problems in early family relationships. This type of therapy is very intensive (involving fifty-minute sessions several times a week), lengthy (usually lasting several years) and quite expensive. Furthermore, it has been found to be useful only for people with mild depressive symptoms, or who have already improved with other treatments.[35]

What to do if you are depressed

Amazingly, despite the existence of several highly effective treatments for depression, very few depressed people actually partake of them. For example, in the United States, of those meeting criteria for major depression (that is, those with the most severe symptoms and disability) only 22 per cent of whites and 11 per cent of Mexican-Americans receive treatment.[36] The percentages are undoubtedly even lower for people whose symptoms are less severe. If you suffer from depression, I strongly encourage you to try one of the immensely effective treatments that exist. The first step towards getting treatment is to make an appointment with your GP. A full physical examination is necessary because many medications and illnesses (such as infections) can have symptoms that are very similar to depression and these need to be ruled out. If they *are* ruled out, then the doctor (or a psychiatrist or psychologist) will complete a psychological evaluation, asking you questions about the history of your symptoms, your family history, and possible substance use problems and suicidal thinking. Your speech, reasoning and memory may be tested as well, as sometimes these types of abilities are affected by depressive illness. If a diagnosis of depression is made, then you and your doctor will decide on the first-line treatment.

The cure for unhappiness is happiness

⁓

'The cure for unhappiness is happiness, I don't care what anyone says.'

ELIZABETH McCRACKEN

⁓

If you are deeply depressed, you may wonder and perhaps question how a book about how to become happier can help you. On the one hand, you would be right to be sceptical. Most people need to get a reprieve from the most troubling symptoms of their depression before they are able to muster the energy and motivation to embark on a happiness-increasing programme. On the other hand, as Seligman has demonstrated, even the most severely depressed individuals can improve by doing a simple daily happiness-increasing exercise. (His study essentially involved an optimism strategy – taking time to recall three things that went well each day.) Indeed, other studies from Seligman's laboratory are demonstrating parallel results.[37] For example, in one, researchers conducted a six-week course of group 'positive psychotherapy', meeting for two hours per week with eight to eleven depressed individuals at a time. Each week, the participants were prompted to do a different 'positive exercise', such as expressing gratitude, savouring or using their signature strengths. Compared to participants who hadn't received any treatment, the positive psychotherapy groups showed significant relief from their depressive symptoms over the course of the six-week therapy. Indeed, amazingly, their levels of happiness not only increased reliably throughout treatment, but continued rising long after the intervention was over, reaching an all-time high after one year. In a subsequent study, patients diagnosed with major depression participated in a ten- to twelve-week individual positive psychotherapy. Patients encouraged to focus on their strengths rather than on their pathologies experienced significantly greater relief from depression compared with those receiving 'treatment as usual' and even compared with those taking antidepressant medication.

The positive psychotherapy recently developed and applied by Seligman and his collaborators uses some happiness-enhancing strategies that are similar to those described in this book. In this way, their research bolsters our confidence in the value of doing happiness activities that bolster positive emotions, positive thoughts and positive experiences in order to begin to relieve mild, moderate and even severe depression. Although the activities illustrated in Part II are not designed to 'cure' depression, if you are depressed, trying one or more of these activities affords a strong chance of lightening the burden and darkness of depression and producing positive feelings.

Furthermore, you might consider trying one of several existing psychotherapies for depression that aim to increase well-being rather than only to relieve symptoms. These psychotherapies are relatively widely tested and established. For example, the goal of one such treatment, the short-term 'well-being therapy', is to improve patients' positive functioning – their sense of life purpose, positive relationships, self-acceptance, etc. – and to increase their experiences of mastery and pleasure. This therapy has been shown to be highly effective at reducing so-called 'residual symptoms' of people who've recovered from depression.[38] Other promising positive-focused therapies for depressive and other psychological disorders include 'Quality of Life Therapy',[39] hope therapy,[40] positive psychotherapy and personal growth therapy.[41]

Surmounting setbacks

A final point needs to be made. Most people experience at least one tragedy or major setback in their lives. Researchers have shown that people are remarkably resilient and, after an initial bout of misery, eventually return to their previous level of well-being.[42] However, while in the throes of their misfortune, some become depressed, insecure and unable to perceive a brighter future. This type of unhappiness is temporary or 'reactive', and the happiness exercises described in this book may be particularly helpful at alleviating it. Committed engagement to happiness activities can lift a person out of the rut, first to a neutral point and then onto higher ground.

During the 2004 US presidential campaign, vice-presidential candidate John Edwards revealed having endured the tragedy of losing his sixteen-year-old son, with whom he had been extremely close. After a period of depression and grief, he appeared to have come out of the experience a different person, with new priorities and goals: 'I have learned two great lessons,' Edwards wrote in his memoir, 'that there will always be heartache and struggle, and that people of strong will can make a difference. One is a sad lesson; the other is inspiring. I choose to be inspired.'[43] Out of depression, if we beat it, we can emerge stronger, happier, more engaged in life.

Additional happiness activities that may fit

The grid below summarizes which happiness-increasing strategies go together. Ideally, first try your four best-fitting happiness
activities established for you by the Person-Activity Fit Diagnostic
(see Chapter 3). After exhausting this list of four, use the grid
below to help you find additional helpful happiness activities.

If you benefit from this activity:

Expressing gratitude (Happiness Activity No. 1)

Cultivating optimism (Happiness Activity No. 2)

Avoiding overthinking and social comparison (Happiness Activity No. 3)

Practising acts of kindness (Happiness Activity No. 4)

Nurturing social relationships (Happiness Activity No. 5)

Developing strategies for coping (Happiness Activity No. 6)

Learning to forgive (Happiness Activity No. 7)

Increasing 'flow' experiences (Happiness Activity No. 8)

Savouring life's joys (Happiness Activity No. 9)

Committing to your goals (Happiness Activity No. 10)

Practising religion and spirituality (Happiness Activity No. 11)

Taking care of your body (Happiness Activity No. 12)

You may want to try this one:	Or this one:
Practising acts of kindness (Happiness Activity No. 4)	Learning to forgive (Happiness Activity No. 7)
Savouring life's joys (Happiness Activity No. 9)	Learning to forgive (Happiness Activity No. 7)
Developing strategies for coping (Happiness Activity No. 6)	Committing to your goals (Happiness Activity No. 10)
Savouring life's joys (Happiness Activity No. 9)	Increasing 'flow' experiences (Happiness Activity No. 8)
Practising acts of kindness (Happiness Activity No. 4)	Taking care of your body (Happiness Activity No. 12)
Committing to your goals (Happiness Activity No. 10)	Learning to forgive (Happiness Activity No. 7)
Developing strategies for coping (Happiness Activity No. 6)	Cultivating optimism (Happiness Activity No. 2)
Savouring life's joys (Happiness Activity No. 9)	Committing to your goals (Happiness Activity No. 10)
Increasing 'flow' experiences (Happiness Activity No. 8)	Committing to your goals (Happiness Activity No. 10)
Savouring life's joys (Happiness Activity No. 9)	Developing strategies for coping (Happiness Activity No. 6)
Taking care of your body (Happiness Activity No. 12)	Developing strategies for coping (Happiness Activity No. 6)
Committing to your goals (Happiness Activity No. 10)	Savouring life's joys (Happiness Activity No. 9)

Notes

INTRODUCTION

1 Lyubomirsky, S., King, L., and Diener, E. (2005), 'The benefits of frequent positive affect: Does happiness lead to success?' *Psychological Bulletin, 131*, 803–855.
2 Seligman, M. E. P., and Csikszentmihalyi, M. (2000), 'Positive psychology: An introduction', *American Psychologist, 55*, 5–14.
3 Ivins, M. (2000, September 22), 'The manufactured public schools crisis', *The Fort-Worth Star Telegram*.

CHAPTER 1

1 (1) Diener, E. (2000), 'Subjective well-being: The science of happiness and a proposal for a national index', *American Psychologist, 55*, 34–43. (2) Diener, E., Suh, E. K., Smith, H., and Shao, L. (1995), 'National differences in reported well-being: Why do they occur?' *Social Indicators Research, 34*, 7–32.
2 Keyes, C. L. M. (2005), 'Mental illness and/or mental health? Investigating axioms of the complete state model of health', *Journal of Consulting and Clinical Psychology, 73*, 539–548.
3 This study was conducted by Martin Seligman, Professor of Psychology at the University of Pennsylvania, and Jeff Levy. Seligman, M. E. P. (2002), *Authentic happiness*, New York: Free Press.
4 (1) Wilson, T. D., and Gilbert, D. T. (2005), 'Affective forecasting: Knowing what to want', *Current Directions in Psychological Science, 14*, 131–134. (2) Gilbert, T. D. (2006), *Stumbling on happiness*, New York: A. A. Knopf.
5 This quote is from Harvard University social psychologist Dan Gilbert. Goldberg, C. (2006, February 6), 'Too much of a good thing', *Boston Globe*, F1.
6 The stories of Neil (this chapter) and Judith (Chapter 2) (not their real names) are presented in the television documentary *In Pursuit of Happiness* (www.happycanadians.com), made by Canadian Television (CTV), with Sarah Spinks as producer, Jon Dore as host and myself as expert. It first aired on CTV on 17 June 2006.
7 Lyubomirsky, S., Sheldon, K. M., and Schkade, D. (2005), 'Pursuing

happiness: The architecture of sustainable change', *Review of General Psychology, 9*, 111–131.

8 (1) Lykken, D., and Tellegen, A. (1996), 'Happiness is a stochastic phenomenon', *Psychological Science, 7*, 186–189. (2) Tellegen, A., Lykken, D. T., Bouchard, T. J., Wilcox, K. J., Segal, N. L., and Rich, S. (1988), 'Personality similarity in twins reared apart and together', *Journal of Personality and Social Psychology, 54*, 1031–1039.

9 Stallone, D. D., and Stunkard, A. J. (1991), 'The regulation of body weight: Evidence and clinical implications', *Annals of Behavioral Medicine, 13*, 220–230.

10 Diener, E., Suh, E. M., Lucas, R. E., and Smith, H. L. (1999), 'Subjective well-being: Three decades of progress', *Psychological Bulletin, 125*, 276–302.

11 Diener, E., Horwitz, J., and Emmons, R. A. (1985), 'Happiness of the very wealthy', *Social Indicators Research, 16*, 263–274.

12 (1) Inglehart, R. (1990), *Culture shift in advanced industrial society*, Princeton, NJ: Princeton University Press. (2) DePaulo, B. M., and Morris, W. L. (2005), 'Singles in society and in science', *Psychological Inquiry, 16*, 57–83.

13 (1) Lyubomirsky, S. (2001), 'Why are some people happier than others?: The role of cognitive and motivational processes in well-being', *American Psychologist, 56*, 239–249. (2) Ibid, Diener et al. (1999). (3) Myers, D. G. (2000), 'The funds, friends, and faith of happy people', *American Psychologist, 55*, 56–67. (4) Diener, E., and Lucas, R. E. (1999), 'Personality and subjective well-being', in D. Kahneman, E. Diener, and N. Schwartz (Eds.), *Well-being: The foundations of hedonic psychology* (pp. 213–229). New York: Russell Sage. (5) Argyle, M. (1999), 'Causes and correlates of happiness', in D. Kahneman, E. Diener, and N. Schwarz (Eds.), *Well-being: The foundations of hedonic psychology* (pp. 353–373). New York: Russell Sage Foundation.

14 (1) Ibid, Lyubomirsky, Sheldon, et al. (2005), (2) Tkach, C. (2005), *Unlocking the treasury of human kindness: Enduring improvements in mood, happiness, and self-evaluations.* Unpublished doctoral dissertation, Department of Psychology, University of California, Riverside. (3) Lyubomirsky, S., Sousa, L., and Dickerhoof, R. (2006), 'The costs and benefits of writing, talking, and thinking about life's triumphs and defeats', *Journal of Personality and Social Psychology, 90*, 692–708. (4) Sheldon, K. M., and Lyubomirsky, S. (2006a), 'How to increase and sustain positive emotion: The effects of expressing gratitude and visualizing best possible selves', *Journal of Positive Psychology, 1*, 73–82. (5) Dickerhoof, R. (2007), *Expressing gratitude and optimism: A longitudinal investigation of cognitive activities to increase well-being.* Unpublished doctoral dissertation, Department of Psychology, University of California, Riverside. For interventions from other laboratories, see also (1) Seligman, M. E., Steen, T. A., Park, N., and Peterson, C. (2005),

'Positive psychology progress: Empirical validation of interventions', *American Psychologist, 60*, 410–421. (2) Fordyce, M. W. (1977), 'Development of a program to increase happiness', *Journal of Counseling Psychology, 24*, 511–521. (3) Fordyce, M. W. (1983), 'A program to increase happiness: Further studies', *Journal of Counseling Psychology, 30*, 483–498.

15 Ibid, Lyubomirsky, King, et al. (2005).

16 Diener, E., Nickerson, C., Lucas, R. E., and Sandvik, E. (2002), 'Dispositional affect and job outcomes', *Social Indicators Research, 59*, 229–259.

17 Harker, L., and Keltner, D. (2001), 'Expressions of positive emotions in women's college yearbook pictures and their relationship to personality and life outcomes across adulthood', *Journal of Personality and Social Psychology, 80*, 112–124.

CHAPTER 2

1 Names, identifying information and details about interviews have been changed for some of the examples offered in this book.

2 Ed Diener, the most distinguished and most widely published researcher in the field of subjective well-being, told me once that he coined the term 'subjective well-being' because he didn't think he would be promoted with tenure if his research was perceived as focusing on something so fuzzy and soft as 'happiness'. The label caught on.

3 However, it's worth noting that 'well-being' is a broader, more holistic construct than happiness, encompassing people's physical and mental health, in addition to their emotional well-being.

4 Lyubomirsky, S., and Lepper, H. S. (1999), 'A measure of subjective happiness: Preliminary reliability and construct validation', *Social Indicators Research, 46*, 137–155.

5 Ibid, Lyubomirsky and Lepper (1999).

6 Radloff, L. (1977), 'The CES-D Scale: A self-report depression scale for research in the general population', *Applied Psychological Measurement, 1*, 385–401.

7 Nezu, A. M., Nezu, C. M., McClure, K. S., and Zwick, M. L. (2002), 'Assessment of depression', in I. H. Gotlib and C. L. Hammen (Eds.), *Handbook of depression* (pp. 61–85), New York: Guilford.

8 (1) Chwastiak, L., Ehde, D. M., Gibbons, L. E., Sullivan, M., Bowen, J. D., and Kraft, G. H. (2002), 'Depressive symptoms and severity of illness in multiple sclerosis: Epidemiologic study of a large community sample', *The American Journal of Psychiatry, 159*, 1862–1868. (2) Unützer, J., Patrick, D. L., Marmon, T., Simon, G. E., and Katon, W. J. (2002), 'Depressive symptoms and mortality in a prospective study of 2,558 older adults', *American Journal of Geriatric Psychiatry, 10*, 521–530.

9 Burt, V. K., and Stein, K. (2002), 'Epidemiology of depression:

Throughout the female life cycle', *Journal of Clinical Psychiatry, 63*, 9–15.

10 Kessler, R. C., McGonagle, K. A., Zhao, S., Nelson, C. B., Hughes, M., Eshlman, S., Wittchen, H. U., and Kendler, K. S. (1994), 'Lifetime and 12-month prevalence rates of DSM-III-R psychiatric disorders in the United States: Results from the National Comorbidity Survey', *Archives of General Psychiatry, 51*, 8–19. (UK statistic from http://www.patient.co.uk/showdoc/23068720)

11 Klerman, G. L. (1988), 'The current age of youthful melancholia: Evidence for increase in depression among adolescents and young adults', *British Journal of Psychiatry, 152*, 4–14.

12 Üstün, T. B., Ayuso-Mateos, J. L., Chatterji, S., Mathers, C., and Murray, C. J. L. (2004), 'Global burden of depressive disorders in the year 2000', *British Journal of Psychiatry, 184*, 386–392. Disease burden is measured by the World Health Organization via the number of disability adjusted life years. In Africa, the share of disease burden for unipolar depressive disorders is 1.2 per cent; in the Americas, they are the leading cause, representing 8 per cent of the total burden. The ranking of depression as a disease burden is thirteenth in Africa, fifth in the Eastern Mediterranean region, fourth in South East Asia, first in the Americas, third in Europe, and second in the Western Pacific.

13 Murray, J. L., and Lopez, A. D. (1996), 'The global burden of disease: A comprehensive assessment of mortality and disability from diseases, injuries and risk factors in 1990 and projected to 2020', Summary. Boston: Harvard School of Public Health: *World Health Organization.*

14 (1) Schwartz, B. (2000), 'Pitfalls on the road to a positive psychology of hope', in Schwartz, B., and Gillham, J. (Eds.), *The science of optimism and hope: Research essays in honor of Martin E. P. Seligman* (pp. 399–412), Philadelphia, PA: Templeton Foundation Press. (2) O'Connor, R. (1999), *Undoing depression*, New York: Berkley. (3) Machoian, L. (2005), *The disappearing girl: Learning the language of teenage depression*, New York: Dutton. (4) Charney, D. S. and Nemeroff, C. B. (2004), *The peace of mind prescription: An authoritative guide to finding the most effective treatment for anxiety and depression*, New York: Houghton Mifflin. (5) Seligman, M. E. P. (1990), 'Why is there so much depression today? The waxing of the individual and the waning of the commons', in Ingram, R. (Ed.), *Contemporary psychological approaches to depression: Theory, research, and treatment* (pp. 1–9), New York: Plenum.

15 (1) Klerman, G. L., and Weissman, M. M. (1989), 'Increasing rates of depression', *Journal of the American Medical Association, 261*, 2229–2235. (2) Lavori, P. W., Warshaw, M., Klerman, G. L., Mueller, T. I., Leon, A., Rice, J., and Akiskal, H. (1993), 'Secular trends in lifetime onset of MDD stratified by selected sociodemographic risk factors', *Journal of Psychiatric Research, 27*, 95–109. (3) Lavori, P. W., Klerman, G. L., Keller, M. B., Reich, T., Rice, J., and Endicott, J.

(1987), 'Age-period-cohort analysis of secular trends in onset of major depression: Findings in siblings of patients with major affective disorder', *Journal of Psychiatric Research, 21*, 23–35.

16 Weber, R. (1991, June 3), 'I can't wait to grow up and be happy', *New Yorker*.

17 Ibid, Diener et al. (1999).

18 In 2005, the national median household income for a family of four was 46,326 dollars. DeNavas-Walt, C., Proctor, B. D., and Lee, C. H. (August, 2005), 'U.S. Census Bureau, Current Population Reports', P60–231, *Income, poverty, and health insurance coverage in the United States: 2005*, Washington DC: US Government Printing Office.

19 Paul Bellew, executive director for market and industry analysis at General Motors, quoted in Scott, J., and Leonhardt, D. (2005, May 15), 'Class in America: Shadowy lines that still divide', *New York Times*.

20 Goodwin, D. K. (1994), *No Ordinary Time*, New York: Touchstone, pp. 42–43.

21 Lane, R. E. (2000), *The loss of happiness in market democracies*, New Haven, CT: Yale University Press. See Figure 1.1, p. 5.

22 Ibid, Lane (2000).

23 It's worth noting that people whose basic needs *aren't* being met – needs for such requisites as safety, food and shelter – report being very unhappy. For this group, more money (for medical care, nutrition, toys for their children, etc.) does indeed make a substantial difference to their well-being and quality of life. So, the small correlation between happiness and wealth holds only for individuals above the 'basic needs', or poverty threshold. For example, see Biswas-Diener, R., and Diener, E. (2001), 'Making the best of a bad situation: Satisfaction in the slums of Calcutta', *Social Indicators Research, 55*, 329–352.

24 Lopez, S. (2004, May 26), 'Neighbors' ire equals scale of Ovitz plan', *Los Angeles Times*, B1.

25 *The Sun*, August, 2002.

26 Nickerson, C., Schwarz, N., Diener, E., and Kahneman, D. (2003), 'Zeroing on the dark side of the American Dream: A closer look at the negative consequences of the goal for financial success', *Psychological Science, 14*, 531–536.

27 Cohen, P., and Cohen, J. (1996), *Life values and adolescent mental health*, Mahwah, NJ: Erlbaum.

28 Sheldon, K. M., and Kasser, T. (1998), 'Pursuing personal goals: Skills enable progress, but not all progress is beneficial', *Personality and Social Psychology Bulletin, 24*, 1319–1331.

29 Richins, M. L. (1995), 'Social comparison, advertising, and consumer discontent', *American Behavioral Scientist, 38*, 593–607.

30 Campbell, A. (1981), *The sense of well-being in America*, New York: McGraw-Hill.

31 Pryor, J. H., Hurtado, S., Saenz, V. B., Lindholm, J. A., Korn, W. S., and Mahoney, K. M. (2006), 'The American Freshman – National

Norms for Fall 2005', Working paper, Higher Education Research Institute.

32 (1) 'Rich think big about living well' (1987, September 24), *Chicago Tribune*, 3. (2) 'Pay nags at workers' job views' (1987, October 18), *Chicago Tribune*, 10B.

33 Kristof, K. M. (2005, January 14), 'Study: Money can't buy happiness, security either', *Los Angeles Times*, C1.

34 Kahneman, D., Krueger, A. B., Schkade, D., Schwarz, N., and Stone, A. A. (2006), 'Would you be happier if you were richer? A focusing illusion', *Science, 312*, 1908–1910.

35 The quote is attributed to Warren Buffett. O'Brien, T. L. (2006, September 17), 'Fortune's fools: Why the rich go broke', *New York Times*.

36 American Society for Aesthetic Plastic Surgery (2004), *Cosmetic surgery Quick facts: 2004 ASAPS statistics*. Retrieved November 16, 2005 from the World Wide Web: http://www.surgery.org/press/statistics-2004.php ('Britons spend more on plastic surgery than tea ...' Retrieved from the World Wide Web: http://www.nortonfinance.co.uk/news/Britons-spend-more-on-plastic-surgery-than-tea)

37 (1) Wengle, H. (1986), 'The psychology of cosmetic surgery: A critical overview of the literature 1960–1982. Part I', *Annals of Plastic Surgery, 16*, 435–443. (2) Young, V. L., Nemecek, J. R., and Nemecek, D. A. (1994), 'The efficacy of breast augmentation: Breast size increase, patient satisfaction, and psychological effects', *Plastic and Reconstructive Surgery, 94*, 958–969. Indeed, women with cosmetic breast implants have been reported to have an increased risk of death from suicide. For example, see McLaughlin, J. K., Wise, T. N., and Lipworth, L. (2004), 'Increased risk of suicide among patients with breast implants: Do the epidemiologic data support psychiatric consultation', *Psychosomatics, 45*, 277–280.

38 Schkade, D. A., and Kahneman, D. (1998), 'Does living in California make people happy? A focusing illusion in judgments of life satisfaction', *Psychological Science, 9*, 340–346..

39 Diener, E., Wolsic, B., and Fujita, F. (1995), 'Physical attractiveness and subjective well-being', *Journal of Personality and Social Psychology, 69*, 120–129.

40 (1) Argyle, M. (1999), 'Causes and correlates of happiness', in D. Kahneman, E. Diener, and N. Schwarz (Eds.), *Well-being: The foundations of hedonic psychology* (pp. 353–375), New York: Russell Sage Foundation. (2) Campbell, A., Converse, P. E., and Rodgers, W. L. (1976), *The quality of American life*, New York: Russell Sage Foundation. (3) Lyubomirsky, S., and Tucker, K. L. (1998), 'Implications of individual differences in self-reported happiness for perceiving, thinking about, and recalling life events', *Motivation and Emotion, 22*, 155–186.

41 Frederick, S., and Loewenstein, G. (1999), 'Hedonic adaptation', in D.

Kahneman, E. Diener, and N. Schwarz (Eds.), *Well-being: The founda-tions of hedonic psychology* (pp. 302–329), New York: Russell Sage Foundation.

42 Ibid, Lyubomirsky, King, et al. (2005).

43 Lucas, R. E., Clark, A. E., Georgellis, Y., and Diener, E. (2003), 'Reexamining adaptation and the set point model of happiness: Reactions to changes in marital status', *Journal of Personality and Social Psychology, 84*, 527–539.

44 Brickman, P., Coates, D., and Janoff-Bulman, R. (1978), 'Lottery win-ners and accident victims: Is happiness relative?' *Journal of Personality and Social Psychology, 36*, 917–927.

45 Riis, J., Loewenstein, G., Baron, J., Jepson, C., Fagerlin, A., and Ubel, P. A. (2005), 'Ignorance of hedonic adaptation to hemodialysis: A study using ecological momentary assessment', *Journal of Experimental Psychology: General, 134*, 3–9.

46 Schneider, C. E. (1998), *The practice of autonomy*, New York: Oxford University Press, p. 71.

47 Lykken, D., and Tellegen, A. (1996), 'Happiness is a stochastic phe-nomenon', *Psychological Science, 7*, 186–189.

48 To protect confidentiality, names and identifying information about participants of research studies have been changed here and through-out the book.

49 Thomas Bouchard compiled and analysed this fascinating sample.

50 Segal, N. (2000), *Entwined lives*, New York: Plume.

51 Headey, B., and Wearing, A. (1989), 'Personality, life events, and sub-jective well-being: Toward a dynamic equilibrium model', *Journal of Personality and Social Psychology, 57*, 731–739.

52 Suh, E. M., Diener, E., and Fujita, F. (1996), 'Events and subjective well-being: Only recent events matter', *Journal of Personality and Social Psychology, 70*, 1091–1102.

53 Bilger, B. (2004, April 5), 'The height gap: Why Europeans are get-ting taller and taller – and Americans aren't', *New Yorker*.

54 Sternberg, R. J., Grigorenko, E. L., and Kidd, K. K. (2005), 'Intelligence, race, and genetics', *American Psychologist, 60*, 46–59.

55 Caspi, A., Sugden, K., Moffitt, T. E., Taylor, A., Craig, I. W., Harrington, H. L., McClay, J., Mill, J., Martin, J., Braithwaite, A., and Poulton, R. (2003), 'Influence of life stress on depression: Moderation by a polymorphism in the 5–HTT gene', *Science, 301*, 386–389.

56 For every single gene, each person has two alleles – one from the mother and one from the father. The short allele of the 5-HTTLPR gene decreases the brain supply of the neurotransmitter serotonin, a brain chemical that is needed to mitigate depression. Indeed, drugs like Prozac are called selective serotonin reuptake inhibitors (SSRIs) because they increase levels of serotonin and thereby lift depressive symptoms.

57 Taylor, S. E., Way, B. M., Welch, W. T., Hilmert, C. J., Lehman, B. J.,

and Eisenberger, N. I. (2006), 'Early family environment, current adversity, the serotonin transporter promoter polymorphism, and depressive symptomatology', *Biological Psychiatry, 60*, 671–676.

58 A typical participant in Davidson's experiments is outfitted with electrodes – metal conductors about the size of a dime – that envelop his head, looking like a great big shower cap. The electrodes are attached to wire leads and an electric current runs through those leads from the participant's scalp to Davidson's measuring instruments. The current comes from biological electrical signals, called biopotentials.

59 (1) Tomarken, A. J., Davidson, R. J., Wheeler, R. E., and Doss, R. C. (1992), 'Individual differences in anterior brain asymmetry and fundamental dimensions of emotion', *Journal of Personality and Social Psychology, 62*, 676–687. (2) Urry, H. L., Nitschke, J. B., Dolski, I., Jackson, D. C., Dalton, K. M., Mueller, C. J., Rosenkranz, M. A., Ryff, C. D., Singer, B. H., and Davidson, R. J. (2004), 'Making a life worth living: Neural correlates of well-being', *Psychological Science, 15*, 367–372. However, see also van Honk, J., and Schutter, D. J. L. G. (2006), 'From affective valence to motivational direction: The frontal asymmetry of emotion revised', *Psychological Science, 17*, 963–965.

60 This remark was made by Nobel Prize winner and Princeton University professor Daniel Kahneman.

61 Mroczek, D. K., and Spiro, A., III. (2005), 'Change in life satisfaction during adulthood: Findings from the Veterans Affairs Normative Aging Study', *Journal of Personality and Social Psychology, 88*, 189–202.

62 Nolen-Hoeksema, S. (2005), *Eating, drinking, overthinking: The toxic triangle of food, alcohol, and depression – and how women can break free*, New York: Henry Holt.

63 This quote is from Benjamin Disraeli. Disraeli, B. (2000), *Lothair* (Vol. III), Cambridge, England: Chadwyck-Healey Ltd., p. 206.

CHAPTER 3

1 (1) Harackiewicz, J. M., and Sansone, C. (1991), 'Goals and intrinsic motivation: You can get there from here', in M. L. Maehr and P. R. Pintrich (Eds.), *Advances in motivation and achievement* (Vol. 7, pp. 21–49), Greenwich, CT: JAI Press. (2) Brunstein, J. C., Schultheiss, O. C., and Grässman, R. (1998), 'Personal goals and emotional well-being: The moderating role of motive dispositions', *Journal of Personality and Social Psychology, 75*, 494–508. (3) Diener, E., and Fujita, F. (1995), Resources, personal strivings, and subjective well-being: A nomothetic and idiographic approach, *Journal of Personality and Social Psychology, 68*, 926–935. (4) Higgins, E. T., (2005), 'Value from regulatory fit', *Current Directions in Psychological Science, 14*, 209–213. (5) Brandstätter, H. (1994), 'Well-being and motivated person-environment fit: A time-sampling study of emotions', *European Journal of Personality, 8*, 75–93. (6) Pervin, L. A. (1968), 'Performance

and satisfaction as a function of individual-environment fit',
Psychological Bulletin, 69, 56–68.

2 With the exception of the 'natural' item, the measure of self-concordant
motivation presented here was based on a methodology developed by
Ken Sheldon and his colleagues. The four reasons to engage in a
happiness activity tap four different kinds of motivation: 1) intrinsic
motivation (assessed by the item 'enjoy', though the item 'natural' is
closely related), defined as doing something because it is inherently
interesting and enjoyable; 2) identified motivation ('value'), defined as
doing something in order to express important values and beliefs; 3)
introjected motivation ('guilty'), defined as acting to avoid guilt or
anxiety; and 4) external motivation ('situation'), defined as doing
something for a reward or to please others. According to Ed Deci and
Rich Ryan, these four motivations lie along a continuum, from internal (or autonomous) to external (or controlled by others). Hence, an
aggregate self-concordant motivation score is computed by averaging
the identified and intrinsic ratings and subtracting the external and
introjected ratings. This score assesses the extent to which a person's
behaviour is inspired by his or her lifelong interests and deeply held
values. The greater the self-concordant motivation for a particular goal
(whether that goal is to become thinner, more productive or more
optimistic), the healthier, happier and more successful is the person in
attaining that goal. Relevant reading: (1) Deci, E. L., and Ryan, R. M.
(2000), 'The "what" and "why" of goal pursuits: Human needs and
the self-determination of behavior', *Psychological Inquiry, 4*, 227–268.
(2) Sheldon, K. M., and Elliot, A. J. (1999), 'Goal striving, need-
satisfaction, and longitudinal wellbeing: The Self-Concordance Model',
Journal of Personality and Social Psychology, 76, 482–497. (3) Sheldon, K.
M., and Kasser, T. (1995), 'Coherence and congruence: Two aspects of
personality integration', *Journal of Personality and Social Psychology, 68*,
531–543.

3 (1) Sheldon, K. M., and Houser-Marko, L. (2001), 'Self-concordance,
goal-attainment, and the pursuit of happiness: Can there be an upward
spiral?' *Journal of Personality and Social Psychology, 80*, 152–165. (2) Ibid,
Sheldon and Kasser (1998). (3) Ibid, Sheldon and Lyubomirsky
(2006a).

4 Ibid, Dickerhoof (2007).

5 For corroborating results with respect to the importance of fit in
increasing well-being, see (1) Ibid, Fordyce (1977, 1983). (2) Ibid,
Sheldon and Lyubomirsky (2006a).

6 Klem, M. L., Wing, R. R., McGuire, M. T., Seagle, H. M., and Hill,
J. O. (1997), 'A descriptive study of individuals successful at long-term
maintenance of substantial weight loss', *American Journal of Clinical
Nutrition, 66*, 239–246.

7 Ibid, Dickerhoof (2007).

INTRODUCTION TO PART II

1 The Oxford Happiness Inventory has been widely used in many nations, especially in Europe. Reference: Argyle, M., Martin, M., and Crossland, J. (1989), 'Happiness as a function of personality and social encounters', in J. P. Forgas and J. M. Innes (Eds.), *Recent advances in social psychology: An international perspective* (pp. 189–203), Amsterdam: Elsevier Science Publishers.

2 It's worth noting that I have modified the original version of this questionnaire by eliminating response options that seemed to me wouldn't be endorsed by any sane person (e.g., 'I am completely satisfied with everything in my life', 'I can make all decisions very easily', and 'I love everybody'). I have also slightly altered the wording of a few items to enhance clarity.

CHAPTER 4

1 Emmons, R. A., and Shelton, C. M. (2002), 'Gratitude and the science of positive psychology', in C. R. Snyder and S. J. Lopez (Eds.), *Handbook of positive psychology* (pp. 459–471), Oxford: Oxford University Press.

2 (1) McCullough, M. E., Emmons, R. A., and Tsang, J. (2002), 'The grateful disposition: A conceptual and empirical topography', *Journal of Personality and Social Psychology, 82*, 112–127. (2) McCullough, M. E., Tsang, J., and Emmons, R. A. (2004), 'Gratitude in intermediate affective terrain: Links of grateful moods to individual differences and daily emotional experience', *Journal of Personality and Social Psychology, 86*, 295–309. (3) Algoe, S., and Haidt, J. (2006), *Witnessing excellence in action: The 'other-praising' emotions of elevation, gratitude, and admiration.* Manuscript submitted for publication. (4) Bartlett, M. Y., and DeSteno, D. (2006), 'Gratitude: Helping when it really costs you', *Psychological Science*, 17, 319–325. (5) For an accessible review, see Robert Emmons' recent book: Emmons, R. A. (2007), *THANKS! How the New Science of Gratitude Can Make You Happier*, New York: Houghton Mifflin Company.

3 Emmons, R. A., and McCullough, M. E. (2003), 'Counting blessings versus burdens: An experimental investigation of gratitude and subjective well-being in daily life', *Journal of Personality and Social Psychology, 84*, 377–389.

4 Ibid, Emmons (2007).

5 Fredrickson, B. L., Tugade, M. M., Waugh, C. E., and Larkin, G. R. (2003), 'What good are positive emotions in crises?: A prospective study of resilience and emotions following the terrorist attacks on the United States on September 11, 2001', *Journal of Personality and Social Psychology, 84*, 365–376.

6 Watkins, P. C., Grimm, D. L., and Kolts, R. (2004), 'Counting your blessings: Positive memories among grateful persons', *Current Psychology: Developmental, Learning, Personality, Social, 23*, 52–67.

7 Ibid, Fredrickson et al. (2003).

8 Malin, A. (2003, September), 'Maximum joy: 14 ways to feel lucky you're alive', *Prevention*.

9 Casey, M. J. (2006, October 20), 'A survivor's optimism', *New York Times*.

10 Bartlett, M. Y., and DeSteno, D. (2006), 'Gratitude and prosocial behavior: Helping when it costs you', *Psychological Science, 17*, 319–325.

11 (1) Ibid, McCullough et al. (2001). (2) Ibid, Emmons and McCullough (2003).

12 Algoe, S. B., Haidt, J., Gable, S. L., and Strachman, A. (2007), *Beyond reciprocity: Gratitude and relationships in everyday life*. Manuscript submitted for publication.

13 Ibid, Lyubomirsky, King, et al. (2005).

14 Ibid, McCullough et al. (2002).

15 Quote from psychiatrist Roger Walsh.

16 See the 'What I Know To Be True' exercise in MacDonald, L. (2004), *Learn to be an optimist*, San Francisco, CA: Chronicle Books.

17 Miller, T. (1995), *How to want what you have*, New York: Avon.

18 Ibid, Tkach (2005).

19 Seligman, M. E., Steen, T. A., Park, N., and Peterson, C. (2005), 'Positive psychology progress: Empirical validation of interventions', *American Psychologist, 60*, 410–421.

20 Ibid, Dickerhoof (2007).

21 This distinction comes from the most thoughtful paper on optimism that I've ever read: Peterson, C. (2000), 'The future of optimism', *American Psychologist, 55*, 44–55.

22 Franken, A. (1992), *I'm good enough, I'm smart enough, and doggone it, people like me!: Daily affirmations by Stuart Smalley*, New York: Dell. Personal disclosure: I love Al Franken.

23 (1) Tiger, L. (1979), *Optimism: The biology of hope*, New York: Simon and Schuster. (2) Scheier, M. F., and Carver, C. S. (1993), 'On the power of positive thinking: The benefits of being optimistic', *Current Directions in Psychological Science, 2*, 26–30.

24 Ibid, Scheier and Carver (1993).

25 (1) Abramson, L. Y., Seligman, M. E. P., and Teasdale, J. D. (1978), 'Learned helplessness in humans: Critique and reformulation', *Journal of Abnormal Psychology, 87*, 49–74. (2) Peterson, C. (1991), 'Meaning and measurement of explanatory style', *Psychological Inquiry, 2*, 1–10.

26 Snyder, C. R. (1994), *The psychology of hope: You can get there from here*, New York: Free Press.

27 King, L. A. (2001), 'The health benefits of writing about life goals', *Personality and Social Psychology Bulletin, 27*, 798–807.

28 Ibid, Sheldon and Lyubomirsky (2006a).

29 For the benefits of writing, see (1) Pennebaker, J. W., and Graybeal, A. (2001), 'Patterns of natural language use: Disclosure, personality, and social integration', *Current Directions in Psychological Science, 10*, 90–93.

(2) Singer, J. A. (2004), 'Narrative identity and meaning making across the adult lifespan: An introduction', *Journal of Personality, 72*, 437–459.

30 Segerstrom, S. C. (2001), 'Optimism, goal conflict, and stressor-related immune change', *Journal of Behavioral Medicine, 24*, 441–467.

31 Snyder, C. R., Harris, C., Anderson, J. R., Holleran, S. A., Irving, L. M., Sigmon, S. T., Yoshinobu, L., Gibb, J., Langelle, C., and Harney, P. (1991), 'The will and the ways: Development and validation of an individual-differences measure of hope', *Journal of Personality and Social Psychology, 60*, 570–585.

32 (1) Scheier, M. F., Weintraub, J. K., and Carver, C. S. (1986), 'Coping with stress: Divergent strategies of optimists and pessimists', *Journal of Personality and Social Psychology, 51*, 1257–1264. (2) Nes, L. S., and Segerstrom, S. C. (2006), 'Dispositional optimism and coping: A meta-analytic review', *Personality and Social Psychology Review, 10*, 235–251.

33 Ibid, Scheier and Carver (1993).

34 Helweg-Larsen, M., Sadeghian, P., and Webb, M. A. (2002), 'The stigma of being pessimistically biased', *Journal of Social and Clinical Psychology, 21*, 92–107.

35 This general suggestion about how to develop hope – and analysis of 'barrier hopes' – has been made by the late psychologist C.R. Snyder.

36 See the 'Look for the Silver Lining' exercise in MacDonald (2004).

37 Gillham, J. E., and Reivich, K. J. (1999), 'Prevention of depressive symptoms in school children: A research update', *Psychological Science, 10*, 461–462.

38 This technique is called ABCDE disputation, described in greater detail in Chapter 8. A = adversity (the issue that you face). B = belief (the negative belief engendered by the adversity. C = consequence (how you feel in response to the adversity). D = disputation (challenging the negative belief). E = Energize (note how more optimistic explanations can give you more energy and make you feel better). References: Seligman's (1991) *Learned Optimism* and (2002) *Authentic Happiness*.

39 Aspinwall, L. G., and Brunhart, S. M. (1996), 'Distinguishing optimism from denial: Optimistic beliefs predict attention to health threats', *Personality and Social Psychology Bulletin, 22*, 993–1003.

40 Seligman, M. (1998), *Learned optimism*, (p. 292) New York: Free Press.

41 For reviews, see (1) Lyubomirsky, S., and Tkach, C. (2003), 'The consequences of dysphoric rumination', in C. Papageorgiou and A. Wells (Eds.), *Rumination: Nature, theory, and treatment of negative thinking in depression* (pp. 21–41), Chichester, England: John Wiley and Sons. (2) Nolen-Hoeksema, S. (2003), *Women who think too much*, New York: Henry Holt.

42 Lyubomirsky, S., Dickerhoof, R., Kasri, F., and Zehm, K. (2007), *The cognitive and hedonic costs of excessive self-reflection*. Manuscript submitted for publication.

43 Ibid, Lyubomirsky et al. (2007). See also Lyubomirsky, S., Kasri, F., and

Zehm, K. (2003), 'Dysphoric rumination impairs concentration on academic tasks', *Cognitive Therapy and Research, 27*, 309–330.

44 (1) Festinger, L. (1954), 'A theory of social comparison processes', *Human Relations, 7*, 114–140. (2) Taylor, S.E., and Lobel, M. (1989), 'Social comparison activity under threat: Downward evaluation and upward contacts', *Psychological Review, 96*, 569–575. (3) Major, B., Testa, M., and Bylsma, W.H. (1991), 'Responses to upward and downward social comparisons: The impact of esteem-relevance and perceived control', in J. Suls, and T.A. Wills, *Social comparison: Contemporary theory and research* (pp. 237–260), Hillsdale, NJ: Erlbaum. (4) Affleck, G., and Tennen, H. (1991), 'Social comparison and coping with major medical problems', in J. Suls and T. A. Wills (Eds.), *Social comparison: Contemporary theory and research* (pp. 369–393), Hillsdale, NJ: Erlbaum.

45 Lyubomirsky, S., and Ross, L. (1997), 'Hedonic consequences of social comparison: A contrast of happy and unhappy people', *Journal of Personality and Social Psychology, 73*, 1141–1157.

46 Unscrambled, they are *basis, snowy* and *toxin*.

47 Ibid, Nolen-Hoeksema (2003).

48 Fredrickson, B. L. (2001), 'The role of positive emotions in positive psychology: The broaden-and-build theory of positive emotions', *American Psychologist, 56*, 218–226.

49 Carlson, R. (1997), *Don't Sweat the Small Stuff – and it's all small stuff*, New York: Hyperion.

50 Tedeschi, R. G., Park, C. L., and Calhoun, L. G. (Eds.) (1998), *Posttraumatic growth: Positive changes in the aftermath of crisis*, Mahwah, NJ: Erlbaum.

CHAPTER 5

1 Berscheid, E. (2003), 'The human's greatest strength: Other humans', in L. G. Aspinwall and U. M. Staudinger (Eds.), *A psychology of human strengths: Fundamental questions and future directions for a positive psychology* (pp. 37–47), Washington, DC: American Psychological Association. The quote appears on p. 39.

2 Ibid, Lyubomirsky, King, et al. (2005).

3 For review, see Lyubomirsky, King, et al. (2005).

4 This study is described in Lyubomirsky, Sheldon, et al. (2005).

5 Ibid, Tkach (2005).

6 All the studies conducted in my laboratory (and described in this book) include at least one control group. The control group in this particular study were participants who didn't perform any extra acts of kindness but were instructed simply to list various events that happened to them weekly.

7 Williamson, G. M., and Clark, M. S. (1989), 'Providing help and desired relationship type as determinants of changes in moods and self-evaluations', *Journal of Personality and Social Psychology, 56*, 722–734.

8 In M. C. Clark (Ed.), *Prosocial behavior: Review of personality and social psychology* (Vol. 12, pp. 238–264), Newbury Park, CA: Sage.

9 Trivers, R. (1971), 'The evolution of reciprocal altruism', *Quarterly Review of Biology, 46*, 35–57.

10 For a review of the literature on volunteering and well-being, see Piliavin, J. A. (2003), 'Doing well by doing good: Benefits for the benefactor', in C. L. M. Keyes, and J. Haidt (Eds.), *Flourishing: Positive psychology and the life well-lived* (pp. 227–247), Washington DC: APA.

11 Schwartz, C. E., and Sendor, M. (1999), 'Helping others helps oneself: Response shift effects in peer support', *Social Science and Medicine, 48*, 1563–1575.

12 Unfortunately, five participants is too few a number ('too small a sample size', in scientific terms) to allow researchers to generalize their findings to the community at large. In all of the studies that I have done with my students and collaborators – and, indeed, in almost all of the research cited in this book – the sample sizes have been large enough to permit such generalization and large enough to permit comparisons across groups (e.g., to answer such questions as 'Is the kindness group happier than the control group?') and across time (e.g., 'Is the kindness group happier in May than it was in January?').

13 Here's a sampling: (1) Pay the toll of the car behind you or put change into an expired parking meter; (2) Pick up litter in your neighbourhood, beach or park; (3) Paint a neighbour's home; (4) Volunteer at a soup kitchen, homeless shelter or church/temple/mosque; (5) Teach an illiterate adult to read; (6) Cook a special meal for a busy family member, neighbour or friend; (7) Spend time with an elderly relative or neighbour, or visit a nursing home; (8) Give up your seat on the bus or train; (9) Do a household chore, even when it's not your turn; (10) Rescue an animal; (11) Open the door for someone or let them ahead of you in a queue; (12) Help someone carry a bag or package; (13) Donate to a charity your money, your time or your blood; (14) Call, write or travel to see a friend in need; (15) Tutor or be a mentor to a younger person; and (16) Leave a thank-you note for your postie, rubbish collector or other individual who simplifies your life.

14 Some of these suggestions are borrowed from Carlson (1997).

15 Ibid, Algoe and Haidt (2006).

16 Glynn, S. A., Busch, M. P., Schreiber, G. B., Murphy, E. L., Wright, D. J., Tu, Y., Kleinman, S. H., and NHLBI REDS study group (2003), 'Effect of a national disaster on blood supply and safety: The September 11 experience', *Journal of the American Medical Association, 289*, 2246–2253.

17 Esterling, B. A., Kiecolt-Glaser, J. K., Bodnar, J. C., and Glaser, R. (1994), 'Chronic stress, social support, and persistent alterations in the natural killer cell response to cytokines in older adults', *Health Psychology, 13*, 291–298.

18 Weitzenkamp, D. A., Gerhart, K. A., Charlifue, S. W., Whiteneck, G.

G., and Savic, G. (1997), 'Spouses of spinal cord injury survivors: The added impact of caregiving', *Archives of Physical Medicine and Rehabilitation, 78*, 822–827

19 Specter, M. (2005, October 24), 'What money can buy', *New Yorker*.

20 For review, see Lyubomirsky, King, et al. (2005). See also Myers (2000).

21 Baumeister, R.F., and Leary, M.R. (1995), 'The Need to Belong: Desire for interpersonal attachments as a fundamental human motivation', *Psychological Bulletin, 117*, 497–529.

22 (1) House, J. S., Landis, K. R., and Umberson, D. (1988), 'Social relationships and health', *Science, 241*, 540–545. (2) Kaplan, R. M., and Toshima, M. T. (1990), 'The functional effects of social relationships on chronic illnesses and disability', in B.R. Sarason, I.G. Sarason, and G. R. Pierce (Eds.), *Social support: An interactional view* (pp. 427–453), Oxford, England: John Wiley and Sons. (3) Verbrugge, L. M. (1979), 'Marital status and health', *Journal of Marriage and the Family, 41*, 267–285. (4) Lynch, J. J. (1977), *The broken heart: The medical consequences of loneliness*, New York: Basic Books.

23 The other three factors the Sardinians, Okinawans and Seventh Day Adventists had in common were 'don't smoke', 'stay physically active', and 'eat a plant-based diet'. Buettner, D. (2005, November), 'New wrinkles on aging', *National Geographic*, pp. 2–27.

24 Berscheid, E., and Reis, H. T. (1998), 'Attraction and close relationships', in D. T. Gilbert, S. T. Fiske, and G. Lindzey (Eds.), *The handbook of social psychology* (fourth ed., Vol. 2, pp. 193–281), New York: McGraw-Hill.

25 Rainwater, L. (1994), 'Family equivalence as a social construction', in D. Ekert-Jaffe (Ed.), *Standards of living and families: Observation and analysis* (pp. 25–39), Montrouge, France: John Libbey Eurotext.

26 Easterlin, R.A. (2005), 'A puzzle for adaptive theory', *Journal of Economic Behavior and Organization, 56*, 513–521.

27 Gottman, J.M., and Silver, N. (1999), *The Seven Principles For Making Marriage Work*, New York: Three Rivers Press.

28 Gottman, J.M. (1994), *What predicts divorce: The relationship between marital processes and marital outcomes*, Hillsdale, NJ: Lawrence Erlbaum.

29 Ibid, Gottman (1994).

30 (1) Drigotas, S. M., Rusbult, C. E., Wieselquist, J., and Whitton, S. W. (1999), 'Close partner as sculptor of the ideal self: Behavioral affirmation and the Michelangelo phenomenon', *Journal of Personality and Social Psychology, 77*, 293–323. (2) Drigotas, S. M. (2002), 'The Michelangelo phenomenon and personal well-being', *Journal of Personality, 70*, 59–77

31 Murray, S. L., Holmes, J. G., and Griffin, D. W. (1996), 'The self-fulfilling nature of positive illusions in romantic relationships: Love is not blind, but prescient', *Journal of Personality and Social Psychology, 71*, 1155–1180.

32 This compelling work has been conducted by Shelly Gable, Harry Reis and their colleagues: Gable, S. L., Reis, H. T., Asher, E. R. and Impett, E. A. (2004), 'What do you do when things go right? The intrapersonal and interpersonal benefits of sharing positive events', *Journal of Personality and Social Psychology, 87*, 228–245.

33 Schueller, S. M. (2006), *Personality fit and positive interventions. Is extraversion important?* Unpublished manuscript, Department of Psychology, University of Pennsylvania.

34 Ibid, Gottman and Silver (1999).

35 Keil, C. P. (1998), 'Loneliness, stress, and human-animal attachment among older adults', in C. C. Wilson and D. C. Turner (Eds.), *Companion animals in human health* (pp. 123–134), Thousand Oaks, CA: Sage Publications.

36 These studies on singles were compiled in a recent influential piece by psychologists Bella DePaulo and Wendy Morris, who challenge what they call the Ideology of Marriage and Family: DePaulo, B. M., and Morris, W. L. (2005), 'Singles in society and in science', *Psychological Inquiry, 16*, 57–83. See also DePaulo, B. (2006), *Singled out: How singles are stereotyped, stigmatized, and ignored, and still live happily ever after*, New York: St. Martin's Press.

37 A number of these suggestions are from McGinnis, A. L. (1979), *The friendship factor*, Minneapolis, MN: Augsburg. The magic number of 'three' was suggested by Stanford University professor Laura Carstensen.

38 A Russian proverb.

39 Argyle, M., and Henderson, M. (1984), 'The rules of friendships', *Journal of Social and Personal Relationships, 1*, 211–237.

40 Clipman, J. M. (1999, March). *A hug a day keeps the blues away: The effect of daily hugs on subjective well-being in college students.* Paper presented at the Seventieth Annual Meeting of the Eastern Psychological Association, Boston, MA.

41 In a subsequent study, Jane Marie Clipman gave students the opportunity to wink or to give compliments instead of hugging. Winking and complimenting also increased well-being.

42 Doehring, K. M. (1989), 'Relieving pain through touch', *Advancing Clinical Care, 4*, 32–33.

CHAPTER 6

1 Ozer, E. J., and Weiss, D. S. (2004), 'Who develops post-traumatic stress disorder?' *Current Directions in Psychological Science, 13*, 169–172.

2 Billings, A. G., and Moos, R. H. (1984), 'Coping, stress, and social resources among adults with unipolar depression', *Journal of Personality and Social Psychology, 46*, 887–891.

3 Carver, C. S., Scheier, M. F., and Weintraub, J. K. (1984), 'Assessing coping strategies: A theoretically based approach', *Journal of Personality and Social Psychology, 56*, 267–283.

4 Nolen-Hoeksema, S., and Morrow, J. (1991), 'A prospective study of depression and posttraumatic stress symptoms after a natural disaster: The 1989 Loma Prieta earthquake', *Journal of Personality and Social Psychology, 61*, 115–121.

5 Schut, H. A. W., Stroebe, M. S., van den Bout, J., and de Keijser, J. (1997), 'Intervention for the bereaved: Gender differences in the efficacy of two counselling programmes', *British Journal of Clinical Psychology, 36*, 63–72.

6 McQueeney, D. A., Stanton, A. L., and Sigmon, S. (1997), 'Efficacy of emotion-focused and problem-focused group therapies for women with fertility problems', *Journal of Behavioral Medicine, 20*, 313–331.

7 Lynn's story was profiled by the *Los Angeles Times*: Foreman, J. (2006, January 16), 'The mystery that is mourning', *Los Angeles Times*, F4.

8 Tennen, H., and Affleck, G. (1999), 'Finding benefits in adversity', in C. R. Snyder (Ed.), *Coping: The psychology of what works* (pp. 279–304), New York: Oxford University Press.

9 Nolen-Hoeksema, S., and Davis, C. G. (2002), 'Positive responses to loss: Perceiving benefits and growth', in C. R. Snyder and S. J. Lopez (Eds.), *Handbook of positive psychology* (pp. 598–606), New York: Oxford University Press.

10 Taylor, S. E., Lichtman, R. R., and Wood, J. V. (1984), 'Attributions, beliefs about control, and adjustment to breast cancer', *Journal of Personality and Social Psychology, 46*, 489–502. See also, Collins, R. L., Taylor, S. E., and Skokan, L. A. (1990), 'A better world or a shattered vision? Changes in life perspectives following victimization', *Social Cognition, 8*, 263–285.

11 For a review, see Taylor, S. E., and Armor, D. A. (1996), 'Positive illusions and coping with adversity', *Journal of Personality, 64*, 873–898.

12 The quotes in this subsection are from bereaved participants in a study reported in Davis, C. G., Nolen-Hoeksema, S., and Larson, J. (1998), 'Making sense of loss and benefiting from the experience: Two construals of meaning', *Journal of Personality and Social Psychology, 75*, 561–574.

13 Shearer, L. (2001, September), 'When the friendly skies are not so friendly', *Georgia Magazine*, 80.

14 Affleck, G., Tennen, H., Croog, S., and Levine, S. (1987), 'Causal attributions, perceived benefits, and morbidity after a heart attack: An 8 year study', *Journal of Consulting and Clinical Psychology, 55*, 29–35.

15 Ibid, Nolen-Hoeksema and Davis (2002), p. 602.

16 (1) Tedeschi, R. G., and Calhoun, L. G. (1995), *Trauma and transformation: Growing in the aftermath of suffering*, Thousand Oaks, CA: Sage. (2) O'Leary, V. E., and Ickovics, J. R. (1995), 'Resilience and thriving in response to challenge: An opportunity for a paradigm shift in women's health', *Women's Health: Research on Gender, Behavior, and Policy, 1*, 121–142.

17 There are many good descriptions of this work, but a particularly good

reference is Tedeschi, R. G., and Calhoun, L. G. (2004), 'Posttraumatic growth: Conceptual foundations and empirical evidence', *Psychological Inquiry, 15*, 1–18.

18 Ibid, O'Leary and Ickovics (1995).

19 Ibid, O'Leary and Ickovics (1995).

20 Langer, L. L. (1990), *Holocaust testimonies: The ruins of memory*, New Haven, CT: Yale University Press, p. 59. Quoted in O'Leary and Ickovics (1995).

21 (1) Engh, A. L., Beehner, J. C., Bergman, T. J., Whitten, P. L., Hoffmeier, R. R., Seyfarth, R. M., and Cheney, D. L. (2006), 'Behavioural and hormonal responses to predation in female chacma baboons (*Papio hamadryas ursinus*)', *Proceedings of the Royal Society B, 273*, 707–712. (2) Dreilinger, R. (2006, April), 'No monkey, no cry', *Observer*, p. 12.

22 Pennebaker, J. W., and O'Heeron, R. C. (1984), 'Confiding in others and illness rate among spouses of suicide and accidental-death victims', *Journal of Abnormal Psychology, 93*, 473–476.

23 Levy, S. M., Herberman, R. B., Whiteside, T., Sanzo, K., Lee, J., and Kirkwood, J. (1990), 'Perceived social support and tumor estrogen/progesterone receptor status as predictors of natural killer cell activity in breast cancer patients', *Psychosomatic Medicine, 52*, 73–85. See also Kiecolt-Glaser, J. K., Dura, J. R., Speicher, C. E., Trask, O. J., and Glaser, R. (1991), 'Spousal caregivers of dementia victims: Longitudinal changes in immunity and health', *Psychosomatic Medicine, 53*, 345–362.

24 Spiegel, D., Bloom, J. R., Kraemer, H. C., and Gottheil, E. (1989), 'Effect of psychosocial treatment on survival of patients with metastatic breast cancer', *Lancet, 2*, 888–891.

25 Gilligan, C. (1982), *In a different voice: Psychological theory and women's development*, Cambridge, MA: Harvard University Press.

26 (1) Rook, K. S. (1984), 'The negative side of social interaction: Impact on psychological well-being', *Journal of Personality and Social Psychology, 46*, 1097–1108. (2) Windholz, M. J., Marmar, C. R., and Horowitz, M. J. (1985), 'A review of the research on conjugal bereavement: Impact on health and efficacy of intervention', *Comprehensive Psychiatry, 26*, 433–447.

27 Janoff-Bulman, R. (1992), *Shattered assumptions: Towards a new psychology of trauma*, New York: Free Press.

28 Lerner, M. J. (1980), *The belief in a just world*, New York: Plenum.

29 Quotes are from Davis et al. (1998).

30 Ibid, Davis et al. (1998).

31 Bower, J. E., Kemeny, M. E., Taylor, S. E., and Fahey, J. L. (1998), 'Cognitive processing, discovery of meaning, CD4 decline, and AIDS-related mortality among bereaved HIV-seropositive men', *Journal of Consulting and Clinical Psychology, 66*, 979–986.

32 A wonderfully readable summary of this work is in Pennebaker, J. W.

(1997), *Opening up: The healing power of expressing emotions*, New York: The Guilford Press.

33 For reviews, see (1) Pennebaker, J. W. (1997), 'Writing about emotional experiences as a therapeutic process', *Psychological Science, 8*, 162–166. (2) Frattaroli, J. (2006), 'Experimental disclosure and its moderators: A meta-analysis', *Psychological Bulletin, 132*, 823–865.

34 Pennebaker, J. W., Mayne, T. J., and Francis, M. E. (1997), 'Linguistic predictors of adaptive bereavement', *Journal of Personality and Social Psychology, 72*, 863–871.

35 Pennebaker, J. W., and Seagal, J. D. (1999), 'Forming a story: The health benefits of narrative', *Journal of Clinical Psychology, 55*, 1243–1254 (p. 1244).

36 Ibid, Seligman (1990).

37 McCullough, M. E., and Witvliet, C. V. (2002), 'The psychology of forgiveness', in C. R. Snyder and S. J. Lopez (Eds.), *Handbook of positive psychology* (pp. 446–458), New York: Oxford University Press.

38 McCullough, M. E., Pargament, K. I., and Thoresen, C. T. (Eds.) (2000), *Forgiveness: Theory, research, and practice*, New York: Guilford.

39 McCullough, M. E., Rachal, K. C., Sandage, S. J., Worthington, E. L., Jr., Brown, S. W., and Hight, T. L. (1998), 'Interpersonal forgiving in close relationships. II. Theoretical elaboration and measurement', *Journal of Personality and Social Psychology, 75*, 1586–1603.

40 For excellent reviews of this research, see McCullough and Witvliet (2002) and McCullough, M. E. (2001), 'Forgiveness: Who does it and how do they do it?' *Current Directions in Psychological Science, 10*, 194–197.

41 Hebl, J. H., and Enright, R. D. (1993), 'Forgiveness as a psychotherapeutic goal with elderly females', *Psychotherapy: Theory, Research, Practice, Training, 30*, 658–667.

42 (1) Worthington, E. L., Jr., Sandage, S. J., and Berry, J. W. (2000), 'Group interventions to promote forgiveness: What researchers and clinicians ought to know', in M. E. McCullough, K. I. Pargament, and C. T. Thoresen (Eds.), *Forgiveness: Theory, research, and practice* (pp. 228–253), New York: Guilford. (2) Harris, A. H. S., and Thoresen, C. E. (2006), 'Extending the influence of positive psychology interventions into health care settings: Lessons from self-efficacy and forgiveness', *Journal of Positive Psychology, 1*, 27–36.

43 Karremans, J. C., Van Lange, P. A. M., and Holland, R. W. (2005), 'Forgiveness and its associations with prosocial thinking, feeling, and doing beyond the relationship with the offender', *Personality and Social Psychology Bulletin, 31*, 1315–1326.

44 This exercise is adapted from one developed by Martin Seligman and Tracy Steen.

45 Witvliet, C. V., Ludwig, T. E., and Vander Laan, K. L. (2001), 'Granting forgiveness or harboring grudges: Implications for emotion, physiology, and health', *Psychological Science, 12*, 117–123.

46 See http://www.forgivenessday.org/hero.htm for examples of such 'heroes of forgiveness', including both famous individuals and extraordinary ordinary people.

47 McCullough, M. E., Worthington, E. L., and Rachal, K. C. (1997), 'Interpersonal forgiving in close relationships', *Journal of Personality and Social Psychology, 73*, 321–336.

48 Shapiro, D. L. (1991), 'The effects of explanations on negative reactions to deceit', *Administrative Science Quarterly, 36*, 614–630.

49 Ibid, McCullough et al. (1997); McCullough et al. (1998).

50 McCullough, M. E., Bellah, C. G., Kilpatrick, S. D., and Johnson, J. L. (2001), 'Vengefulness: Relationships with forgiveness, rumination, well-being, and the Big Five', *Personality and Social Psychology Bulletin, 27*, 601–610.

51 Remnick, D. (2006, September 18), 'The wanderer', *New Yorker*, p. 66.

CHAPTER 7

1 Gregory, A. (2005, March 21), '(Man at work thinking about golf, golfing thinking about sex, having sex, thinking about work.)' *New Yorker*.

2 The best treatment of flow, in my opinion, is in Csikszentmihalyi, M. (1990), *Flow: The psychology of optimal experience*, NY: Harper and Row.

3 Nakamura, J., and Csikszentmihalyi, M. (2002), 'The concept of flow', in C. R. Snyder and S. J. Lopez (Eds.), *Handbook of positive psychology* (pp. 89–105), Oxford: Oxford University Press.

4 Csikszentmihalyi, M., Rathunde, K., and Whalen, S. (1993), *Talented teenagers*, Cambridge, England: Cambridge University Press.

5 Ibid, Csikszentmihalyi (1990), p. 10.

6 LeFevre, J. (1988), 'Flow and the quality of experience during work and leisure', in M. Csikszentmihalyi and I. Csikszentmihalyi (Eds.), *Optimal experience* (pp. 307–318), New York: Cambridge University Press.

7 Csikszentmihalyi, M. (2000), *Beyond boredom and anxiety*, San Francisco: Jossey-Bass. (Original work published 1975.)

8 This exercise was developed by Marty Seligman and Tracy Steen.

9 Wrzesniewski, A., McCauley, C., Rozin, P., and Schwartz, B. (1997), 'Jobs, careers, and callings: People's relations to their work', *Journal of Research in Personality, 31*, 21–33.

10 Wrzesniewski, A., and Dutton, J. E. (2001), 'Crafting a job: Revisioning employees as active crafters of their work', *Academy of Management Review, 26*, 179–201.

11 In addition, some people find flow in vandalism, physical violence or exerting tyrannical control over a group, organization or nation. Others experience flow while risk-taking in reckless driving, gambling, shoplifting or committing fraud. Therein lies another potential negative side of flow. Although these activities might make you feel joyful

and self-possessed in the short term, the long-term costs are very high and the happiness will not endure. Use your judgement.

12 David Lodge coined a wonderful term for this phenomenon – 'future nostalgia'.

13 Fred Bryant and Joseph Veroff were the first to study and describe the phenomenon of savouring. For an updated and accessible overview, see Bryant, F. B., and Veroff, J. (2006), *Savoring: A new model of positive experience*, Nahwah, N. J.: Erlbaum. Their work is also described in the following papers: (1) Bryant, F. B. (1989), 'A four-factor model of perceived control: Avoiding, coping, obtaining, and savoring', *Journal of Personality*, 57, 773–797. (2) Bryant, F. B. (2003), 'Savoring beliefs inventory (SBI): A scale for measuring beliefs about savoring', *Journal of Mental Health, 12*, 175–196.

14 Ibid, Bryant (2003).

15 Ibid, Bryant, p. 195 (2003).

16 Seligman, M. E. P., Rashid, T., and Parks, A. C. (in press), 'Positive psychotherapy', *American Psychologist*.

17 Ibid, Schueller (2006).

18 Attributed to Robert Brault.

19 Pasupathi, M., and Carstensen, L. L. (2003), 'Age and emotional experience during mutual reminiscing', *Psychology and Aging, 18*, 430–442.

20 Havighurst, R. J., and Glasser, R. (1972), 'An exploratory study of reminiscence', *Journal of Gerontology, 27*, 245–253.

21 Bryant, F. B., Smart, C. M., and King, S. P. (2005), 'Using the past to enhance the present: Boosting happiness through positive reminiscence', *Journal of Happiness Studies, 6*, 227–260.

22 Ibid, Bryant et al. (2005).

23 Ibid, Bryant et al. p. 237(2005).

24 Humphrey Bogart says this to Ingrid Bergman in the last scene of *Casablanca*, before she boards a plane to Lisbon, never to see him again.

25 Ibid, Lyubomirsky, Sousa, et al. (2006).

26 Langston, C. A. (1994), 'Capitalizing on and coping with daily-life events: Expressive responses to positive events', *Journal of Personality and Social Psychology, 67*, 1112–1125. See also Gable et al. (2004).

27 Ibid, Bryant and Veroff (2006).

28 Haidt, J., and Keltner, D. (2004), 'Appreciation of beauty and excellence [Awe, Wonder, Elevation]', in C. Peterson and M. E. P. Seligman (Eds.), *Character strengths and virtues: A handbook and classification* (pp. 537–551), Washington DC: APA.

29 This wonderful example was cited by Haidt and Keltner (2004), p. 537.

30 Brown, K. W., and Ryan, R. M. (2003), 'The benefits of being present: Mindfulness and its role in psychological well-being', *Journal of Personality and Social Psychology, 84*, 822–848.

31 James, W. (1924), *Memories and studies*, New York: Longmans, Green, and Co. (Original work published 1911.)

32 Jon Kabat-Zinn, founder of the Stress Reduction Clinic at the

University of Massachusetts Medical Center, has been a pioneer in this field. For an overview of these studies, see Kabat-Zinn, J. (2005), *Full catastrophe living: Using the wisdom of your body and mind to face stress, pain, and illness: Fifteenth anniversary edition*, New York: Bantam Dell.

33 Ibid, Bryant and Veroff (2006).

34 LeBel, J. L., and Dubé, L. (2001, June), 'The impact of sensory knowledge and attentional focus on pleasure and on behavioral responses to hedonic stimuli.' Paper presented at the thirteenth annual American Psychological Society Convention, Toronto, Ontario, Canada.

35 This story is quoted in Kubovy, M. (1999), 'On the pleasures of the mind', in D. Kahneman, E. Diener, and N. Schwarz (Eds.), *Well-being: The foundations of hedonic psychology* (pp. 134–154), New York: Russell Sage Foundation.

36 This idea was suggested by social psychologist Jaime Kurtz.

37 Kurtz, J. L. and Wilson, T. D. (2007), *Looking to the future to appreciate the present: The function of bittersweet emotions.* Manuscript in preparation.

38 Boehm, J. K., Dickerhoof, R., and Lyubomirsky, S. (2007), *Endowing versus contrasting life events: The relationship between thought perspective and well-being.* Unpublished data, Department of Psychology, University of California, Riverside.

39 Attributed to Jim Holliday. Caen, H. (1975, April 15) [Editorial], *San Francisco Chronicle*.

40 Wildschut, T., Sedikides, C., Arndt, J., and Routledge, C. (2006), 'Nostalgia: Content, triggers, functions', *Journal of Personality and Social Psychology, 91*, 975–993.

41 Ibid, Lyubomirsky, Sousa, et al. (2006).

42 Epel, E. S., Bandura, A., and Zimbardo, P. G. (1999), 'Escaping homelessness: The influences of self-efficacy and time perspective on coping with homelessness', *Journal of Applied Social Psychology, 29*, 575–596.

43 Kessler, L. (2004, August 22), 'Dancing with Rose: A strangely beautiful encounter with Alzheimer's patients provides insights that challenge the way we view the disease', *Los Angeles Times Magazine*, 29.

44 For reviews, see (1) Zimbardo, P. G. and Boyd, J. N. (1998), 'Putting time in perspective: A valid, reliable individual-difference metric', *Journal of Personality and Social Psychology, 77*, 1271–1288. (2) Boyd, J. N., and Zimbardo, P. G. (2005), 'Time perspective, health, and risk taking', in A. Strathman and J. Joireman (Eds.), *Understanding behavior in the context of time: Theory, research, and application* (pp. 85–107), Mahwah, N. J.: Erlbaum.

45 For evidence that people are capable of doing both – that is, of living in the present while also being oriented towards the future – see Liu, W., and Aaker, J. (2007), 'Do you look to the future or focus on today? The impact of life experience on intertemporal decisions', *Organizational Behavior and Human Decision Processes, 102*, 212–225

46 The quote is from former US President Bill Clinton. Ibid, Remnick (2006, September 18), p. 53.

1 Wolfe, W. B. (2001), *How to be happy though human*, London: Routledge. (Original work published in 1932.)

2 For a review, see Cantor, N., and Sanderson, C. A. (1999), 'Life task participation and well-being: The importance of taking part in daily life, in D. Kahneman, E. Diener, and N. Schwarz (Eds.), *Well-being: The foundations of hedonic psychology* (pp. 230–243), New York: Russell Sage Foundation.

3 Brunstein, J. C. (1993), 'Personal goals and subjective well-being: A longitudinal study', *Journal of Personality and Social Psychology, 65*, 1061–1070.

4 Swed, M. (2004, June 7), 'At Disney, a soaring tribute; Esa-Pekka Salonen's "Wing on Wing" is a stirringly heartfelt work honoring Frank Gehry', *Los Angeles Times*, E1.

5 Cantor, N. (1990), 'From thought to behavior: "Having" and "doing" in the study of personality and cognition', *American Psychologist, 45*, 735–750.

6 For a review, see Ryan, R. M., and Deci, E. L. (2000), 'Self-determination theory and the facilitation of intrinsic motivation, social development, and well-being', *American Psychologist, 55*, 68–78.

7 (1) Kasser, T., and Ryan, R. M. (1993), 'A dark side of the American dream: Correlates of financial success as a central life aspiration', *Journal of Personality and Social Psychology, 65*, 410–422. (2) Kasser, T., and Ryan, R. M. (1996), 'Further examining the American dream: Differential correlates of intrinsic and extrinsic goals', *Personality and Social Psychology Bulletin, 22*, 280–287. (3) Sheldon, K. M., and Kasser, T. (1995), 'Coherence and congruence: Two aspects of personality integration', *Journal of Personality and Social Psychology, 68*, 531–543.

8 For two excellent reviews, see (1) Sheldon, K. M. (2002), 'The self-concordance model of healthy goal-striving: When personal goals correctly represent the person', in E. L. Deci and R. M. Ryan (Eds.), *Handbook of self-determination theory* (pp. 65–86), Rochester, NY: University of Rochester Press. (2) Sheldon, K. M., and Elliot, A. J. (1999), 'Goal striving, need satisfaction, and longitudinal well-being: The self-concordance model', *Journal of Personality and Social Psychology, 76*, 546–557.

9 (1) Elliot, A. J., and Sheldon, K. M. (1998), 'Avoidance personal goals and the personality-illness relationship', *Journal of Personality and Social Psychology, 75*, 1282–1299. (2) Elliot, A. J., Sheldon, K. M., and Church, M. A. (1997), 'Avoidance personal goals and subjective well-being', *Personality and Social Psychology Bulletin, 23*, 915–927.

10 Elliot, A. J., and McGregor, H. A. (2001), 'A 2 X 2 achievement goal framework', *Journal of Personality and Social Psychology, 80*, 501–519.

11 Strachman, A., and Gable, S. L. (2006), 'What you want (and do not

want) affects what you see (and do not see): Avoidance social goals and social events', *Personality and Social Psychology Bulletin, 32,* 1446–1458.

12 This phenomenon is essentially what happens in a 'rebound effect', when you are trying so hard to *not* think about or do something that you end up thinking or doing it. For a review, see Wegner, D. M. (1994), 'Ironic processes of mental control', *Psychological Review, 101,* 34–52.

13 (1) Ibid, Sheldon and Kasser (1995). (2) Emmons, R. A., and King, L. A. (1988), 'Conflict among personal strivings: Immediate and long-term implications for psychological and physical well-being', *Journal of Personality and Social Psychology, 54,* 1040–1048.

14 Ibid, Cantor and Sanderson (1999).

15 Carstensen, L. L., Isaacowitz, D. M., and Charles, S. T. (1999), 'Taking time seriously: A theory of socioemotional selectivity', *American Psychologist, 54,* 165–181.

16 Fredrickson, B. L., and Carstensen, L. L. (1990), 'Choosing social partners: How old age and anticipated endings make people more selective', *Psychology and Aging, 5,* 335–347.

17 Sheldon, K. M., and Lyubomirsky, S. (2006b), 'Achieving sustainable gains in happiness: Change your actions, not your circumstances', *Journal of Happiness Studies, 7,* 55–86.

18 The instructions for this task are adapted from Kaiser, R. T., and Ozer, D. J. (1997), 'Emotional stability and goal-related stress', *Personality and Individual Differences, 22,* 371–379.

19 Kahneman, D., Krueger, A. B., Schkade, D., Schwarz, N., and Stone, A. A. (2004), 'A survey method for characterizing daily life experience: The Day Reconstruction Method', *Science, 306,* 1776–1780.

20 Ibid, Csikszentmihalyi et al. (1993).

21 These suggestions were adapted from two exercises developed by Martin Seligman and Tracy Steen.

22 Quote by Robert Peter Tristram Coffin.

23 Sheldon, K. M., Kasser, T., Smith, K., and Share, T. (2002), 'Personal goals and psychological growth: Testing an intervention to enhance goal attainment and personality integration', *Journal of Personality, 70,* 5–31.

24 Bearman, P. S., and Brückner, H. (2001), 'Promising the future: Virginity pledges and first intercourse', *American Journal of Sociology, 106,* 859–912.

25 Greenwald, A. G., Carnot, C. G., Beach, R., and Young, B. (1987), 'Increasing voting behavior by asking people if they expect to vote', *Journal of Applied Psychology, 72,* 315–318.

26 Norcross, J. C., Mrykalo, M. S., and Blagys, M. D. (2002), 'Auld Lang Syne: Success predictors, change processes, and self-reported outcomes of New Year's resolvers and nonresolvers', *Journal of Clinical Psychology, 58,* 397–405. See also Brunstein (1993).

27 Norcross, J. C., Ratzin, A. C., and Payne, D. (1989), 'Ringing in the

New Year: The change processes and reported outcomes of resolutions', *Addictive Behaviors, 14*, 205–212.

28 For an excellent review, see David Myer's social psychology textbook: Myers, D. G. (2005), *Social psychology*, New York: McGraw-Hill.

29 Ibid, Sheldon and Houser-Marko (2001).

30 Norcross, J. C., and Vangarelli, D. J. (1989), 'The resolution solution: Longitudinal examination of New Year's change attempts', *Journal of Substance Abuse, 1*, 127–134.

31 Brandtstädter, J., and Renner, G. (1990), 'Tenacious goal pursuit and flexible goal adjustment: Explication and age-related analysis of assimilative and accommodative strategies of coping', *Psychology and Aging, 5*, 58–67.

32 Heckhausen, J., and Schulz, R. (1995), 'A life-span theory of control', *Psychological Review, 102*, 284–304.

33 Lepper, M. R., Greene, D., and Nisbett, R. E. (1973), 'Undermining children's intrinsic interest with extrinsic reward: A test of the "overjustification" hypothesis', *Journal of Personality and Social Psychology, 28*, 129–137.

34 Gollwitzer, P. M. (1999), 'Implementation intentions', *American Psychologist, 54*, 493–503.

35 Dubé, M., Lapierre, S., Bouffard, L., and Alain, M. (in press), 'Impact of a personal goals management program on the subjective well-being of young retirees', *European Review of Applied Psychology*. For a similar study that confirmed these findings, see Green, L. S., Oades, L. G., and Grant, A. M. (2006), 'Cognitive-behavioral, solution-focused life coaching: Enhancing goal striving, well-being, and hope', *The Journal of Positive Psychology, 1*, 142–149.

36 Ibid, Dubé et al. (in press). The case study of Mrs M is presented on pp. 17–20.

CHAPTER 9

1 For an excellent review, see Ellison, C. G., and Levin, J. S. (1998), 'The religion-health connection: Evidence, theory, and future directions', *Health Education and Behavior, 25*, 700–720. Another very readable review is Myers (2000).

2 McIntosh, D. N., Silver, R. C., and Wortman, C. B. (1993), 'Religion's role in adjustment to a negative life event: Coping with the loss of a child', *Journal of Personality and Social Psychology, 65*, 812–821.

3 Examples of studies showing that religion is related to superior health include (1) Oman, D., and Reed, D. (1998), 'Religion and mortality among the community dwelling elderly', *American Journal of Public Health, 88*, 1469–1475. (2) Koenig, H. G., Hays, J. C., George, L. K., Blazer, D. G., Larson, D. B., and Landerman, L. R. (1997), 'Modeling the cross-sectional relationships between religion, physical health, social support, and depressive symptoms', *American Journal of Geriatric*

Psychology, 5, 131–144. (3) Oxman, T. E., Freeman, D. H., and Manheimer, E. D. (1995), 'Lack of social participation or religious strength and comfort as risk factors for death after cardiac surgery in the elderly', *Psychosomatic Medicine, 57,* 5–15. (4) Strawbridge, W. J., Cohen, R. D., Shema, S. J., and Kaplan, G. A. (1997), 'Frequent attendance at religious services and mortality over 28 years', *American Journal of Public Health, 87,* 957–961.

4 Ibid, Oxman et al. (1995).

5 Ibid, Koenig et al. (1997).

6 Ibid, Ellison and Levin (1998).

7 This finding comes from analyses of National Opinion Research Center General Social Survey data. Ibid, Myers (2000).

8 Ibid, Ellison and Levin (1998).

9 Pollner, M. (1989), 'Divine relations, social relations, and well-being', *Journal of Health and Social Behavior, 30,* 92–104.

10 Koenig, H. G., George, L. K., and Siegler, I. C. (1988), 'The use of religion and other emotion-regulating coping strategies among older adults', *Gerontologist, 28,* 303–310.

11 Quoted in Pargament, K. I., and Mahoney, A. (2002), 'Spirituality: Discovering and conserving the sacred', in C. R. Snyder and S. J. Lopez (Eds.), *Handbook of positive psychology* (pp. 646–659), New York: Oxford University Press.

12 Jenkins, R. A., and Pargament, K. I. (1988), 'Cognitive appraisals in cancer patients', *Social Science and Medicine, 26,* 625–633.

13 Baumeister, R. F. (1991), *Meanings of life,* New York: Guilford Press.

14 McCullough, M. E., and Worthington, E. L. (1999), 'Religion and the forgiving personality', *Journal of Personality, 67,* 1141–1164.

15 Vaillant, G. E. (in press), *Faith, hope, and joy,* New York: Morgan Road Books.

16 Saucier, G. and Skrzypiñska, K. (2006), 'Spiritual but not religious? Evidence for two independent dispositions', *Journal of Personality, 74,* 1257–1292.

17 Pargament, K. I. (1999), 'The psychology of religion and spirituality? Yes and no', *International Journal for the Psychology of Religion, 9,* 3–16.

18 Ibid, Pargament and Mahoney (2002).

19 Pollner, M. (1989), 'Divine relations, social relations, and well-being', *Journal of Health and Social Behavior, 30,* 92–104.

20 Ibid, Pargament and Mahoney (2002).

21 Poloma, M. M., and Gallup, G. H., Jr. (1991), *Varieties of prayer: A survey report,* Philadelphia: Trinity Press International.

22 For a review of this research, see Compton, W. C. (2004), 'Religion, spirituality, and well-being', in *An introduction to positive psychology* (pp. 196–216), Belmont, CA: Wadsworth.

23 Freud, S. (1964), *The future of an illusion* (p. 71), Garden City, NY: Doubleday. (Original work published 1928.)

24 For example, see Klonoff, E. A., and Landrine, H. (1996), 'Belief in

the healing power of prayer: Prevalence and health correlates for African-Americans', *Western Journal of Black Studies, 20,* 207–210.

25 For example, see Koenig, H. G., Pargament, K. I., and Nielsen, J. (1998), 'Religious coping and health status in medically ill hospitalized older adults', *Journal of Mental and Nervous Disease, 186,* 513–521.

26 Glock, C. Y., and Stark, R. (1966), *Christian beliefs and anti-semitism,* New York: Harper and Row.

27 Altemeyer, B., and Hunsberger, B. (1992), 'Authoritarianism, religious fundamentalism, quest, and prejudice', *International Journal for the Psychology of Religion, 2,* 113–133.

28 Ibid, Compton (2004).

29 Blanton, D. (2005, December 1), '12/01/05 FOX poll: Courts driving religion out of public life; Christianity under attack'. Retrieved June 26, 2006 from the World Wide Web: http://www.foxnews.com/story/0,2933,177355,00.html (UK Home Office report retrieved from World Wide Web: http://news.bbc.co.uk/1/hi/uk/3725801.stm)

30 (1) Hoge, D. R. (1996), 'Religion in America: The demographics of belief and affiliation', in E. P. Shafranske (Ed.), *Religion and the clinical practice of psychology* (pp. 21–42), Washington DC: American Psychological Association. (2) Johnson, B., Bader, C., Dougherty, K., Froese, P., Stark, R., Mencken, C., and Park, J. (2006, September 11), 'Losing my religion? No, says Baylor religion survey'. Retrieved September 16, 2006 from the World Wide Web: http://www.baylor.edu/pr/news.php?action=story&story=41678 (Ibid for UK statistics).

31 Shapiro, S. L., Schwartz, G. E. R., and Santerre, C. (2002), 'Meditation and positive psychology', in C. R. Snyder and S. J. Lopez (Eds.), *Handbook of positive psychology* (pp. 632–645), New York: Oxford University Press.

32 Kabat-Zinn, J. (1990), *Full catastrophe living,* New York: Delacorte Press.

33 Many of these studies – described in this section – are well reviewed in Shapiro et al. (2002).

34 Davidson, R. J., Kabat-Zinn, J., Schumacher, J., Rosenkranz, M., Muller, D., Santorelli, S. F., Urbanowaki, F., Harrington, A., Bonus, K., and Sheridan, J. F. (2003), 'Alterations in brain and immune function produced by mindfulness meditation', *Psychosomatic Medicine, 65,* 564–570.

35 Smith, W. P., Compton, W. C., and West, W. B. (1995), 'Meditation as an adjunct to a happiness enhancement program', *Journal of Clinical Psychology, 51,* 269–273.

36 See also a study that found that a sixteen-week training programme in transcendental meditation led to improved blood pressure, insulin resistance and the reduction of other risk factors for coronary heart disease: Paul-Labrador, M., Polk, D., Dwyer, J. H., Velasquez, I., Nidich, S., Rainforth, M., Schneider, R., and Merz, N. B. (2006), 'Effects of a randomized controlled trial of transcendental meditation on compo-

nents of the metabolic syndrome in subjects with coronary heart disease', *Archives of Internal Medicine, 166*, 1218–1224.

37 Fredrickson, B. L., Cohn, M. A., Coffey, K., Pek, J., and Finkel, S. (2007), *Open hearts build lives: Positive emotions, induced through meditation, build consequential personal resources.* Manuscript under review.

38 Blumenthal, J. A., Babyak, M. A., Moore, K. A., Craighead, E., Herman, S., Khatri, P., Waugh, R., Napolitano, M. A., Forman, L. M., Appelbaum, M., Doraiswamy, P. M., and Krishnan, K. R. (1999), 'Effects of exercise training on older patients with major depression', *Archives of Internal Medicine, 159*, 2349–2356.

39 Babyak, M. A., Blumenthal, J. A., Herman, S., Khatri, P., Doraiswamy, M., Moore, K., Craighead, W. E., Baldewicz, T. T., and Krishnan, K. R. (2000), 'Exercise treatment for major depression: Maintenance of therapeutic benefit at 10 months', *Psychosomatic Medicine, 62*, 633–638.

40 See numerous sources, including (1) Biddle, S. J. H., Fox, K. R., and Boutcher, S. H. (Eds.) (2000), *Physical activity and psychological well-being*, London: Routledge. (2) Kahn, E. B., Ramsey, L. T., Brownson, R. C., Heath, G. W., Howze, E. H., and Powell, K. E., Stone, E. J., Rajab, M. W., Corso, P., and the Task Force on Community Preventive Services (2002), 'The effectiveness of interventions to increase physical activity – A systematic review', *American Journal of Preventive Medicine, 22*, 73–107. (3) Centers for Disease Control and Prevention (1999, November 17), 'Physical activity and health: A report of the Surgeon General'. Retrieved June 27, 2006 from the World Wide Web: http://www.cdc.gov/nccdphp/sgr/sgr.htm

41 Motl, R. W., Konopack, J. F., McAuley, E., Elavsky, S., Jerome, G. J., and Marquez, D. X. (2005), 'Depressive symptoms among older adults: Long-term reduction after a physical activity intervention', *Journal of Behavioral Medicine, 28*, 385–394.

42 (1) Thayer, R. E., Newman, J. R., and McClain, T. M. (1994), 'Self-regulation of mood: Strategies for changing a bad mood, raising energy, and reducing tension', *Journal of Personality and Social Psychology, 67*, 910–925. (2) Biddle, S. J. H. (2000), 'Emotion, mood, and physical activity', in S. J. H. Biddle, K. R. Fox, and S. H. Boutcher (Eds.), *Physical activity and psychological well-being* (pp. 63–87), London: Routledge.

43 (1) Bahrke, M. S., and Morgan, W. P. (1978), 'Anxiety reduction following exercise and meditation', *Cognitive Therapy and Research, 2*, 323–333. (2) Harte, J. L., Eifert, G. H., and Smith, R. (1995), 'The effects of running and meditation on beta-endorphin, corticotrophin-releasing hormone, and cortisol in plasma, and on mood', *Biological Psychology, 40*, 251–256.

44 Carter-Morris, P., and Faulkner, G. (2003), 'A football project for service users: The role of football in reducing social exclusion', *Journal of Mental Health Promotion, 2*, 24–30 (p. 27).

45 Meeusen, R., and De Meirleir, K. (1995), 'Exercise and brain neuro-transmission', *Sports Medicine, 20*, 160–188.

46 Biddle, S. J. H., and Ekkekakis, P. (2006), 'Physically active lifestyles and well-being', in F. A. Huppert, N. Baylis, and B. Keverne (Eds.), *The science of well-being* (pp. 141–168), New York: Oxford University Press.

47 Mutrie, N., and Faulkner, G. (2004), 'Physical activity: Positive psychology in motion', in A. Linley, and S. Joseph (Eds.), *Positive psychology in practice* (pp. 146–164), Hoboken, NJ: John Wiley and Sons.

48 To measure your heart rate during exercise without disrupting your work-out too much, stop what you're doing and count the number of times you feel a pulse in your wrist or neck during a precise six-second period. Multiply by ten and you have your heart rate. To increase accuracy, use a longer time period – for example, take a ten-second pulse then multiply by six, or a thirty-second pulse then multiply by two.

49 Bailey, C. (1994), *Smart exercise*, New York: Houghton Mifflin.

50 Stanford University School of Medicine professor William Dement: Dement, W. C., and Vaughan, C. (2000), *The promise of sleep*, New York: Dell.

51 Ibid, Lyubomirsky, King, et al. (2005).

52 Darwin, C. R. (1896), *The expression of emotions in man and animals*, New York: Appleton (p. 365).

53 Strack, F., Martin, L. L., and Stepper, S. (1988), 'Inhibiting and facilitating conditions of the human smile: A nonobtrusive test of the facial feedback hypothesis', *Journal of Personality and Social Psychology, 54*, 768–777.

54 Levenson, R. W., Ekman, P., and Friesen, W. V. (1990), 'Voluntary facial action generates emotion-specific autonomic nervous system activity', *Psychophysiology, 27*, 363–384.

55 Cole, J. (1998), *About face* (p. 127), Cambridge, MA: MIT Press.

56 Finzi, E., and Wasserman, E. (2006), 'Treatment of depression with botulinum toxin A: A case series', *Dermatologic Surgery, 32*, 645–650.

57 Fromm, E. (1956), *The art of loving* (p. 49), New York: Harper and Row. The other findings described in this paragraph are reviewed in Lyubomirsky, King, et al. (2005).

58 Keltner, D., and Bonanno, G. A. (1997), 'A study of laughter and dissociation: Distinct correlates of laughter and smiling during bereavement', *Journal of Personality and Social Psychology, 73*, 687–702.

59 Berk, L. S., Tan, S. A., and Westengard, J. (2006, April), 'Beta-Endorphin and HGH increase are associated with both the anticipation and experience of mirthful laughter'. Paper presented at the annual Experimental Biology meeting, San Francisco, CA.

CHAPTER 10

1 (1) Diener, E., Sandvik, E., and Pavot, W. (1991), 'Happiness is the fre-

quency, not the intensity, of positive versus negative affect', in F. Strack, M. Argyle, and N. Schwarz (Eds.), *Subjective well-being: An interdisciplinary perspective* (pp. 119–139), Elmsford, NY: Pergamon Press. (2) Urry, H. L., Nitschke, J. B., Dolski, I., Jackson, D. C., Dalton, K. M., Mueller, C. J., Rosenkranz, M. A., Ryff, C. D., Singer, B. H., and Davidson, R. J. (2004), 'Making a life worth living: Neural correlates of well-being', *Psychological Science, 15*, 367–372.

2 Ibid, Fredrickson (2001).

3 Proust, M. (1982), *Remembrance of things past, Volume I: Swann's way and within a budding grove* (C. K. S. Moncrieff and T. Kilmartin, Trans.), New York: First Vintage. (Original work published 1913–1918.)

4 (1) Davidson, R. J. (1993), 'The neuropsychology of emotion and affective style', in M. Lewis and J. M. Haviland (Eds.), *Handbook of emotion* (pp.143–154), New York: Guilford Press. (2) Watson, D., Clark, L. A., and Carey, G. (1988), 'Positive and negative affectivity and their relations to anxiety and depressive disorders', *Journal of Abnormal Psychology, 97*, 346–353.

5 (1) MacLeod, A. K., Tata, P., Kentish, J., and Jacobsen, H. (1997), 'Retrospective and prospective cognitions in anxiety and depression', *Cognition and Emotion, 11*, 467–479. (2) MacLeod, A. K., Pankhania, B., Lee, M., and Mitchell, D. (1997), 'Depression, hopelessness and future-directed thinking in parasuicide', *Psychological Medicine, 27*, 973–977. (3) MacLeod, A. K., and Byrne, A. (1996), 'Anxiety, depression and the anticipation of future positive and negative experiences', *Journal of Abnormal Psychology, 105*, 286–289. For a review, see MacLeod, A. K., and Moore, R. (2000), 'Positive thinking revisited: Positive cognitions, well-being, and mental health', *Clinical Psychology and Psychotherapy, 7*, 1–10.

6 Joormann, J., Siemer, M., and Gotlib, I. H. (2006), *Mood regulation in depression: Differential effects of distraction and recall of happy memories on sad mood*. Manuscript submitted for publication.

7 Brown, G. W., Lemyre, L., and Bifulco, A. (1992), 'Social factors and recovery from anxiety and depressive disorders: A test of specificity', *British Journal of Psychiatry, 161*, 44–54. See also Taylor et al. (2006).

8 (1) Fredrickson, B. L., and Levenson, R. W. (1998), 'Positive emotions speed recovery from the cardiovascular sequelae of negative emotions', *Cognition and Emotion, 12*, 191–220. (2) Fredrickson, B. L., Mancuso, R. A., Branigan, C., and Tugade, M. M. (2000), 'The undoing effect of positive emotions', *Motivation and Emotion, 24*, 237–258.

9 (1) Ibid, Fredrickson and Levenson (1998). (2) Ibid, Fredrickson et al. (2000).

10 Ibid, Dickerhoof (2007).

11 Ibid, Fredrickson (2001). See also Ong, A. D., Bergeman, C. S., Bisconti, T. L., and Wallace, K. A. (2006), 'Psychological resilience, positive emotions, and successful adaptation to stress in later life', *Journal of Personality and Social Psychology, 91*, 730–749.

12 Namely, cognitive theory and hopelessness theory.

13 Ibid, Dickerhoof (2007).

14 Behavioural therapy, which aims at getting the depressed person to increase the number of pleasant experiences in his or her daily life, is a clear exception.

15 Ibid, Keyes (2005).

16 Ibid, Lyubomirsky, King, et al. (2005).

17 King, L. A., Hicks, J. A., Krull, J. L., and Del Gaiso, A. K. (2006), 'Positive affect and the experience of meaning in life', *Journal of Personality and Social Psychology, 90*, 179–196.

18 Ibid, Lyubomirsky, Sheldon, et al. (2005).

19 It's relevant here to consider the work of Leaf Van Boven at the University of Colorado, who has found that people are happier if they invest their money and resources in *experiences* (which, of course, include a wide variety of activities) rather than *possessions*. He posits three reasons for this: 1) Experiences, relative to material things, are more likely to improve with time; 2) People are less likely to unfavourably compare their experiences (as opposed to their possessions) with those of more fortunate others; and 3) Experiences have more social value and are more likely to promote relationships. I would add a fourth benefit – experiences (including activities) are relatively less prone to hedonic adaptation. For a review, see Van Boven, L. (2005), 'Experientialism, materialism, and the pursuit of happiness', *Review of General Psychology, 9*, 132–142.

20 (1) Berlyne, D. (1970), 'Novelty, complexity, and hedonic value', *Perception and Psychophysics, 8*, 279–286. (2) McAlister, L. (1982), 'A dynamic attribute satiation model of variety-seeking behavior', *Journal of Consumer Research, 9*, 141–150. (3) Ratner, R. K., Kahn, B. E., and Kahneman, D. (1999), 'Choosing less-preferred experiences for the sake of variety', *Journal of Consumer Research, 26*, 1–15. (4) Berns, G. (2005), *Satisfaction: The science of finding true fulfillment*, New York: Henry Holt and Co.

21 Ibid, Tkach, 2005.

22 Robert Jeffery, Division of Epidemiology and Community Health, University of Minnesota. Personal communication, July 17, 2006.

23 Eugenides, J. (2003), *Middlesex* (p. 69), New York: Picador.

24 Brown, G. W., and Harris, T. (1978), *Social origins of depression: A study of psychiatric disorder in women*, New York: Free Press.

25 Ibid, Dubé et al. (in press).

26 Gladwell, M. (2005, September 12), 'The cellular church: How Rick Warren's congregation grew', *New Yorker*.

27 Friedman, H. S. (2002), *Health psychology* (2nd ed.), Upper Saddle River, NJ: Prentice Hall.

28 Caplan, R. D., Robinson, E. A. R., French, J. R. P., Jr., Caldwell, J. R., and Shinn, M. (1976), *Adhering to medical regimens: Pilot experiments in patient education and social support*, Ann Arbor: Research Center for Group

Dynamics, Institute for Social Research, University of Michigan.

29 Ibid, Norcross and Vangarelli (1989).

30 Wing, R. R., and Jeffery, R. W. (1999), 'Benefits of recruiting participants with friends and increasing social support for weight loss and maintenance', *Journal of Consulting and Clinical Psychology, 67*, 132–138.

31 Ibid, Dickerhoof (2007).

32 Ibid, Sheldon and Lyubomirsky (2006a).

33 (1) Ibid, Seligman et al. (2005). (2) Ibid, Sheldon and Lyubomirsky (2006a).

34 Attributed to seventeenth-century scholar and mathematician Isaac Barrow: 'Nothing of worth or weight can be achieved with half a mind, with a faint heart, and with a lame endeavor.'

35 Oishi, S., Diener, E., and Lucas, R. E. (in press), 'Optimum level of well-being: Can people be too happy?', *Perspectives in Psychological Science*.

36 (1) Ibid, Lyubomirsky, King, et al. (2005). (2) Ibid, Fredrickson (2001).

37 For example, Wood, W., Tam, L., and Witt, M. G. (2005), 'Changing circumstances, disrupting habits', *Journal of Personality and Social Psychology, 88*, 918–933. For a review of the psychological literature on habits, see Neal, D. T., Wood, W., and Quinn, J. M. (2006), 'Habits – A repeat performance', *Current Directions in Psychological Science, 15*, 198–202.

38 Shiffrin, R. M., and Schneider, W. (1977), 'Controlled and automatic human information processing: II. Perceptual learning, automatic attending and a general theory', *Psychological Review, 84*, 127–190.

39 (1) Centers for Disease Control (1993), 'Smoking cessation during previous year among adults – United States, 1990 and 1991', *MMWR, 42*, 504–507. (2) McGuire, M., Wing, R. and Hill, J. (1999), 'The prevalence of weight loss maintenance among American adults', *International Journal of Obesity, 23*, 1314–1319. (3) Kassirer, J., and Angell, M. (1998), 'Losing weight – an ill-fated New Year's resolution', *New England Journal of Medicine, 338*, 52–54.

40 Schachter, S. (1982), 'Recidivism and self-cure of smoking and obesity', *American Psychologist, 37*, 436–444.

41 Ibid, Klem et al. (1997).

POSTSCRIPT

1 American Psychiatric Association (2000), *Diagnostic and statistical manual of mental disorders* (fourth ed., text rev.), Washington DC: Author.

2 Kessler, R. C. (2005, August), 'Population perspectives on the epidemiology and use of services for behavioral health disorders'. Paper presented at the Annual Convention of the American Psychological Association, Washington, DC.

3 Schatzberg, A. F. (2000), 'New indications for antidepressants', *Journal of Clinical Psychiatry, 61*, 9–17.

4 Kessler, R. C., Michelson, K. D., Barber, C. B., and Wang, P. (2001),

'The association between chronic medical conditions and work impairment', in A. S. Rossi (Ed.), *Caring and doing for others: Social responsibility in the domain of the family, work, and community* (pp. 403–426), Chicago: University of Chicago Press.

5 Greenberg, P., Kessler, R. C., Nells, T., Finkelstein, S., and Berndt, E. R. (1996), 'Depression in the workplace: An economic perspective', in J. P. Feighner and W. F. Boyer (Eds.), *Selective serotonin reuptake inhibitors: Advances in basic research and clinical practice* (pp. 327–363), New York: Wiley. (English statistic retrieved from the World Wide Web: http://www.mind.org.uk/Information/Factsheets/Statistics/Statistics+5.html)

6 This is called the diathesis-stress model. Diathesis represents a genetic susceptibility or predisposition. Stress represents an environmental trigger or precipitating event.

7 Kendler, K., Neale, M., Kessler, R., Heath, A., and Eaves, L. (1992), 'Major depression and generalized anxiety disorder', *Archives of General Psychiatry, 49*, 716–722.

8 Sullivan, P. F., Neale, M. C., and Kendler, K. S. (2000), 'Genetic epidemiology of major depression: Review and meta-analysis', *American Journal of Psychiatry, 157*, 1552–1562.

9 Thase, M. E., Jindal, R., and Howland, R. H. (2002), 'Biological aspects of depression', in I. H. Gotlib and C. L. Hammen (Eds.), *Handbook of depression* (pp. 192–218), New York: Guilford Press. See also Carlson, P. J., Singh, J. B., Zarate, C. A., Drevets, W. C., and Manji, H. K. (2006), 'Neural circuitry and neuroplasticity in mood disorders: Insights for novel therapeutic targets', *The Journal of the American Society for Experimental NeuroTherapeutics, 3*, 22–41.

10 Mayberg, H. S., Lozano, A. M., Voon, V., McNeeley, H. E., Seminowicz, D., Hamani, C., Schwalb, J. M., and Kennedy, S. H. (2005, March 3), 'Deep brain stimulation for treatment-resistant depression', *Neuron, 45*, 651–660.

11 Monroe, S. M., and Hadjiyannakis, K. (2002), 'The social environment and depression: Focusing on severe life stress', in I. H. Gotlib and C. L. Hammen (Eds.), *Handbook of depression* (pp. 314–340), New York: Guilford Press.

12 (1) Abramson, L. Y., Alloy, L. B., Hogan, M. E., Whitehouse, W. G., Donovan, P., Rose, D., Panzarella, C., and Raniere, D. (1999), 'Cognitive vulnerability to depression: Theory and evidence', *Journal of Cognitive Psychotherapy: An International Quarterly, 13*, 5–20. (2) Alloy, L. B., Abramson, L. Y., Whitehouse, W. G., Hogan, M. E., Tashman, N., Steinberg, D., Rose, D. T., and Donovan, P. (1999), 'Depressogenic cognitive styles: Predictive validity, information processing and personality characteristics, and developmental origins', *Behaviour Research and Therapy, 37*, 503–531.

13 National Institute of Mental Health. Depression. Bethesda (MD): National Institute of Mental Health, National Institutes of Health, US

Department of Health and Human Services; 2002 [updated 2004]. (NIH Publication Number: 02–3561.) Twenty-five pages. Available from: http://www.nimh.nih.gov/publicat/depression.cfm

14 (1) Nolen-Hoeksema, S. (2003), *Women who think too much*, New York: Henry Holt. (2) Ibid, Lyubomirsky and Tkach (2003).

15 Hollon, S. D., Haman, K. L., and Brown, L. L. (2002), 'Cognitive-behavioral treatment of depression', in I. H. Gotlib and C. L. Hammen (Eds.), *Handbook of depression* (pp. 383–403), New York: Guilford Press.

16 (1) DiMascio, A., Weissman, M. M., Prusoff, B. A., Neu, C., Zwilling, M., and Klerman, G. L. (1979), 'Differential symptom reduction by drugs and psychotherapy in acute depression', *Archives of General Psychiatry, 36*, 1450–1456. (2) Weissman, M. M., Prusoff, B. A., DiMascio, A., Neu, C., Goklaney, M., and Klerman, G. L. (1979), 'The efficacy of drugs and psychotherapy in the treatment of acute depressive episodes', *American Journal of Psychiatry, 136*, 555–558. (3) Elkin, I., Shea, M. T., Watkins, J. T., Imber, S. D., Sotsky, S. M., Collins, J. F., Glass, D. R., Pilkonis, P. A., Leber, W. R., Docherty, J. P., Fiester, S. J., and Parloff, M. B. (1989), 'National Institute of Mental Health Treatment of Depression Collaborative Research Program: General effectiveness of treatments', *Archives of General Psychiatry, 46*, 971–982.

17 Whisman, M. A. (2001), 'The association between depression and marital dissatisfaction', in S. R. H. Beach (Ed.), *Marital and family processes in depression: A scientific foundation for clinical practice* (pp. 3–24), Washington DC: American Psychological Association.

18 Lovejoy, M. C., Gracyk, P. A., O'Hare, E., and Neuman, G. (2000), 'Maternal depression and parenting behavior: A meta-analytic review', *Clinical Psychology Review, 20*, 561–592.

19 Stress-generation theory was developed by Constance Hammen of the University of California, Los Angeles. Hammen, C. (1991), *Depression runs in families: The social context of risk and resilience of children of depressed mothers*, New York: Springer-Verlag.

20 Beach, S. R. H., and Jones, D. B. (2002), 'Marital and family therapy for depression in adults', in I. H. Gotlib and C. L. Hammen (Eds.), *Handbook of depression* (pp. 422–440), New York: Guilford Press.

21 Markman, H., Stanley, S., and Blumberg, S. I. (1994), *Fighting for your marriage*, San Francisco: Jossey-Bass.

22 Patterson, G. R. (1982), *Coercive family processes*, Eugene, OR: Castilia.

23 (1) Beach, S. R. H., and O'Leary, K. D. (1992), 'Treating depression in the context of marital discord: Outcome and predictors of response for marital therapy versus cognitive therapy', *Behavior Therapy, 23*, 507–528. (2) Jacobson, N. S., Dobson, K., Fruzzetti, A. E., Schmaling, K. B., and Salusky, S. (1991), 'Marital therapy as a treatment of depression', *Journal of Consulting and Clinical Psychology, 59*, 547–557.

24 Ibid, Beach and Jones (2002).

25 IMS Health, Inc. (2006, February), '2005 Year-end U.S. prescription

and sales information and commentary'. Retrieved September 29, 2006, from http://www.imshealth.com/ims/portal/front/articleC/0,2777,6599_18731_77056778,00.html

26 Klein, D. F., Gittelman-Klein, R., Quitkin, F. M., and Rifkin, A. (1980), *Diagnosis and drug treatment of psychiatric disorders*, Baltimore: Williams and Wilkins.

27 Gelenberg, A. J., and Chesen, C. L. (2000), 'How fast are antidepressants?' *Journal of Clinical Psychiatry, 61*, 712–721. However, in the most recent major published study on the effectiveness of antidepressants, half of approximately 3,000 patients did not show benefits until eight to ten weeks. Reference: Rush, A. J., Trivedi, M. H., Wisniewski, S. R., Stewart, J. W., Nierenberg, A. A., Thase, M. E., Ritz, L., Biggs, M. M., Warden, D., Luther, J. F., Shores-Wilson, K., Niederehe, G., Fava, M., and STAR★D Study Team (2006), 'Bupropion-SR, Sertraline, or Venlafaxine-XR after failure of SSRIs for depression', *New England Journal of Medicine, 354*, 1231–1242.

28 (1) Moffitt, T. E., Caspi, A., and Rutter, M. (2006), 'Measured gene-environment interactions in psychopathology', *Perspectives on Psychological Science, 1*, 5–27. (2) McMahon, F. J., Buervenich, S., Charney, D., Lipsky, R., Rush, A. J., Wilson, A. F., Sorant, A. J., Papanicolaou, G. J., Laje, G., Fava, M., Trivedi, M. H., Wisniewski, S. R., and Manji, H. (2006), 'Variation in the gene encoding the serotonin 2A receptor is associated with outcome of antidepressant treatment', *The American Journal of Human Genetics, 78*, 804–814.

29 In most states in the US, only medical doctors (who have MD degrees) can prescribe medication. Psychotherapists cannot, but will refer you to someone who can.

30 Ibid, Rush et al. (2006). See also Trivedi, M. H., Fava, M., Wisniewski, S. R., Thase, M. E., Quitkin, F., Warden, D., Ritz, L., Nierenberg A. A., Lebowitz, B. D., Biggs, M. M., Luther, J. F., Shores-Wilson, K., Rush, A. J., and STAR★D Study Team (2006), 'Medication augmentation after the failure of SSRIs for depression', *New England Journal of Medicine, 354*, 1243–1252.

31 (1) Frank, E., Kupfer, D. J., Perel, J. M., Cornes, C., Jarrett, D. B., Mallinger, A. G., Thase, M. E., McEachran, A. B., and Grochocinski, V. J. (1990), 'Three-year outcomes for maintenance therapies in recurrent depression', *Archives of General Psychiatry, 47*, 1093–1099. (2) Kupfer, D. J., Frank, E., Perel, J. M., Cornes, C., Mallinger, A. G., Thase, M. E., McEachran, A. B., and Grochocinski, V. J. (1992), 'Five-year outcome for maintenance therapies in recurrent depression', *Archives of General Psychiatry, 49*, 769–773.

32 (1) Keller, M. B., Gelenberg, A. J., Hirschfeld, R. M. A., Rush, A. J., Thase, M. E., Kocsis, J. H., Markowitz, J. C., Fawcett, J. A., Koran, L. M., Klein, D. N., Russell, J. M., Kornstein, S. G., McCullough, J. P., Davis, S. M., and Harrison, W. M. (1998), 'The treatment of chronic depression: Part 2. A double-blind randomized trial of sertraline and

imipramine', *Journal of Clinical Psychiatry, 59*, 598–606. (2) Kocsis, J. H., Friedman, R. A., Markowitz, J. C., Leon, A. C., Miller, N. L., Gniwesch, L., Parides, M., Kupfer, D. J., and Frank, E. (1996), 'Maintenance therapy for chronic depression: A controlled clinical trial of desipramine', *Archives of General Psychiatry, 53*, 769–774.

33 Linde, K., Ramirez, G., Mulrow, C. D., Pauls, A., Weidenhammer, W., and Melchart, D. (1996), 'St. John's wort for depression: An overview and meta-analysis of randomized clinical trials', *British Medical Journal, 313*, 253–258.

34 Shelton, R. C., Keller, M. B., Gelenberg, A., Dunner, D. L., Hirschfield, R., Thase, M. E., Russell, J., Lydiard, R. B., Crist-Christoph, P., Gallop, R., Todd, L., Hellerstein, D., Goodnick, P., Keitner, G., Stahl, S. M., and Halbreich, U. (2001), 'Effectiveness of St. John's wort in major depression: A randomized controlled-trial', *JAMA, 285*, 1978–1986.

35 (1) Ibid, National Institute of Mental Health. (2) Covi, L., and Lipman, R. S. (1987), 'Cognitive behavioral group psychotherapy combined with imipramine in major depression', *Psychopharmacology Bulletin, 23*, 173–177.

36 Hough, R. L., Landsverk, J. A., Karno, M., Burnam, M. A., Timbers, D. M., Escobar, J. I., and Regier, D. A. (1987), 'Utilization of health and mental health services by Los Angeles Mexican-Americans and Non-Hispanic Whites', *Archives of General Psychiatry, 44*, 702–709.

37 Ibid, Seligman, Rashid, and Parks (in press).

38 Fava, G. A., Rafanelli, C., Cazzaro, M., Conti, S., and Grandi, S. (1998), 'Well-being therapy: A novel psychotherapeutic approach for residual symptoms of affective disorders', *Psychological Medicine, 28*, 475–480. For an overview of well-being therapy, see Fava, G. A., and Ruini, C. (2003), 'Development and characteristics of a well-being enhancing psychotherapeutic strategy: Well-being therapy', *Journal of Behavior Therapy and Experimental Psychiatry, 34*, 45–63.

39 Frisch, M. B. (2005), *Quality of Life Therapy: Applying a life satisfaction approach to positive psychology and cognitive therapy*, New York: Wiley.

40 Hope therapy was developed over a number of years by the late C.R. Snyder. See Lopez, S. J., Snyder, C.R., Magyar-Moe, J. L., Edwards, L. M., Pedrotti, J. T., Janowski, K., Turner, J. L., and Pressgrove, C. (2004), 'Strategies for accentuating hope', in P. A. Linley and S. Joseph (Eds.), *Positive psychology in practice* (pp. 388–404), Hoboken, NJ: John Wiley and Sons.

41 Positive psychotherapy was developed by Nossrat Peseschkian and personal growth therapy by Christine Robitschek. For brief descriptions of these positively focused therapies, see Compton, W. C. (2004), 'Positive psychology interventions', in *An introduction to positive psychology* (pp. 182–195), Belmont, CA: Wadsworth.

42 (1) Ibid, Lucas et al. (2003). (2) Masten, A. S. (2001), 'Ordinary magic:
    Resilience processes in development', *American Psychologist, 56*, 227–238.
43 Edwards, J. (2004), *Four trials*, New York: Simon and Schuster.

Index